Vietnam Envy and the Emerging Iraq Syndrome

Vietnam Envy and the Emerging Iraq Syndrome

HOW THE MODERN ANTIWAR PROTEST MOVEMENT PREVENTS THE UNITED STATES FROM WINNING MILITARY CONFLICTS

Michael E. Ginsberg

For Andrew

ISBN: 0997233702
ISBN 13: 9780997233704
Library of Congress Control Number: 2016901283
Michael E. Ginsberg, Fairfax, VA

This book solely reflects the opinions of the author.

Table of Contents

Chapter 1 The Iraq Syndrome and Its Foundations: Vietnam Envy and the Antiwar Movement · 1
Chapter 2 The Vietnam Essentials · 11
Chapter 3 September 11, the War on Terror, and the Antiwar Movement's Next Generation · 21
Chapter 4 As the Movement Turns: Growth of the Antiwar Movement in the Early Stages of the Iraq Occupation · · · · · · 41
Chapter 5 Fetishizing Multilateralism · 72
Chapter 6 The Beginning of the Iraq Occupation and Abu Ghraib: Renewed Antiwar Sentiment and Finding Iraq's My Lai · 86
Chapter 7 Vietnam Envy in Full: The Antiwar Movement's Vietnam Pantomime Reaches Full Flower · · · · · · · · · · · · · · · 98
Chapter 8 Treating Soldiers as Victims: What the Antiwar Movement Learned from Vietnam · 139
Chapter 9 Pouring Partisan Gasoline on the Antiwar Fire: How Iraq Was Worse than Vietnam · 150
Chapter 10 The Wrong Lessons Learned and the Emergence of the Iraq Syndrome: The 2008 Campaign and the Iran Nuclear Deal · 158

Chapter 11 Consequences: The Enduring Aftermath of the Antiwar Movement, the Emerging Iraq Syndrome, and Recommendations for the Future 182
Chapter 12 Being Prepared for the Next War....221

About the Author....225

CHAPTER 1

The Iraq Syndrome and Its Foundations: Vietnam Envy and the Antiwar Movement

SINCE THE LAST AMERICANS LEFT the US embassy in Saigon on those desperate helicopters in 1975, the United States has engaged in a variety of armed conflicts around the world. Some were full-fledged wars, such as the 1991 Gulf War, the invasion of Afghanistan, and the Iraq War. Others were shorter or more limited military interventions: the invasion of Grenada in 1983, the bombing of Libya in 1986, the invasion of Panama in 1989, and the air war in Yugoslavia in the mid-1990s.

Virtually every time the United States engages in military conflict, the same questions arise: How will the United States avoid another Vietnam? Will this conflict become a quagmire? What is the United States' exit strategy? When General Colin Powell was the chairman of the Joint Chiefs of Staff under President George H. W. Bush, he developed a military doctrine that came to be known as the Powell Doctrine, a doctrine that reflected America's and his own experience in Vietnam and that attempted to answer these questions before the United States engaged in military action.

It has been forty years since that fateful day the helicopters left the roof of the US embassy in Saigon. Since then, the Cold War has ended and new threats, particularly radical Islamic terrorism and the proliferation of weapons of mass destruction among rogue states, have risen to take the Cold War's place. Nevertheless, politicians, policy makers, the media, and other analysts, with metronomic regularity, continue to cite the Powell doctrine and other post-Vietnam military, diplomatic, and political lessons and doctrines when analyzing a prospective American military action.

Policy makers are not the only Americans who fall back on the Vietnam experience when confronted with prospective US military action. In nearly every instance in which America engages in significant, prolonged military action, protest movements reminiscent of the 1960s heyday spring into existence.

The Vietnam War colored an entire generation's view of when and how the United States should engage in military conflict. For years, the United States suffered from a Vietnam syndrome that made it extremely cautious in the deployment and use of force. It was said that after the American victory in the 1991 Gulf War, which liberated Kuwait from Saddam Hussein's Iraq, Vietnam syndrome had been broken and the United States had regained its confidence in its ability to fight and win wars. After all, the Gulf War was the first major hot war involving large numbers of ground troops since Vietnam and was a stunning victory for the coalition led by the United States.

In the wake of the Iraq War, there now appears to be a very real possibility that the United States will suffer from an "Iraq syndrome" similar to the Vietnam syndrome of an earlier generation. Much of the United States' foreign policy since 2008 has been predicated on not repeating the supposed mistakes of Iraq. America's engagement in world crises, from the Syrian civil war to the Libyan civil war to the rise of the Islamic State in Iraq and Syria (ISIS), has been defined by an expressed unwillingness of American political leaders to deploy large numbers of ground troops. In proposing strategies for approaching foreign policy problems, policy makers regularly insist from the outset they will not deploy large-scale ground forces. The thinly veiled implication is that they will not get the United States into another Iraq War and will not repeat the mistakes the United States made during the Iraq War.

The Iraq War thus threatens to become for the current generation what the Vietnam War was for an earlier generation: the basis for a deep reluctance to deploy American forces and project American power across the globe in defense of American interests. The perceived mistakes in launching and prosecuting the Iraq War have already influenced American policy to an immense degree since 2008. Just as one generation reflexively looked to the supposed lessons of Vietnam in making decisions about going to war, the current generation is poised to reflexively look to the supposed lessons of Iraq every time the United States contemplates military action.

American policy makers will always be faced with decisions about whether to engage in military action. How they make these decisions in the near future will be governed, at least in part, by the answers to the following questions: Will an Iraq syndrome reminiscent of the Vietnam syndrome take hold of the United States? Has the Iraq War experience, like Vietnam before it, created a generation of antiwar activism that will color America's involvement in world affairs and its deployment of force for years to come? What will this mean for the United States' ability to counter threats in the coming years?

To answer these questions, this book looks at the history of the opposition to the Iraq War and compares it to the opposition to the Vietnam War. As this book will describe, the protests prior to the Iraq War in the fall of 2002 and winter of 2003, the international opposition to the war in the United Nations in 2002 and 2003, the adoption of the antiwar position by a major American political party in 2004, and the continued protests during the war from 2005 through 2007 acted as a positive feedback loop that continuously amplified opposition to the Iraq War. The 2002–2003 protests convinced politicians in 2004—and ultimately an entire political party—to adopt the antiwar position, which in turn encouraged the domestic and international protests that took place from 2005 through 2007 as the Iraq War continued. Over time, in the cacophony of negative assessments of the war from protesters, activists, politicians, artists, and members of the media, the American people soured on the war. The antiwar movement and the politicians that joined the antiwar camp in the face of the antiwar movement's pressure stirred such a negative storm around the war that American political leaders had extreme difficulty prosecuting the war.

In order to understand this feedback loop, it is necessary to unpack each element within it. The theory of this book is that each stage of this feedback loop is highly analogous to elements within the Vietnam-era antiwar movement. Therefore, this book compares each element in the Iraq War opposition feedback loop to the Vietnam War protests. The similarities and differences between the opposition to the Vietnam War and the Iraq War are illuminating and bear ominous signs that an Iraq syndrome may be taking hold within the United States.

Vietnam Envy: The Antiwar Protests

The first thread this book will explore is the notion of Vietnam envy, the idea that the protesters of the Iraq War wanted to be part of a protest movement as exciting and historic as the antiwar protests of the 1960s. The Iraq War opponents—protesters, artists, members of the media, and politicians—consciously or unconsciously wanted to recreate the protest atmosphere of the 1960s and saw themselves as the next great generation of antiwar protesters. The Vietnam-era protests, as we shall see, were never very far from the minds of the Iraq War protesters.

The attitude toward protest and protesters that first took shape during the 1960s continues to this day, contributing to the quick rise of antiwar opposition and protest movements after—and in the case of the Iraq War, even before—the United States engages in military conflict. Protesters are celebrated for speaking truth to power and having the courage to speak out in opposition against US military action. Opponents of the 2003 Iraq War regularly reminded Americans that "dissent is the highest form of patriotism."[1] *Wall Street Journal* columnist Dan Henninger once wrote that protesters have come to be viewed as "holy people." In effect, every time America enters into a conflict, an element of American society sets to work recreating the 1960s protest movement. The media amplifies

---

1 For example, see Sen. John Kerry, Commencement Address to Emerson College, May 15, 2006, The Democratic Daily, accessed January 27, 2016, http://blog.thedemocraticdaily.com/?p=2993; FoxNews.com, "Raw Data: Kennedy Speech on Iraq War," September 27, 2004, http://www.foxnews.com/story/2004/09/27/raw-data-kennedy-speech-on-iraq-war.html; Howard Zinn, "Dissent in Pursuit of Equality, Life, Liberty, and Happiness," HowardZinn.org, July 3, 2002, http://howardzinn.org/dissent-in-pursuit-of-equality-life-liberty-and-happiness/; Greg Hengler, "Krauthammer: During Bush Dissent Was The Highest Form of Patriotism & Now It's The Lowest Form of Racism," TownHall.org, September 17, 2009, http://townhall.com/tipsheet/greghengler/2009/09/17/krauthammer_during_bush_dissent_was_the_highest_form_of_patriotism__now_its_the_lowest_form_of_racism.

these protests with exaggerated coverage of them out of all proportion to their size and scope.

In addition, Americans live in a culture that lionizes protesters and reveres the 1960s protest movement. Members of younger generations are always on the lookout for opportunities to protest in the same way their forebears protested in the 1960s and, in effect, reenact the 1960s. This impulse was on display in late 2015 on college campuses. In November 2015, student protesters at the University of Missouri forced the resignation of the university president and university system chancellor over a handful of alleged incidents of racism for which they deemed the university's response inadequate. The protesters shouted through bullhorns, repeated the signature "Hey hey, ho ho, [insert name here] has got to go" chants of the 1960s protesters, and engaged in hunger strikes and other attention-grabbing activities reminiscent of the 1960s. The football team even went on strike. Students at Virginia Commonwealth University demanding an increase in African American professors and more "cultural competency training" took over the university president's office, another favored tactic of 1960s campus radicals.[2] Yale students launched a "March of Resilience" in protest of a professor who suggested that free speech might permit individuals to wear Halloween costumes that might be provocative or offensive.[3] The same impulse animated Occupy Wall Street and its various spin-off movements; the protestors in New York occupied the city's Zuccotti Park for a number of months in 2011 in protest of capitalism and income inequality. Occupy Wall Street featured street theater and visits by celebrities, including actors Mark Ruffalo, Russell Simmons, Alec Baldwin, Roseanne Barr, Yoko Ono, and others.[4] Protest, in short, is trendy.

---

2 Louis Llovio, "Black Students Take Over VCU's Office to Demand Changes," *Richmond Times-Dispatch*, November 12, 2015, http://www.richmond.com/news/local/city-of-richmond/article_4a05d70e-99fe-539f-9097-8415205caafd.html.

3 Liam Stack, "Yale's Halloween Advice Stokes a Racially Charged Debate," *New York Times*, November 8, 2015, http://www.nytimes.com/2015/11/09/nyregion/yale-culturally-insensitive-halloween-costumes-free-speech.html?_r=0; Jon Victor, Monica Wang, and Victor Wang, "More than 1,000 Gather in Solidarity," *Yale News*, November 10, 2015, http://yaledailynews.com/blog/2015/11/10/more-than-1000-gather-in-solidarity/.

4 *Huffington Post*, "Occupy Wall Street: Celebrities Show Support," October 2, 2011, http://www.huffingtonpost.com/2011/10/02/occupy-wall-street-celebrities-_n_991066.html.

Protests also represent opportunities for artists and the media. Artists have the opportunity to make edgy antiwar art in movies, music, and books. It is an opportunity for them to "speak truth to power" and to play in the political sandbox. And, of course, antiwar activism means publicity. For reporters who take an antiwar position, it is an opportunity to shape events, not merely report on them.

The opportunity to protest a war—not a short military action but a full-scale, potentially years-long war—is an extraordinary temptation for those seeking to recreate the Vietnam-era protests. This is particularly true when those in power are the natural ideological opponents of the protesters. Such protests, and the extensive media coverage they receive, represent a significant risk to the United States' ability to successfully prosecute a war that national political leadership has determined to be in the national interest.

Politicians as Antiwar Followers

The second key thread of this book is that with both Vietnam and Iraq, politicians were followers, not leaders, of the antiwar movement. On both Vietnam and Iraq, the antiwar movement was in the vanguard of opposition to the war and drove political parties and their candidates to adopt the antiwar position, not the other way around. The antiwar movement in both wars united behind a single presidential candidate, which ultimately forced that presidential candidate's party to adopt the antiwar position. In the case of both Iraq and Vietnam, the antiwar opposition proved so strong that in time it effectively captured an entire political party. The resulting political schism between those supporting the war and opposing the war greatly affected the United States' ability to fight and demonstrate resolve in the face of the enemy.

Moreover, many of the politicians opposing the Iraq War came of age during the Vietnam War. These politicians expressly compared Iraq to their own experiences in and understanding of the Vietnam War. In so doing, they breathed life into the Vietnam syndrome that was thought to be dead after the 1991 Gulf War. Raising the specter of Vietnam during the Iraq War made explicit the connection of those two wars.

International Protests

Protests of American military actions are not confined to the United States. The opportunity to protest American military actions (and foreign policy in general) is a temptation to international protesters as well. Just as protests broke out in Europe against the Vietnam War, protests similar in size and opposition to the United States broke out in response to the Iraq War. In the case of both Vietnam and Iraq, worldwide opposition contributed to the feeling among Americans that the United States made a mistake in engaging in military action.

Moreover, just as in the United States, overseas politicians seized upon the opportunity that the antiwar movement presented to publicly break with the United States. By hitching their star to the antiwar movement in Europe, these politicians enhanced their own domestic political popularity and received worldwide acclaim.

International protests and the support they received from international politicians fed further into the positive feedback loop. Domestic politicians and protesters seized upon the international opposition to further discredit the war in the minds of the American public.

Avoiding a Full-Fledged Iraq Syndrome

Recent American foreign policy has been defined as much by what the United States has expressly stated it will not do (i.e., deploy large numbers of ground troops) as what it says it is willing to do. This suggests that a nascent Iraq syndrome is taking hold. Where previous generations worried about whether a potential military engagement would turn into another Vietnam, the current generation now worries whether foreign military engagements will turn into another Iraq.

But it does not have to be this way. There are indeed lessons to be learned from the Iraq War (and Vietnam before it) that should bear on the thinking of policy makers deciding whether to engage in military action. The final part of this book focuses on those lessons and how to counter the protests and opposition to any contemplated military conflict.

What this book argues is that modern American wars require not only an effective military strategy but a full-fledged, robust domestic political strategy. An aggressive political strategy must be a major component of any significant, extended military commitment. American political leaders cannot simply make the case for war, obtain congressional approval, and assume that the country and the political class will support the war to its successful conclusion.

We live in an era in which news travels at speeds unthinkable in any previous military conflict. Reporters embedded with US troops can instantly file stories from the front lines. Troops can report home about how they are doing instantly through e-mail, Skype, and cellular telephones. In short, Americans can obtain information from the battlefield in nearly real time. As a result, Americans can form opinions quickly about military conflicts. Just as Vietnam was the first war fought on Americans' television screens, the Iraq War was the first major war fought in the era of instant Internet communications. And just as support for the Vietnam War eroded over time as television news broadcast apparent setbacks in the war into Americans' homes, Americans became increasingly disenchanted with the Iraq War as modern media reported setbacks in the war back to the United States.

Because setbacks can be so quickly communicated to the world, those opposed to a particular conflict can seize upon setbacks immediately to demonstrate why their opposition is correct and why the conflict should be ended. The reaction to this amplification of opposition to a conflict is an erosion of support for a war. This cycle repeats itself until support for a conflict has eroded to the point where the war cannot be sustained domestically, and commanders do not have the opportunity to change strategy before the American public has given up on the war.

This conundrum calls for a complete rethinking of domestic political strategies regarding military conflict. It is no longer sufficient to put the best military minds to work to strategize to win a conflict. It is now necessary to create a comprehensive and sustained domestic political strategy to maintain support for American military conflicts, one that relentlessly reminds Americans of the rationale for the conflict and why it is important to national security. As will be seen later in this book, political leaders cannot allow false narratives to enter the mainstream and become accepted fact. Falsehoods about American military conflicts must be confronted immediately before they become accepted as facts. The 1992 Clinton presidential campaign famously featured a war room that responded to any attack immediately and forcefully. Political leaders and military commanders today must apply this same war room strategy to communicating the prosecution of an actual war.

Nor can political leaders and military commanders rely on third parties in the media and the commentariat to make their points for them. The media cannot be relied upon to present the battlefield and political successes of a military conflict with the same vigor and emphasis as they will report upon failures. The lessons of first Vietnam and later Iraq are that the media often will misunderstand the military consequences of individual battles and events during a conflict. Members of the media and the commentariat opposed to a conflict—and there are often many—will seize upon any setback as another piece of evidence indicting the entire enterprise as a failure. Political leaders and military commanders must respond immediately before the American people conclude that the conflict is a failure before the goals of the conflict are achieved.

This does not mean that political leaders and military commanders should be Pollyannaish about reporting the truth of what is taking place in combat and in the political sphere of those countries in which conflicts are occurring. In fact, by honestly reporting setbacks and providing answers about how the United States will respond to those setbacks (without compromising operational security), political and military leaders will enjoy enhanced credibility with the American public. Of course, some level of emphasis on battlefield successes is important for troop morale and to maintain support for the conflict; if the conflict is truly not succeeding and the political and military leadership believe they cannot develop new strategies to reverse those losses and achieve the goals of the conflict, the United States should consider ending the conflict. But by reporting the bad with the good, US policy makers can enhance their credibility when they speak of the aims and status of the war.

The single greatest failure of the Bush administration's prosecution of the Iraq War was not developing a comprehensive, persistent, and forceful domestic strategy to respond to the Vietnam-style protest movement and the politicians who aligned themselves with that movement and gradually rose up in opposition to the war. This failure, more than any other, nearly sank the Iraq War effort. To save the Iraq War, President Bush was forced to buck popular opinion in 2007 and execute the now-famous surge of troops into Iraq, which pacified that country to an extent the majority of Americans thought impossible at the end of 2006. The Bush administration's failure to persistently and robustly defend the Iraq War allowed matters to reach the point where changes to US strategy had to be made in the face of loud public opposition rather than with public support.

As this book will show, given the antiwar movements that arose in response to Vietnam and later to Iraq, future presidents and their administrations can be assured that any major military action they contemplate will be opposed by a vocal and aggressive antiwar movement. That movement will drive at least some politicians to an antiwar position, even if they originally supported the conflict.

The experience in Iraq and the late 2015 protests on college campuses across the nation is that protest culture simply is baked into a segment of the population. That antiwar movement will alight upon any battlefield reversal in order to discredit the military action. If the president and administration do not respond immediately and as forcefully and loudly as that opposition, then the military action, if it extends beyond six months to a year, will gradually lose the support of the American people. This will be true whether or not American forces are making progress toward achieving the goals of the conflict or if American leaders, sensing a lack of success in the initial stages of the conflict, alter their strategy for the conflict. American policy makers must develop a domestic strategy for reporting on the war every bit as sophisticated and comprehensive as the military strategies they plan for the battlefield. Otherwise, the antiwar protest movement and the politicians that hitch their stars to this movement will make it impossible for the United States to sustain a long-term military commitment, no matter how vital the commitment is to the national interest.

CHAPTER 2

The Vietnam Essentials

THERE ARE A NUMBER OF lessons Americans commonly draw from Vietnam. A Google search for "lessons of Vietnam" calls up thousands of links to newspapers, online periodicals, personal websites, and other sources. Identifying the lessons of Vietnam is practically a cottage industry. One opinion writer in *U.S. News and World Report* stated that the lesson of Vietnam was "that a foreign war without a clear rationale and popular support will only tear the country in two, at home and abroad."[5] A writer for *Salon* suggested that the lesson of Vietnam was the failure of the United States to appreciate the misery and suffering of the local population the war created, which Americans "have seldom found of the slightest interest."[6] There is simply no shortage of opinions about what constitute the true "lessons of Vietnam."

General David Petraeus, the former CENTCOM commander and CIA director whose PhD dissertation studied the lessons of Vietnam on the military, stated that the "conventional wisdom" held that the lessons of Vietnam comprised the following:

Don't commit US troops unless

- you really have to (in which case, presumably, vital US interests are at stake);

5 Jamie Stiehm, "The Lessons Dick Cheney Never Learned," *U.S. News & World Report*, July 7, 2014, http://www.usnews.com/opinion/blogs/jamie-stiehm/2014/07/07/in-iraq-dick-cheney-forgot-the-lessons-of-vietnam.

6 Nick Turse, "Have We Really Learned the Lessons of Vietnam?," *Salon*, January 8, 2013, http://www.salon.com/2013/01/08/have_we_really_learned_the_lessons_of_vietnam/.

- you have established clear-cut, attainable military objectives for American forces (that is, more than just some fuzzy political goals);
- you provide the military commander sufficient forces and the freedom to accomplish his mission swiftly (remember, this may necessitate mobilization of the reserve components—perhaps even a declaration of war); and
- you can ensure sufficient public support to permit carrying the commitment through to its conclusion.[7]

General Colin Powell, when he was the chairman of the Joint Chiefs of Staff under President George H. W. Bush, made famous his Powell doctrine, which consisted of eight questions:

- Is a vital national security interest threatened?
- Do we have a clear attainable objective?
- Have the risks and costs been fully and frankly analyzed?
- Have all other nonviolent policy means been fully exhausted?
- Is there a plausible exit strategy to avoid endless entanglement?
- Have the consequences of our action been fully considered?
- Is the action supported by the American people?
- Do we have genuine broad international support?[8]

The Powell doctrine requires all eight of these questions to be answered in the affirmative before the United States commits troops to war. Although policy makers do not explicitly say it in every instance, they—or politicians, analysts, and members of the media—generally ask some combination of these questions when the United States is contemplating military action of some kind.

---

7 David H. Petraeus, "The American Military and the Lessons of Vietnam: A Study of Military Influence and the Use of Force in the Post-Vietnam Era" (PhD diss., Princeton University, 1987), 132.

8 Stephen M. Walt, "Applying the 8 Questions of the Powell Doctrine to Syria," *Foreign Policy*, September 3, 2013, http://foreignpolicy.com/2013/09/03/applying-the-8-questions-of-the-powell-doctrine-to-syria/.

Looking at these questions, one cannot help but recognize that they are heavily influenced by America's experience in Vietnam. In fact, the questions more or less flow directly from the Vietnam experience. This is not surprising, as Powell was a Vietnam veteran who "stressed the 'lessons learned' in Vietnam."[9]

This book is not another entry in the veritable library of publications attempting to identify the lessons of Vietnam that the United States might apply to future wars and conflicts to avoid the perceived failures of the Vietnam War. Rather, this book identifies the lingering effects of Vietnam on how the American public views the use of force and how American leaders' options and capabilities for deploying military force are circumscribed by the lingering memories and experiences of the Vietnam era and how those experiences affect public opinion regarding the use of force today. This book looks at the Iraq War protest movement, the ways in which it was similar to and different from the Vietnam War movement, and how those similarities and differences suggest the onset of an Iraq syndrome among Americans.

The last of General Petraeus's "conventional wisdom" lessons is where Vietnam envy can have the most dramatic impact, for this last lesson is the lesson over which policy makers have the least control and the most competition. In understanding how Vietnam envy affects our ability to fight and win wars in the present, it is important to appreciate certain essential aspects of the Vietnam War and the protest movement that it spawned. These must be understood when comparing the protests surrounding and coverage of the Iraq War and present-day circumstances.

First, protests against the Vietnam War were driven greatly by the young; as the protests grew larger toward the end of the 1960s, the dissent took on a "cool" factor. The Vietnam protest movement merged with the general rise of the counterculture—the sexual revolution, increased drug use, the revolution in music, and the synthesis of all these trends into Woodstock—that represented a breaking away from the past. It was exciting for people who were a part of it, and understandably so. These students were at the forefront of great

9 Jim Mokhiber and Rick Young, "The Uses of Military Force," *Frontline* (PBS), http://www.pbs.org/wgbh/pages/frontline/shows/military/force/.

social change and in many ways drove this change. Those who lived through the 1960s felt like they were part of something exciting, something larger. Think of Amy Madigan's character in *Field of Dreams* as she leaves the high school after standing up to the parents who want to remove a book from the school's curriculum. She is cheery and pugnacious as she walks through the high school hallway, exclaiming that the experience was "just like the sixties!" Many a veteran of the protest movements of the 1960s looks back on that period as a halcyon time in his or her life. Or think of Cynthia at the party at the moon tower in *Dazed and Confused*, recounting how the fifties were "boring," "the sixties rocked," and the seventies "obviously suck."

A second key aspect of the war was the feeling among many that the US government could not be trusted to provide accurate information. From the murky circumstances of the Gulf of Tonkin incident to the emphasis on body counts, Americans had difficulty believing the information the US government provided. The press referred to the daily briefings by the US military in Vietnam as the "five o'clock follies" because they viewed them as overly rosy and untrustworthy, overestimating American successes and underestimating American setbacks.[10]

Third, the American public misunderstood the day-to-day facts of the war and came to reject the theory underlying the war's importance to American policy makers. These misunderstandings were the result of a number of factors. Perhaps most importantly, Americans often received incomplete or simply inaccurate information about the progress of the Vietnam War from the mass media. Vietnam was the first American war covered daily by television news. Television networks and newscasters played a tremendous role in how Americans perceived the war effort. However, the media's often inaccurate and incomplete representations of the war effort turned Americans against the

10 Mitchel P. Roth and James Stuart Olsen, *Historical Dictionary of War Journalism* (Greenwood Publishing Group), Google Books edition, https://books.google.com/books?id=Og8-5_oqumYC&pg=PA105&lpg=PA105&dq=the+five+o%27clock+follies+during+the+vietnam+war+was&source=bl&ots=_eNhSsmaWZ&sig=fW6D2akrI1wQ4emHJxdGC1JZqc0&hl=en&sa=X&sqi=2&ved=0CF0Q6AEwCWoVChMIo8LM9-3BxwIVhxkeCh0jMQPf#v=onepage&q=the%20five%20o%27clock%20follies%20during%20the%20vietnam%20war%20was&f=false.

war. Perhaps the most consequential of these misrepresentations was Walter Cronkite's reporting of the Tet Offensive as a defeat for South Vietnamese and American forces. Today, it is well known that the Tet Offensive was a devastating military defeat for the North Vietnamese. The North Vietnamese lost over fifty thousand men, many of whom were well-trained noncommissioned officers, and suffered heavy equipment losses.[11] However, Cronkite turned against the war in the wake of Tet, stating that "for it now seems more certain than ever, that the bloody experience in Vietnam is to end in a stalemate."[12] In response to Cronkite's commentary, President Johnson famously said, "If I've lost Cronkite, I've lost Middle America."[13]

Cronkite today is lionized as one of the finest and most influential newspeople of his generation and in the entire history of television news. Cronkite later stated that his statements on the Vietnam War, including calling the war a "stalemate" and saying that "the only way out was to negotiate," were his proudest accomplishment.[14] (He later called for the withdrawal of troops from Iraq.[15]) Cronkite's elevation into the pantheon of antiwar heroes comes, at least in part, from his opposition to Vietnam.[16] Opposing the Vietnam War won Cronkite acclaim, praise, and status. By opposing Vietnam and aligning

---

11 "Vietnam after Ho Chi Minh: An Interview with P. J. Honey," September 13, 1969, http://archive.thetablet.co.uk/article/13th-september-1969/3/vietnam-after-ho-chi-minh.

12 "Final Words: Cronkite's Vietnam Commentary," National Public Radio, July 18, 2009, http://www.npr.org/templates/story/story.php?storyId=106775685.

13 Leigh Ann Caldwell, "Walter Cronkite: The 'Maestro' of News," CBS News, May 27, 2012, accessed October 25, 2015, http://www.cbsnews.com/news/walter-cronkite-the-maestro-of-news/; Douglas Martin, "Walter Cronkite, 92, Dies; Trusted Voice of TV News," *New York Times*, July 17, 2009, http://www.nytimes.com/2009/07/18/us/18cronkite.html?pagewanted=all&_r=0.

14 David Usborne, "Cronkite's Vietnam Moment: 'US Must Leave Iraq,'" April 1, 2009, http://www.independent.co.uk/news/world/americas/cronkites-vietnam-moment-us-must-leave-iraq-6111440.html; Lee Cary, "Walter Cronkite, Vietnam, and the Decline of Media Credibility," *The American Thinker*, February 27, 2008, http://www.americanthinker.com/articles/2008/02/walter_cronkite_vietnam_and_th.html.

15 Ibid.

16 For example, see Edward Kosner, "Too Good to Check," review of *Getting it Wrong*, by W. Joseph Campbell, *Wall Street Journal*, July 12, 2010, http://www.wsj.com/articles/SB10001424052748704535004575349633765738968.

himself with the antiwar camp, Cronkite elevated himself from trusted news anchor to national moral conscience.

Similarly, many in the media, public life, and the protest movement downplayed the notion of the "domino theory," which states that the fall of one country to Communism would threaten its neighbors and ultimately lead to their fall to Communism. Southeast Asia, many reasoned, was thousands of miles away, and the immediate threat to the United States was not apparent. To many Americans, it was a mystery why young American men and women should be sent to jungles thousands of miles away to fight what seemed like someone else's war and, even worse, the remnants of a French colonial war. American political leadership did a poor job of explaining the consequences of a domino-style collapse of Southeast Asia from a strategic or humanitarian perspective. As a result, many Americans did not believe the domino theory, did not understand the threat or appreciate the consequences if the domino theory was true, or did not care about the consequences, whatever they might be.

Fourth, celebrities rose up to loudly and ostentatiously oppose the war. Muhammad Ali, the boxing champion, famously refused to serve in Vietnam as a conscientious objector, helping to elevate his status from champion boxer to cultural icon. Jane Fonda infamously went to North Vietnam and sat on a North Vietnamese antiaircraft gun. Other celebrities opposing the war included Paul Newman (who campaigned for Eugene McCarthy), John Fogerty, Bob Dylan, Joan Baez, Joni Mitchell, and Donald Sutherland.[17] Over time, America made heroes of those celebrities who dared to challenge publicly US policy in Vietnam and foreign policy in general.

Fifth, the Vietnam War got caught up in the romanticizing of the anticolonial and Third World movements of the 1950s and 1960s. The new heroes of the 1960s generation were revolutionary freedom fighters, such as Fidel Castro, Che Guevara, and Ho Chi Minh. Recall the picture of British college students visiting Libya in 1973 and meeting with Gaddafi not long after

---

17 Jennifer Llewellyn, Jim Southey, and Steve Thompson, "The Anti-War Movement," *Alpha History*, http://alphahistory.com/vietnam/anti-war-movement/; Jack Doyle, "1968 Presidential Race, Democrats," PopHistoryDig.com, August 14, 2008, http://www.pophistorydig.com/topics/tag/vietnam-war/.

he deposed the Libyan king and took power in that country in the name of "freedom, socialism, and unity."[18] The leftist radicals that went on to form groups such as Weatherman idolized Third World communists like Castro and Che.[19] Ho Chi Minh—kindly "uncle Ho," as his effective propagandists presented him—fell squarely into this new generation of anticolonial, Third World heroes.[20] Leaders standing up to the Western world and the supposed evils of capitalism and colonialism were received as heroes by those who saw Western influence as malignant and rapacious, including much of the 1960s protest generation. These 1960s protesters were all too willing to overlook or simply deny the monstrous crimes of Communist regimes and their leaders, from Stalin to Mao to Castro, and the brutal treatment of countries and peoples suffering under the yoke of Communist domination in Eastern Europe, Asia, and elsewhere.

Sixth, politicians for the most part represented a trailing edge of antiwar leadership at the onset of war. Only two senators voted against the 1964 Gulf of Tonkin Resolution (Democrats Wayne Morse of Idaho and Ernest Gruening of Alaska).[21] However, recognizing the strain of public opposition to the war, politicians slowly but surely flocked to the antiwar banner. As Vietnam began to deteriorate and opposition to the war grew, antiwar activists searched for a candidate to support in the 1968 presidential election. A "dump Johnson" movement within the Democratic Party sought an antiwar candidate to challenge incumbent president Lyndon Johnson, searching among many candidates (including Sens. Robert F. Kennedy and George McGovern) before Sen.

18 Merle Robillard, "Photos: The Reign of Muammar Gaddafi," October 20, 2011, http://news.nationalpost.com/2011/10/20/moamar-gaddafi-dead-photos-june-7-1942-oct-20-2011/.

19 Brian Burrough, *Days of Rage* (New York: Penguin 2015), 61–63, 84, 85.

20 George Katsiaficas, *The Imagination of the New Left: A Global Analysis of 1968*, Google Books edition, 82, https://books.google.com/books?id=PjCRRVjalVoC&pg=PA82&lpg=PA82&dq=ho+chi+minh+hero+to+the+Left&source=bl&ots=8ANZ5BKQX3&sig=F4B8PiUPIrTiipZqk7RbCOeV-N8&hl=en&sa=X&ei=cJX4VK3lK4qXgwSMjoLoCg&ved=0CEIQ6AEwCDgU#v=onepage&q=ho%20chi%20minh%20hero%20to%20the%20Left&f=false.

21 John Nichols, "Remembering the Folly of 'Blank Check' War and 'Escalation Unlimited,'" *The Nation*, August 7, 2014, https://www.thenation.com/article/remembering-folly-blank-check-war-and-escalation-unlimited/.

Eugene McCarthy agreed to take up the antiwar mantle against Johnson in the Democratic primaries.[22]

As protests against the war grew, McCarthy began to publicly oppose the Vietnam War. He declared his presidential candidacy in November 1967 and made ending the Vietnam War the central plank of his platform. In a December 2, 1967, speech denouncing the war, McCarthy stated "that [the United States] cannot stand apart, attempting to control the world by imposing covenants and treaties and by violent military intervention; that our role is not to police the planet but to use military strength with restraint and within limits, while at the same time we make available to the world the great power of our economy, of our knowledge, and of our good will."[23] In March 1968, after Johnson defeated McCarthy in the New Hampshire primary by only seven points (forty-nine to forty-two), Robert Kennedy entered the presidential race.[24] After these two setbacks, President Johnson announced his withdrawal from the race.[25] The swing of the Democratic Party into the antiwar camp was completed in 1972, when the party nominated Sen. George McGovern for president on an explicit peace platform.[26]

Once the Democratic Party fully embraced the antiwar position, it took affirmative steps to affect President Nixon's conduct of the war with the goal of ending the war. The Senate voted to defund the US bombings of Cambodia in 1973 against the personal pleading of National Security Advisor Henry

---

22 Tim Pugmire, "The Anti-War Candidate," *MPR News*, November 20, 2006, http://www.mprnews.org/story/2006/11/20/mccarthy1b; Robert M. Krim, "Lowenstein: The Making of a Liberal 1968," *The Harvard Crimson*, January 8, 1968, http://www.thecrimson.com/article/1968/1/8/lowenstein-the-making-of-a-liberal/.

23 Eugene McCarthy, "Denouncing the Vietnam War," Speech Vault, December 2, 1967, http://www.speeches-usa.com/Transcripts/eugene_mccarthy-vietnam.html.

24 John Gardner, "Thematic Window: The Election of 1968," PBS, http://www.pbs.org/johngardner/chapters/5a.html.

25 Ibid.

26 Michael A. Cohen, "How Vietnam Haunts the Democrats," *Politico Magazine*, February 17, 2015, http://www.politico.com/magazine/story/2015/02/vietnam-lbj-pleiku-haunts-democrats-115259_Page3.html#.VQRnSY7n9vk.

Kissinger.[27] Senate Majority Leader Mike Mansfield stated that "the only way to face up to our responsibilities, the only way to do it effectively is to cut the purse strings."[28] From 1973 to 1975, the antiwar Congress's reduction in military aid to South Vietnam gravely weakened South Vietnam's ability to maintain morale and defend itself against continued North Vietnamese aggression. These cuts placed the South Vietnamese on what the US Defense Attaché Office in Saigon called a "starvation diet."[29] The cuts included the refusal to replace military equipment that was no longer useable, although the Paris Peace Accords permitted this.

The antiwar Congress of 1973–75 reflected the American public's weariness with the Vietnam conflict and the corruption and weakness of the South Vietnamese government. The Watergate crisis further undermined confidence in American government, allowed Congress to assert itself in foreign affairs, and weakened President Ford's ability to rally support for the beleaguered South Vietnamese government. A badly weakened executive, a strongly antiwar Congress, and a war-weary American public proved to be too much. South Vietnam fell in April 1975.[30]

Finally, an understanding of the Vietnam War would not be complete without an understanding of the aftermath of the war and the triumph of the antiwar movement in forcing America's withdraw from Vietnam and its wholesale abandonment of South Vietnam. Far from leading to a Socialist paradise, the Communist takeover of Vietnam led to a nightmare for hundreds

---

27 "On This Day: May 31," BBC News, http://news.bbc.co.uk/onthisday/hi/dates/stories/may/31/newsid_2481000/2481543.stm.

28 Ibid.

29 James Rothrock, *Divided We Fall: How Disunity Leads to Defeat* (AuthorHouse, 2006), Google Books edition, 312, https://books.google.com/books?id=e6POVwba0oAC&pg=PA311&lpg=PA311&dq=democrats+cut+off+funding+to+South+Vietnam&source=bl&ots=qS6ty-p-VZ&sig=RJ3QAsu1-TYwbsSR-j5KTnUnEcE&hl=en&sa=X&ei=n24EVfaSB4S-ggTLgYHwBw&ved=0CDMQ6AEwBDgU#v=onepage&q=democrats%20cut%20off%20funding%20to%20South%20Vietnam&f=false.

30 Lauren Zanolli, "What Happens When Democrats Cut Off Funding for the War in Iraq?," *History News Network* (George Mason University), April 13, 2007, http://historynewsnetwork.org/article/31400; Barry Sussman, "Cutting the Funding for the Vietnam War: A Precedent for Iraq?," *Nieman Watchdog Blog*, January 9, 2007, http://www.niemanwatchdog.org/blog/?p=63.

of thousands of Vietnamese shipped off to "reeducation camps" or executed. It led to the mass exodus of tens of thousands of "boat people" from Vietnam, many of whom ultimately made their way to the United States and went on to lead productive and prosperous lives. As many predicted, Vietnam's Southeast Asian neighbors, Laos and Cambodia, fell to Communist forces and suffered their own horrific massacres at the hands of their Communist revolutionaries.[31]

Some of today's politicians, academics, educators, and cultural icons grew up during the ferment of the Vietnam War. Increasingly, however, many of them are too young to have lived through the Vietnam period. After all, today's fifty-year-olds were born in 1965. They were ten years old in 1975 when South Vietnam fell. Their college years were the early 1980s, not the 1960s.

It is true that today's fifty-year-olds were taught by professors and raised by parents who came of age in the 1960s and whose world views were shaped by the 1960s. Nevertheless, one might expect that the influence of the Vietnam War on American policy and culture might attenuate with the passage of time and the departure of the Vietnam generation from positions of influence. Regrettably, the most recent wars in Iraq and Afghanistan seem to demonstrate that the legacy and influence of Vietnam, far from diminishing with time, remains as powerful as ever and is in some ways more powerful.

---

31 John Mueller, "The Iraq Syndrome," *Foreign Affairs*, November/December 2005, http://www.foreignaffairs.com/articles/61196/john-mueller/the-iraq-syndrome.

CHAPTER 3

September 11, the War on Terror, and the Antiwar Movement's Next Generation

AMERICANS WHO LIVED THROUGH THE events of September 11, 2001, will never forget where they were or what they were doing when news of the attacks on New York and Washington trickled in and the nature and scope of the attacks came into focus. The days after 9/11 recalled America's times of greatest national trauma, including Pearl Harbor and the Cuban missile crisis. In those dark days, Americans displayed flags, wore flag pins, and unified behind the president and government in a way rarely seen before or since. The French paper *Le Monde* published an editorial declaring that "we are all Americans."[32] Politics, at least for a few weeks and months, took a backseat as the US government considered its options for retaliation.

It didn't last.

The Political Debate over Iraq

In many ways, the movement opposing the Iraq War picked up right where the Vietnam War antiwar protest movement left off, and it did so even as the Iraq War was still being debated in Congress and at the United Nations. Unlike the protests against the Vietnam War, which grew to a crescendo over the course of a decade in combat, the antiwar protest movement of the 2000s

32 Editorial, "Nous sommes tous Américains," *Le Monde*, September 13, 2001, http://www.lemonde.fr/idees/article/2007/05/23/nous-sommes-tous-americains_913706_3232.html.

was born fully formed, organized, and ready to mimic its antiwar predecessor of a generation before.

Although even the United States' invasion of Afghanistan to topple the Taliban and eradicate al-Qaeda met some resistance, the war had tremendous popular support at home and abroad. The United States indisputably had a casus belli; no one on the planet could have expected that the United States would not take action in response to 9/11.

Iraq, however, posed a different set of challenges for the United States. Although the US government did not have evidence directly linking the Iraqi regime of Saddam Hussein to the 9/11 attacks, the United States also had been the victim of bioterror attacks shortly after 9/11, as envelopes laced with anthrax arrived at a number of federal government offices. The attacks caused the illness and death of a number of postal workers and caused enormous fear and disruption, shutting down Senate office buildings and requiring new protocols for handling mail received by the federal government. Policy makers considering al-Qaeda's unorthodox but cataclysmic conventional terrorist attacks of 9/11 had to ask themselves about the possibility of al-Qaeda, another terrorist group, or a state sponsor of terror acquiring weapons of mass destruction (WMD) from a rogue state or other source. The consequences of a successful biological, chemical, or nuclear attack on the US homeland were and still are difficult to contemplate.

The US government was no stranger to concerns about WMD in Iraq. Even after the United States ejected Iraq from Kuwait in the 1991 Gulf War, Iraq remained a source of major WMD concern for the United States. In October 1997, Iraq expelled UN weapons inspectors carrying out the WMD inspection regime established after the Gulf War.[33] Although the Iraqis readmitted the inspectors after the United States and the United Kingdom began to build up forces in the Gulf for a possible invasion, the Iraqis continued to thwart the inspectors' efforts. Most significantly, the Iraqis refused to grant the inspection teams access to Saddam's palaces scattered throughout Iraq.[34]

---

33 US Department of Defense, "Chronology from Desert Storm to Desert Fox," http://archive.defense.gov/specials/desert_fox/timeline.html.

34 Ibid.

Throughout 1998, tensions simmered as Iraq did not cooperate fully with the UN inspections. On December 16, 1998, after two separate Iraqi moves to eject UN inspectors, President Clinton launched Operation Desert Fox.[35] The Pentagon's web page describing Operation Desert Fox states that the mission was "to strike military and security targets in Iraq that contribute to Iraq's ability to produce, store, maintain and deliver weapons of mass destruction."[36]

In 2002, when the United States began to make the case for ending the threat of Iraqi WMD, the world's leading intelligence agencies had reached a consensus that the Iraqis had active WMD programs, certainly in the biological and chemical realm and possibly in the nuclear realm as well. The US, British, French, and Russian intelligence agencies all had reached this conclusion.[37] CIA director George Tenet—who was originally named CIA director by Democrat Bill Clinton and retained by Republican George Bush—famously stated that the CIA believed the case that Iraq had active WMD programs was a "slam dunk."[38]

Congress joined in the chorus of concern about Iraq's WMD program. Democrats in 2002 did not dispute that Iraq had active WMD programs. In September 2002, former vice president Al Gore—less than two years removed from serving as vice president and having access to the most inside information and intelligence—stated that "we know that [Saddam Hussein] has stored away secret supplies of biological weapons and chemical weapons throughout his country."[39] In that same speech, Gore warned that "Iraq's search for weapons of mass destruction has proven impossible to completely deter, and we should assume that it will continue for as long as Saddam is in power."[40]

---

35 Ibid.

36 US Department of Defense, "Operation Desert Fox," http://archive.defense.gov/specials/desert_fox/.

37 Kenneth Pollack, "Spies, Lies, and Weapons: What Went Wrong," *The Atlantic*, January/February 2004, http://www.theatlantic.com/magazine/archive/2004/01/spies-lies-and-weapons-what-went-wrong/302878/.

38 "Woodward: Tenet Told Bush WMD Case Was a 'Slam Dunk,'" CNN, April 19, 2004, http://www.cnn.com/2004/ALLPOLITICS/04/18/woodward.book/.

39 "Text: Gore Assails Bush's Policy," *Washington Post On Politics Blog*, September 23, 2002, http://www.washingtonpost.com/wp-srv/politics/transcripts/gore_text092302.html.

40 Ibid.

Quotations from leading Democrats as the United States moved toward war with Iraq evince the grave concerns they harbored over Iraq's WMD programs. Congress expressed bipartisan alarm at the prospect of active Iraqi WMD programs. Democrats not only voted for the Iraq War resolution; they vociferously denounced Saddam Hussein and his efforts to obtain WMD:

Sen. John Edwards, speech to the Council on Foreign Relations, October 7, 2002: My position is very clear: The time has come for decisive action to eliminate the threat posed by Saddam Hussein's weapons of mass destruction. I am a co-sponsor of the bipartisan resolution we're currently considering.

Saddam Hussein's regime is a grave threat to America and our allies—including our vital ally, Israel. For more than 20 years, Saddam has obsessively sought weapons of mass destruction through every possible means. We know that he has chemical and biological weapons today, that he has used them in the past, and that he is doing everything he can to build more. Every day he gets closer to his longtime goal of nuclear capability. We must not allow him to get nuclear weapons...

Nothing must undermine the central goal of disarming Iraq...

We must make a genuine commitment to help build a democratic Iraq after the fall of Saddam. And let's be clear: a genuine commitment means a real commitment of time, resources, and yes, leadership.[41]

Sen. John Kerry, US Senate floor speech, October 9, 2002: It is clear that in the four years since the UNSCOM inspectors were forced out, Saddam Hussein has continued his quest for weapons of mass destruction. According to the CIA's unclassified report released last Friday, Iraq has chemical and biological weapons as well as missiles

41 Sen. John Edwards, "America's Role in the World," speech to the Center for Strategic and International Studies, October 7, 2002, Council on Foreign Relations, http://www.cfr.org/world/americas-role-world/p5441.

with ranges in excess of the 150 kilometer restriction imposed by the United Nations in the ceasefire resolution…

According to the CIA's report, all US intelligence experts agree that Iraq is seeking nuclear weapons. There is little question that Saddam Hussein wants to develop nuclear weapons…

In the wake of September 11, who among us can discount the possibility that those weapons might be used against our troops or our allies in the region? And while the administration has failed to prove any direct link between Iraq and the events of September 11, can we afford to ignore the possibility that Saddam Hussein might provide weapons of destruction to some terrorist group bent on destroying the United States? Can we really leave this to chance, when we could eliminate this deadly threat by acting now in concert with the international community, or alone if the threat is imminent—which it is not now? In my view, we cannot. The Iraqi regime's record over the decade leaves little doubt that Saddam Hussein wants to retain his arsenal of weapons of mass destruction and to expand it to include nuclear weapons. We cannot allow him to prevail in that quest. The weapons are an unacceptable threat. And if the Iraqi regime refuses to allow the international community to find and destroy those weapons through a non-negotiable, immediate, unfettered and unconditional inspection process, then together with the international community, we will be justified in going to war to eliminate the threat…[42]

Mr. President, I will be voting to give the President of the United States the authority to use force—if necessary—to disarm Saddam Hussein because I believe that a deadly arsenal of weapons of mass destruction in his hands is a real and grave threat to our security and that of our allies in the Persian Gulf region.

42 "Remarks of Senator John Kerry on Iraq," October 9, 2002, http://web.archive.org/web/20040610230230/http://www.johnkerry.com/pressroom/speeches/spc_2002_1009.html.

Sen. Hillary Clinton, US Senate floor speech, October 10, 2002: In the four years since the inspectors left, intelligence reports show that Saddam Hussein has worked to rebuild his chemical and biological weapons stock, his missile delivery capability, and his nuclear program. He has also given aid, comfort, and sanctuary to terrorists, including Al Qaeda members, though there is apparently no evidence of his involvement in the terrible events of September 11, 2001.

It is clear, however, that if left unchecked, Saddam Hussein will continue to increase his capacity to wage biological and chemical warfare, and will keep trying to develop nuclear weapons. Should he succeed in that endeavor, he could alter the political and security landscape of the Middle East, which as we know all too well affects American security.

Now this much is undisputed.[43]

John Kerry, January 23, 2003: Without question, we need to disarm Saddam Hussein. He is a brutal, murderous dictator, leading an oppressive regime. We all know the litany of his offenses. He presents a particularly grievous threat because he is so consistently prone to miscalculation. He miscalculated an eight-year war with Iran. He miscalculated the invasion of Kuwait. He miscalculated America's response to that act of naked aggression. He miscalculated the result of setting oil rigs on fire. He miscalculated the impact of sending Scuds into Israel and trying to assassinate an American President. He miscalculated his own military strength. He miscalculated the Arab world's response to his misconduct. And now he is miscalculating America's response to his continued deceit and his consistent grasp for weapons of mass destruction.[44]

---

43 "Floor Speech of Sen. Hillary Rodham Clinton," October 10, 2002, http://web.archive.org/web/20080723141509/http://clinton.senate.gov/speeches/iraq_101002.html.

44 "Foreign Policy Speech at Georgetown University," January 23, 2003, http://web.archive.org/web/20040411164128/http://www.johnkerry.com/pressroom/speeches/spc_2003_0123.html.

Moreover, although the US government did not emphasize it in the run-up to the Iraq War, Saddam Hussein's regime was one of the world's most brutal. Saddam's Iraq was a charnel house. The regime killed opponents using wood chippers. It used poison gas on the Kurds in northern Iraq. The regime brutally tortured and murdered Iraqi athletes who failed to win at international sporting competitions, including the Olympics.[45] This was no liberal regime the United States proposed to remove. Many of those who voted for the Iraq War resolution cited Saddam's suppression of the Shia, the gassing of the Kurds in Halabja in 1994, and other horrors Saddam Hussein visited on Iraqis during his rule.

Ultimately, future vice president Joe Biden and future secretaries of state Hillary Clinton and John Kerry all voted in support of the Iraq War resolution. However, they and many other politicians included with their vote a criticism that the United States had been acting "unilaterally" in advocating possible military action against Saddam Hussein. They emphasized the need to get UN resolutions and build an international coalition. As Americans were to learn later, hidden within these admonishments and criticisms was an implicit "out clause" for these supporters of the war. If the war was not successful, they could go back in time and claim that all diplomatic avenues had not been exhausted. They could claim that the international coalition was not large enough. They could claim that the United States "rushed to war."

The Antiwar Movement Ramps Up

Despite the ostensible support of the Democrats—the political party that today is generally less disposed to the use of force abroad—for ending Iraq's WMD threat, using force if necessary, the antiwar movement revved up to full speed well before the Iraq War began. Unlike with Vietnam, the antiwar movement

45 Suzanne Goldenberg, "Footballers Who Paid the Penalty for Failure," *The Guardian*, April 18, 2003, http://www.theguardian.com/world/2003/apr/19/iraq.football; Don Yaeger, "Son of Saddam: As Iraq's Top Olympic Official, Uday Hussein Is Accused of the Torture and Murder of Athletes Who Fail to Win," *Sports Illustrated*, March 24, 2003, http://www.si.com/vault/2003/03/24/340225/son-of-saddam-as-iraqs-top-olympic-official-uday-hussein-is-accused-of-the-torture-and-murder-of-athletes-who-fail-to-win.

launched and gained tremendous public attention before the war even began. Nevertheless, the anti–Iraq War protest movement that launched even before the war began mirrored its 1960s forebears in many ways—consciously and unconsciously.

Indeed, it is hard not to think that some of the antiwar opposition that grew up around the Iraq War even before the war began was a self-conscious attempt by entertainers, students, protest veterans, and others to recreate the protest movement and spirit of the 1960s. The Iraq War represented an opportunity for a new generation of campus activists, celebrities in Hollywood and elsewhere, and others to participate in a Vietnam-style antiwar movement, and it gave Vietnam-era activists an opportunity to relive the antiwar movement. Iraq represented a cause and moral crusade they could join, following in the footsteps of their antiwar movement forerunners during the Vietnam era. The Iraq War provided artists who missed the 1960s an opportunity to demonstrate their courage and progressive bona fides.

Entertainers were quick to oppose the war and ostentatiously proclaim their opposition in the most public of forums. During the 2003 Academy Awards, when announcing an Oscar winner, actor Gael Garcia Bernal said that if Frida Kahlo, the artist who at the time was the subject of a popular biopic, was alive, she would be against the Iraq War. Not long after, singer Sheryl Crow wore a guitar strap emblazoned with the words *No War* during a performance at the 2003 Grammy Awards. A lovely sentiment, perhaps, but one to which the 9/11 hijackers, the USS *Cole* bombers, or the 1998 embassy bombers were unlikely to have subscribed.

Even before the Iraq War began, in the run-up to war, a number of Hollywood celebrities organized themselves as the Artists United to Win Without War. Noted leftist celebrities Mike Farrell, Ed Asner, Susan Sarandon, Tim Robbins, Martin Sheen, and others were part of the group.[46] Revitalizing the old criticism of the military-industrial complex, Asner said, "I think that they have keyed and geared the war machine—which is costing us enormous

46 United Press International, "Celebrities Urge Bush to Avoid Iraq War," December 10, 2002, http://www.upi.com/Odd_News/2002/12/10/Celebrities-urge-Bush-to-avoid-Iraq-war/97531039550943/.

billions of dollars—that they've got to unload it someplace. Iraq is the likeliest place."[47] He went on to accuse President Bush of being a warmongering cowboy and the American people of being "sheep," saying that "[the American people] like him enough to credit him with saving the nation after 9/11. Three thousand people get killed, and everybody thinks they're next on the list. The president comes along, and he's got his six-guns strapped on, and people think he's going to save them."[48]

These activists did not speak out during Operation Desert Fox in Iraq in 1998 or the US air war to protect and ultimately liberate Kosovo from Serbia in 1999.[49] These wars, unlike the Iraq War, did not involve significant levels of ground troops. The United States primarily fought these wars from the air. Moreover, these wars did not include a lead-up and debate lasting several months in the same way the Iraq War did.

Antiwar activism is not risky. After all, most people are not "pro-war." Very few people *want* to launch offensive wars. The consequences of opposing wars are not great. Nevertheless, after Vietnam, the US public came to lionize antiwar protesters. The Iraq War presented Hollywood the opportunity to "take a stand" and join the line of proud, ostentatious Hollywood antiwar protesters that began in the Vietnam era.

Tim Robbins's speech to the National Press Club in April 2003, one month after the Iraq War began, is an orgy of martyrdom, self-congratulation, and faux boldness that epitomizes perfectly the frisson these celebrities likely felt when they publicly opposed the Iraq War. It also captures clearly their vision of themselves as the successors to the Vietnam generation of antiwar protesters. Robbins told the Press Club audience,

> In the 19 months since 9/11, we have seen our democracy compromised by fear and hatred. Basic inalienable rights, due process, the sanctity of the home have been quickly compromised in a climate

47 Ibid.

48 Ibid.

49 Peter Baker, "Sean Penn Visits Iraq, Pleads for Peace," *SFGate*, December 16, 2002, http://www.sfgate.com/politics/article/Sean-Penn-visits-Iraq-pleads-for-peace-Actor-2711007.php.

> of fear. A unified American public has grown bitterly divided, and a world population that had profound sympathy and support for us has grown contemptuous and distrustful, viewing us as we once viewed the Soviet Union, as a rogue state.
>
> This past weekend, Susan and I and the three kids went to Florida for a family reunion of sorts. Amidst the alcohol and the dancing, sugar-rushing children, there was, of course, talk of the war. And the most frightening thing about the weekend was the amount of times we were thanked for speaking out against the war because that individual speaking thought it unsafe to do so in their own community, in their own life. Keep talking, they said; I haven't been able to open my mouth…
>
> A chill wind is blowing in this nation. A message is being sent through the White House and its allies in talk radio and Clear Channel and Cooperstown. If you oppose this administration, there can and will be ramifications.
>
> Every day, the air waves are filled with warnings, veiled and unveiled threats, spewed invective and hatred directed at any voice of dissent. And the public, like so many relatives and friends that I saw this weekend, sit in mute opposition and fear.
>
> And in the midst of all this madness, where is the political opposition? Where have all the Democrats gone? Long time passing, long time ago.[50]

One can almost hear Robbins's perception of himself as a martyr, sacrificed in the crusade of what he perceives to be this generation's frothing-at-the-mouth Republican McCarthyites. As if to emphasize and make plain his connection to the antiwar protest movement, he referenced "Where Have All the Flowers Gone," a song written by Pete Seeger that particularly caught on with the

50 "Text of Tim Robbins Speech," *World News Daily*, April 16, 2003, http://www.wnd.com/2003/04/18309/.

1960s antiwar movement in a version sung by Peter, Paul and Mary.[51] Yet it is difficult to understand what country he was talking about. "Warnings"? "Veiled and unveiled threats"? "Spewed invective and hatred"? To what on earth was he referring? Certainly the decision to go to war was contentious. But President Bush *did* go to the United Nations, spending six months there, from October 2002 through March 2003, aiming to win international support. He *did* seek to build an international coalition. Far from stifling voices of dissent, he acceded to the wishes of many of the protesters and much of the American public by seeking international support for action against Iraq.

Moreover, President Bush and other administration officials implored Americans not to retaliate against Muslims living in the United States and repeatedly referred to Islam as a "religion of peace." The US government went out of its way to make clear it was not making war on the Muslim faith but only against terrorists who politicians repeatedly stated relied upon a warped view of Islam. The United States went so far as to change the name of its military operation in Afghanistan from Operation Infinite Justice to Operation Enduring Freedom after Muslim complaints that only G-d can mete out justice.[52]

In any event, Robbins did not seem to have suffered personally from his opposition to the Iraq War. Imbd.com lists Robbins as having twenty-four movie credits since 2004. It is true that, in 2003, at the beginning of the Iraq War, the National Baseball Hall of Fame canceled a fifteenth-anniversary screening of *Bull Durham* to which Robbins and his equally outspoken companion Susan Sarandon had been invited. However, in the ensuing fury, Robbins was interviewed on HBO's *On the Record* by Bob Costas, and the Hall of Fame apologized.[53] Stalinist Russia it wasn't.

---

51 David Hadju, "Where Has 'Where Have All the Flowers Gone?' Gone," *The New Republic*, June 28, 2004, http://www.newrepublic.com/article/where-has-where-have-all-the-flowers-gone.

52 "Infinite Justice, Out—Enduring Freedom, In," BBC News, September 25, 2001, http://news.bbc.co.uk/2/hi/americas/1563722.stm.

53 "*Bull Durham* Stars to Appear in Costas's Premiere," *New York Times*, April 23, 2003, http://www.nytimes.com/2003/04/23/sports/baseball/23hall.html; "Hall President Apologizes to Actors," *New York Times*, April 19, 2003, http://www.nytimes.com/2003/04/19/sports/hall-president-apologizes-to-actors.html.

Sean Penn is another actor who proudly and ostentatiously opposed the war before it even began. Penn went so far as to visit Iraq in December 2002, where he met with officials of the Iraqi government and "challenged President Bush to put up or shut up by disclosing any evidence of weapons of mass destruction held by Iraq."[54]

Despite their outspoken opposition to the Iraq war, Penn and Robbins both appeared in 2003's *Mystic River.* Both Penn and Robbins won Academy Awards in February 2004 for their performances in that movie, Penn for Best Actor and Robbins for Best Supporting Actor. It is difficult to conclude that they suffered for their opposition to the Iraq War when they won Academy Awards within a year of their antiwar protests.

Despite the fact that opponents of the war suffered little professional impact, the idea that the Bush administration was launching an assault on civil liberties and dissent took hold within segments of the American public. Pretty soon, opponents of the war were regularly telling the world that dissent was the highest form of patriotism. They would turn indignant about anyone questioning their patriotism, even when only their opinions were challenged and not their patriotism. Nevertheless, the idea that the Bush administration was systematically attacking and eroding American civil liberties undermined the Bush administration's arguments for bringing democracy to Iraq. It also subtly aligned today's antiwar movement with the victims of the McCarthy Red Scare of the 1950s. Just as the victims of McCarthyism are lionized as heroes today, so too could the antiwar activists supposedly suffering for their outspoken opposition to the war take their place in the pantheon of free speech heroes.

Another organization of artists calling itself Not in Our Name issued a "statement of conscience" opposing the Iraq War in full-page ads in the *New York Times, Los Angeles Times,* and *USA Today* in September and October 2002, several months before the war began. The statement included the following:

> Let it not be said that people in the United States did nothing when their government declared a war without limit and instituted stark new measures of repression…

54 Baker, "Sean Penn Visits Iraq, Pleads for Peace."

We believe that peoples and nations have the right to determine their own destiny, free from military coercion by great powers. We believe that all persons detained or prosecuted by the United States government should have the same rights of due process. We believe that questioning, criticism, and dissent must be valued and protected. We understand that such rights and values are always contested and must be fought for.

We believe that people of conscience must take responsibility for what their own governments do—we must first of all oppose the injustice that is done in our own name. Thus we call on all Americans to RESIST the war and repression that has been loosed on the world by the Bush administration. It is unjust, immoral, and illegitimate. We choose to make common cause with the people of the world.

We too watched with shock the horrific events of September 11, 2001. We too mourned the thousands of innocent dead and shook our heads at the terrible scenes of carnage—even as we recalled similar scenes in Baghdad, Panama City, and, a generation ago, Vietnam. We too joined the anguished questioning of millions of Americans who asked why such a thing could happen.

But the mourning had barely begun, when the highest leaders of the land unleashed a spirit of revenge. They put out a simplistic script of "good vs. evil" that was taken up by a pliant and intimidated media. They told us that asking why these terrible events had happened verged on treason. There was to be no debate. There were by definition no valid political or moral questions. The only possible answer was to be war abroad and repression at home.

In our name, the Bush administration, with near unanimity from Congress, not only attacked Afghanistan but arrogated to itself and its allies the right to rain down military force anywhere and anytime. The brutal repercussions have been felt from the Philippines to Palestine, where Israeli tanks and bulldozers have left a terrible trail of death and destruction. The government now openly prepares to wage all-out war on Iraq—a country which has no connection to the horror of September 11. What kind of world will this become if the US government has a blank check to drop commandos, assassins, and bombs wherever it wants?

In our name, within the US, the government has created two classes of people: those to whom the basic rights of the US legal system are at least promised, and those who now seem to have no rights at all. The government rounded up over 1,000 immigrants and detained them in secret and indefinitely. Hundreds have been deported and hundreds of others still languish today in prison. This smacks of the infamous concentration camps for Japanese Americans in World War 2. For the first time in decades, immigration procedures single out certain nationalities for unequal treatment.

In our name, the government has brought down a pall of repression over society. The President's spokesperson warns people to "watch what they say." Dissident artists, intellectuals, and professors find their views distorted, attacked, and suppressed. The so-called Patriot Act—along with a host of similar measures on the state level—gives police sweeping new powers of search and seizure, supervised if at all by secret proceedings before secret courts.

In our name, the executive has steadily usurped the roles and functions of the other branches of government. Military tribunals with lax rules of evidence and no right to appeal to the regular courts are put in place by executive order. Groups are declared "terrorist" at the stroke of a presidential pen...

President Bush has declared: "you're either with us or against us." Here is our answer: We refuse to allow you to speak for all the American people. We will not give up our right to question. We will not hand over our consciences in return for a hollow promise of safety. We say NOT IN OUR NAME. We refuse to be party to these wars and we repudiate any inference that they are being waged in our name or for our welfare. We extend a hand to those around the world suffering from these policies; we will show our solidarity in word and deed.

> We also draw on the many examples of resistance and conscience from the past of the United States: from those who fought slavery with rebellions and the underground railroad, *to those who defied the Vietnam war by refusing orders, resisting the draft, and standing in solidarity with resisters.*
>
> Let us not allow the watching world today to despair of our silence and our failure to act. Instead, let the world hear our pledge: we will resist the machinery of war and repression and rally others to do everything possible to stop it.[55]

This letter reflects a cornucopia of different strands commonly found within the antiwar protest movement. The statement is thick with references to anticolonialism—for example, the statement that "peoples and nations have the right to determine their own destiny, free from military coercion by great powers" and the notion that "war and repression [had] been loosed on the world by the Bush administration." The reference to "Israeli tanks and bulldozers" leaving a "terrible trail of death and destruction" further evinces the authors' anticolonialist mind-set and gives the letter particular anticolonialist panache. The world is full of tyrants and dictators who commit the grossest human rights violations. But the authors of this letter saw fit to uniquely single out democratic Israel, a country that no one in good faith can claim is less respectful of human rights than North Korea, Cuba, Sudan, Syria, Russia, or Iran.

There is also an overweening sense of martyrdom, as evidenced in the statements that "the government has brought down a pall of repression over society" and that "dissident artists, intellectuals, and professors find their views distorted, attacked, and suppressed." The signatories envision themselves as the next in the line of artists persecuted for their beliefs, the latest victims of McCarthyism.

---

55 "Not in Our Name Statement of Conscience," Artists Network of Refuse and Resist, https://web.archive.org/web/20090106030431/http://artists.refuseandresist.org/news4/news170.html (emphasis added).

The statement also included a level of moral equivalence between the events of 9/11 and previous American wars. The signatories said that they shook their heads at the carnage on 9/11—and then immediately referenced what they implied was American-caused carnage in Baghdad, Panama City, and Vietnam. By lumping 9/11 in with past American wars, they sought to equate those past American military actions with an attack intended to kill as many innocent civilians as possible.

Hovering over all of this, as the authors themselves make clear, is the comparison of themselves "to those who defied the Vietnam war by refusing orders, resisting the draft, and standing in solidarity with resisters." The authors of this protest letter openly associate the September 11 attacks with Vietnam when, in describing their reaction to the September 11 attacks, they state that "we too mourned the thousands of innocent dead and shook our heads at the terrible scenes of carnage—even as we recalled similar scenes in Baghdad, Panama City, and, a generation ago, Vietnam." For these antiwar protesters, it all comes back to Vietnam; it is their alpha and omega.

The statement is also notable for just how overwrought it is. The idea that anything the US government did in the wake of the September 11 attacks was at all similar to the internment of Japanese Americans in World War II is an absurd, hyperbolic calumny. As noted previously, President Bush went to extraordinary lengths to praise Islam as a religion of peace.[56] Politicians from all across the spectrum urged American citizens not to engage in retaliation against American Muslims or, more generally, "Islamophobia." And Americans heeded these calls. No outbreak of Islamophobia occurred.

The signatories to the Not in Our Name statement are a who's who of the antiwar left and antiwar celebrities, including from the Vietnam era. Signatories included Tom Hayden, Noam Chomsky, Daniel Ellsburg, Edward Said, Pete Seeger, Susan Sarandon, John Cusack, Jane Fonda, Howard Zinn,

56 "Islam is Peace, Says President," remarks by the President at Islamic Center of Washington, DC, September 17, 2001, http://georgewbush-whitehouse.archives.gov/news/releases/2001/09/20010917-11.html.

Lawrence Ferlinghetti, Mumia Abu-Jamal, Jesse Jackson, Al Sharpton, Martin Sheen, and Bernardine Dohrn.[57]

Not in Our Name held antiwar rallies in a number of US cities on October 6, 2002. The rally in New York's Central Park drew approximately twenty thousand people to oppose the possibility of war in Iraq.[58] The rally itself was organized by the International Action Center (IAC), which was affiliated with the organizing wing of the Not in Our Name movement, the Not in Our Name Project.[59] The IAC had close ties to a number of radical Communist organizations. It opposed any action against Saddam Hussein, even the containment strategy the West used throughout the 1990s, and believed that the United States had the worst human rights record on earth.[60]

Not in Our Name continued to channel the 1960s protest movement with a rally and concert at the Berkeley Community Theater in Berkeley, California, on January 31, 2003. The concert was a benefit for the Central Committee for Conscientious Objectors and the Not in Our Name campaign.[61]

Artists were not alone in opposing the Iraq War. International Act Now to Stop War and End Racism (International ANSWER) brought together a coalition of traditional protesters to oppose the Iraq War. As one activist said, "Students, anti-globalisation street activists, and old-time peaceniks alike appreciate ANSWER's knack for mobilizing the unaffiliated and turning out the Arab-American community."[62]

International ANSWER, MoveOn.org, and others organized large protests in the fall of 2002 and winter of 2003 opposing the war in Iraq. Approximately 150,000 antiwar protesters took to the streets of Washington, DC, and San

---

57 "A Statement of Conscience: Not in Our Name," Not in Our Name, http://www.envirosagainstwar.org/sayno/NION.pdf.

58 Lisa Featherstone, "Peace Gets a Chance," *The Nation*, October 10, 2002, http://www.thenation.com/article/peace-gets-chance/.

59 Michelle Goldberg, "Peace Kooks," *Salon*, October 16, 2002, http://www.salon.com/2002/10/16/protest_14/.

60 Ibid.

61 http://artists.refuseandresist.org/news7/news327.html.

62 Karen Simonson, "The Antiwar Movement: Waging Peace on the Brink of War," Centre for Applied Studies in International Negotiation, March 2003, 8.

Francisco on October 26, 2002. ANSWER held the Washington, DC, rally near the Vietnam Veterans Memorial. C-SPAN began its coverage of the rally just as a rapper was on stage singing "no blood for oil."[63] Protesters held signs with President Bush's face dripping oil from an oil mustache. It only took ten minutes from the time C-SPAN began covering the protest for a speaker to reference the Gulf of Tonkin Resolution and how it was based on a lie. The very first speaker said that "the people stopped the Vietnam War and we can stop this war [the Iraq War]." Later speakers also said that protesters needed to stop the Iraq War before it started the same way that protesters stopped the Vietnam War. Jesse Jackson, a speaker at the protest, said that "Dr. King would be especially happy to see so many young people energizing a new peace movement in America." Jackson also said that the war would result in the United States controlling Iraqi oil and raising defense contracts. Al Sharpton, also speaking at the protest, said that President Bush was bent on fighting a war over oil.

Massive antiwar protests took place all over the world on February 15, 2003, about a month before the Iraq war began. Millions of people marched in London, New York, San Francisco, Barcelona, Rome, and elsewhere after "calls to action were issued to 'freaks, puppetistas, drummers, musicians, singers and loud hummers, samba bands, jugglers, fire eaters, ravers, Vikings, critical massers, radical rockettes, those united for peace and justice and anybody and everybody who thinks that this war is absurd' in preparation to 'mock the axis of oil'—and they were answered in what many describe as a vibrant, electric, festive, celebration of peace with one serious demand: no war in Iraq."[64]

The February 15, 2003, New York protest featured a caricature of President Bush holding buckets of blood and oil.[65] Richie Havens sang "Freedom," just as he did at Woodstock.[66] The San Francisco protest featured a march-

63 C-SPAN coverage of antiwar rally, October 26, 2002, http://www.c-span.org/video/?173521-1/antiwar-rally.

64 Simonson at 13 and appendix F.

65 "Cities Jammed in Worldwide Protest of Iraq," CNN, February 16, 2003, http://www.cnn.com/2003/US/02/15/sprj.irq.protests.main/.

66 Sue Chan, "Massive Anti-War Outpouring," February 16, 2003, http://www.cbsnews.com/news/massive-anti-war-outpouring/.

er dressed as the Statue of Liberty, bound and gagged by another marcher dressed as Uncle Sam and swigging from a gasoline can.[67] London mayor Ken Livingstone told the assembled crowd in London that "this war is solely about oil. George Bush has never given a damn about human rights."[68] BBC News claimed that anywhere between six and ten million protesters marched all over the world on February 15, 2003, and that the protests were the largest since—you guessed it—the Vietnam War.[69]

One writer described the protests as follows: "Performers did skits, radical cheerleaders danced to anti-war chants, students and grey haired veterans, punks and hippies, street people, and hordes of ordinary citizens took part in the largest ever street party against war that the world has ever witnessed."[70] The first speaker at the Seattle rally on February 15 kicked off the event by addressing the crowd and saying, "There's a hell of a lot of gray ponytails out there."[71] The February 15 protests in New York featured tie-dyed flags with the peace symbol and more American flags with peace symbols replacing the stars, a classic 1960s protest prop.[72] New York City protesters on March 19, 2003, chanted, "George Bush, you can't hide, we charge you with genocide."

Such protests before a war even began were unprecedented. The earliest mass protest against Vietnam took place in 1965, after the United States had already committed to fighting the war, and drew approximately fifteen thousand people.[73] The protests grew as Vietnam escalated, more and more college graduates were drafted into the military, and battlefield success appeared elusive. Comparing the pre–Iraq War protests and the Vietnam protests of

---

67 "Millions Join Global Anti-War Protests," BBC News, February 17, 2003, http://news.bbc.co.uk/2/hi/europe/2765215.stm.

68 Ibid.

69 Ibid.

70 Simonson at 13.

71 "Pre-Iraq War Protest, Seattle, February 15, 2003: 'The World Says No to War,'" MobileUnit.tv, https://www.youtube.com/watch?v=yzhIDzworJA&index=6&list=PLDQB_6XE5ZBJnlBXiteWyt04Rk-pchuSd.

72 "Antiwar Protest in New York: Half a Million Protesters," video taken February 15, 2003, https://www.youtube.com/watch?v=HA8Ef4Lp6Z4.

73 John Ritter, "Voices against War Seem Muted," USA Today, October 6,2002, http://usatoday30.usatoday.com/news/nation/2002-10-06-protests_x.htm.

the mid-1960s, Tom Hayden, one of the protest movement's icons from the 1960s, said, "Right now there's much more anti-war protest than there was on the eve of the Vietnam War."[74]

Watching the protests, the commentary, the outspoken artists, and so on, the protests look like nothing so much as a pantomime of the Vietnam antiwar movement. The protests featured a variety of anticapitalist and anticolonial protesters, all opposing American intervention in foreign affairs. The protests were heavy on street theater and sixties-style chants. Artists and activists expressly compared their antiwar efforts to the movement to end the Vietnam War. The signs they held and the statements they made gave every indication that they planned to treat the Iraq War as this generation's Vietnam.

74 Ibid.

CHAPTER 4

As the Movement Turns: Growth of the Antiwar Movement in the Early Stages of the Iraq Occupation

THE INITIAL SUCCESS OF THE Iraq War led to a period of quiet for the antiwar movement. The joy of Iraqis freed from Saddam's tyrannical rule was undeniable. The images of Iraqis smacking portraits of Saddam with their shoes (a traditional sign of disrespect in Arab culture) and chiseling away at fallen statues of Saddam were genuinely moving. No one could truly suggest that the majority of ordinary Iraqis were saddened by the demise of Saddam and his psychopathic sons Uday and Qusay. Indeed, as the invasion revealed to the world the horrors of life in Saddam's Iraq, the invasion more and more appeared to be a true victory for human rights.

Yet even as the combat phase was winding down, the antiwar movement was already probing for ways to challenge the success of the defeat of the Baathist regime. One early example was the complaints from the arts community about the looting of the Mosul Museum after that city was liberated. Another complaint focused on the fact that a US soldier covered the face of a giant Saddam statue in Baghdad with an American flag as US forces toppled it. In these examples, the United States had achieved the silver lining of liberating Iraq from decades of misrule and government-sponsored human rights atrocities, and the antiwar movement desperately sought the cloud.

Nevertheless, events in Iraq took a turn for the worse as the Iraqi insurgency began in the summer of 2003. As the insurgency gained strength, the antiwar movement was quick to pounce on the war as a mistake and to reignite its criticism of the US action in Iraq.

The reinvigorated antiwar movement paralleled the Vietnam protest movement in critical ways. First, in large measure due to the 2004 presidential election, politicians initially unwilling to criticize the war during the prewar debates gradually became more full-throated critics of the war as it became less popular. Just as they had during the Vietnam era, antiwar activists set about finding a candidate to support and in time took over the Democratic Party. Antiwar politicians followed the protest movement; they did not lead it. In addition, activists and politicians took every opportunity to discredit the war and undermine its legitimacy, seeking an Iraq version of the Gulf of Tonkin Resolution to show that the Bush administration lied to bring the United States into war. Finally, just as in Vietnam, the antiwar movement and its elected supporters refused to acknowledge military successes, working overtime to claim that purported successes were based on false statistics—another Vietnam echo—or that successes could not be attributed to American military forces.

It is apparent from the statements and actions of the antiwar protagonists that Vietnam was never very far from their minds. Just as the prewar protests channeled Vietnam-era antiwar protests, the opposition to the Iraq War in 2004 and beyond reprised many of the same tactics as its Vietnam forebears.

The Iraq Opposition Consolidates: The 2004 Election

What supercharged the reigniting of the antiwar movement after the initial combat phase of the Iraq War ended was the US presidential election of 2004 and, particularly, the 2004 Democratic primaries. Just as in the Vietnam era, in 2004 there was an opening on the Left for an antiwar candidate. A healthy proportion of rank-and-file Democrats opposed the war. Yet many of the leading 2004 candidates—Sen. John Kerry, Sen. John Edwards, Sen. Joe Lieberman, and Rep. Dick Gephardt—all voted in favor of or supported the resolution authorizing the use of force in Iraq.[75] Senator Edwards had even

75 Adam Nagourney and Jodi Wilgoren, "At Debate, Democrats Clash over Middle East," *New York Times*, September 10, 2003, http://www.nytimes.com/2003/09/10/us/at-debate-democrats-clash-over-mideast.html; Glen Johnson and Raja Mishra, "Kerry Campaign Says Bush Misled US on Iraq," *Boston Globe*, July 11, 2004, http://www.boston.com/news/nation/articles/2004/07/11/kerry_campaign_says_bush_misled_us_on_iraq/?page=full.

cosponsored the Senate resolution, and Representative Gephardt had sponsored the House resolution.[76] Senator Kerry and Senator Lieberman had been outspoken on the Senate floor about the need to remove Saddam Hussein and Iraq's WMD threat. This left an opening for an antiwar candidate to claim the large antiwar faction of the Democratic Party, which yearned to find a standard bearer. Just as in Vietnam, the antiwar movement was a movement in search of a candidate and not the other way around. Whoever successfully positioned himself or herself as the antiwar candidate in the 2004 election had a ready-made set of supporters just waiting to flock to his or her banner.

In time, the candidate that won the heart of the antiwar movement was former Vermont governor Howard Dean. While some fringe Democratic candidates, like Rep. Dennis Kucinich and Al Sharpton, also opposed the war, Dean was able to rally the antiwar movement to his side. He told adoring crowds that he represented the "Democratic wing of the Democratic Party," a subtle suggestion that the other first-tier candidates had strayed from the party's roots and supported the Iraq War.[77] In his speech to the Democratic National Committee on February 21, 2003, after greeting his audience, Dean's first line was, "What I want to know is why in the world the Democratic party leadership is supporting the president's unilateral attack on Iraq."[78]

Unquestionably, Dean's antiwar stance made him the darling of Democratic voters in the fall of 2003. The issue of the war, more than any other, distinguished Dean from his rivals for the Democratic nomination. Ron Brownstein, a reporter and commentator for the *Los Angeles Times*, wrote that "opposition to the war in Iraq seems every bit as important to Dean's campaign as opposition to the Vietnam War was to George McGovern's

---

76 Authorization for the Use of Military Force in Iraq, S.J. Res. 46, October 2, 2002, https://www.congress.gov/bill/107th-congress/senate-joint-resolution/46; H.J. Res. 114, Authorization for the Use of Military Force in Iraq, October 2, 2002, https://www.congress.gov/bill/107th-congress/house-joint-resolution/114.

77 Remarks by Howard Dean, Democratic National Committee Winter Meeting, February 21, 2003, http://www.c-span.org/video/?c4456690/howard-dean-dnc-winter-meeting-address-feb-2003.

78 Ibid.

successful bid for the Democratic nomination in 1972."[79] Brownstein cited a CNN/Gallup poll that noted that three-fifths of Democrats thought the United States should never have invaded Iraq, and only 40 percent viewed the Iraq War as part of the war on terror. Perhaps most importantly, the survey—taken in August 2003—found that 70 percent of Americans thought the aftermath of the war was going badly.[80] A writer in the *Guardian* said that "if you had to boil [Dean's] success to a single equation it would probably read: Iraq + passion + internet."[81]

The consequences of the Dean surge immediately were apparent to the veteran political journalist Brownstein, who wrote,

> The force of [the antiwar] current has encouraged all the Democrats to more harshly criticize Bush's handling of the prewar intelligence and postwar reconstruction. In that way, Dean's rise guarantees Bush will face a more aggressive critique of the way he has managed the war and, especially, its aftermath, no matter who wins the Democratic race. After the grass-roots outpouring for Dean, no Democratic nominee can afford to submerge the issue as the party did in the 2002 midterm elections; Bush will have to work to defend his decisions.[82]

In the January 2004 Democratic primary debate at Saint Anselm College in New Hampshire, Dean was asked about a statement he made that his opponents' vote on the Iraq War resolution "call[ed] into question their judgment and ability to sort out complicated issues regarding the most crucial decision any president has to make." He answered,

---

79 Ronald Brownstein, "Dean's Antiwar Stance Creates a Force to be Reckoned With," *Los Angeles Times*, September 1, 2003, http://articles.latimes.com/2003/sep/01/nation/na-outlook1.

80 Ibid.

81 Tom Happold, "'The Democratic Wing of the Democratic Party,'" *The Guardian*, January 20, 2004, http://www.theguardian.com/world/2004/jan/20/uselections2004.usa8.

82 Ronald Brownstein, "Dean's Antiwar Stance Creates a Force to be Reckoned With."

> I do. We were presented with a series of facts. I came to a different conclusion than the senators did on those facts. My conclusion was that there was no Al Qaida in Iraq, as the president intimated. My conclusion was that Iraq was not about to acquire nuclear weapons, as the president intimated. My conclusion was that we'd successfully contained Saddam Hussein.
>
> I was able to sort out that the president was not being candid with the American people. We have lost 500 soldiers and 2,200 wounded. Those soldiers were sent there by the vote of Senator Lieberman and Senator Kerry and Senator Edwards. That is a fact. And I think that's a very serious matter. And it is a matter upon which we differ.[83]

In this statement, Dean made clear his strategy to assume the role of the antiwar candidate. He expressly distinguished himself from his rivals in the primaries, including Senators Kerry, Edwards, and Lieberman, on the issue of the war, holding their votes to authorize the use of force against them. Dean left no doubt that he had seized the antiwar mantle and would use it to separate himself from the pack in the primaries.

Of course, Dean's suggestion that he was more prescient and better able to "sort out" President Bush's alleged lack of candor than the other Democratic candidates regarding Iraq's weapons of mass destruction had the benefit of hindsight. Dean's claims that "we [presumably, the American people] were presented a series of facts" overstated the case. What President Bush and his administration presented the American people was a series of beliefs and concerns based on information American and other intelligence services had gathered over time. These were not conclusively proved facts but the best conclusions based on judgments about a country, Iraq, that was deliberately opaque and secretive about its weapons programs and for years had thwarted weapons inspectors. Moreover, the information Dean cited came not just from the Bush administration but from all of the world's major intelligence services.

---

83 "Howard Dean on War & Peace," *On the Issues*, http://www.ontheissues.org/2004/Howard_Dean_War_+_Peace.htm.

Dean also cleverly parsed his words, suggesting that President Bush "intimated" that Iraq was about to acquire nuclear weapons. Implicit in Dean's use of the term *intimated* was an admission that President Bush had never expressly alleged that Iraq was about to acquire nuclear weapons. Nor did President Bush claim that al-Qaeda was in Iraq or that Iraq had involvement in the 9/11 attacks. Nevertheless, Iraq was the cudgel that Dean used to batter his primary opponents repeatedly on the campaign trail.

As the only mainstream antiwar candidate, Dean drew the bulk of the antiwar Democrats to his campaign. His campaign took off like a rocket, largely on the strength of his anti–Iraq War stance. Before a single voter cast a single vote in the 2004 Democratic primaries, the upstart from Vermont posed a grave threat to the other Democratic candidates. Having assumed the antiwar mantle, the existing antiwar movement flocked to his banner.

With his uncompromising antiwar stance, Dean tapped into an antiwar strain within the Democratic Party that first achieved power and prominence during the Vietnam era and that has never truly gone away. While somewhat forgotten today, the 1991 Authorization for the Use of Military Force in Iraq, which allowed the first President Bush to launch the Gulf War and eject Saddam Hussein from Kuwait, barely passed the Senate by a vote of fifty-two to forty-seven.[84] Only ten of the forty-five Senate Democrats voted in favor of the measure. Sen. Paul Simon said it was the narrowest margin for authorizing the use of force since the War of 1812.[85]

Howard Dean himself was a somewhat unremarkable candidate. He did not have a substantial national following after his six (two-year) terms as governor of Vermont. He initially had no signature issue on which he was running. Dean's campaign manager, Joe Trippi, recalled in an interview that when Dean announced his exploratory committee for the 2004 presidential race, he wanted to make health care, early childhood development, and the

---

84 Sara Fritz and William J. Eaton, "Congress Authorizes Gulf War," *Los Angeles Times*, January 13, 1991, http://articles.latimes.com/1991-01-13/news/mn-374_1_persian-gulf.

85 Ibid.

deficit the issues of his campaign.[86] But as the Iraq War approached in early 2003, Dean's opposition to the war launched him out of the pack. The Pew Research Center released a survey in April 2005 that found that 66 percent of Dean primary voters cited the war in Iraq as the most important factor in supporting Dean.[87] According to the survey, the Iraq War far outpaced any other issue as the most important issue to Dean voters. Importantly, the Pew survey found that 79 percent of Dean supporters were college graduates, 41 percent had postgraduate or professional degrees, and 45 percent had incomes over $75,000.[88] Individuals falling into these categories are the types of individuals who are likely to go into government and policy-making activities or other avenues (journalism, academia, and think tanks) that influence American opinion.

The fact that Howard Dean enjoyed such stunning success in the early stages of the Democratic primary process over the course of 2003 was a testament to the strength of the antiwar movement and how strongly the antiwar protests influenced the 2004 primary process, just as the earlier antiwar movement influenced the 1968 primaries and forced President Johnson out of the race. The 2004 primary process demonstrated that the antiwar strain within the United States and the Democratic Party that developed during the Vietnam era never entirely disappeared. In the aftermath of the September 11 attacks, this antiwar element was understandably muted; it would have been difficult for any mainstream Democrat to have opposed the operation in

---

86 *Campaign for President: The Managers Look at 2004*, the Institute of Politics, the John F. Kennedy School of Government, and Harvard University, eds. (Rowman & Littlefield Publishers, 2005), 2, available at Google Books, https://books.google.com/books?id=N5MbWWz9sGcC&pg=PA2&lpg=PA2&dq=campaign+for+president:+the+managers+look+at+2004+woodruff+dean+trippi+early+childhood+health+care&source=bl&ots=RHaDme1ImU&sig=iKN0ao_T-LWGgmQ5lQFlVTlB3Dc&hl=en&sa=X&ved=0CB8Q6AEwAGoVChMIrcXY25SMyQIVRTM-Ch2oNwVW#v=onepage&q=campaign%20for%20president%3A%20the%20managers%20look%20at%202004%20woodruff%20dean%20trippi%20early%20childhood%20health%20care&f=false.

87 "An In-Depth Look: The Dean Activists; Their Profile and Prospects," Pew Research Center, April 6, 2005, http://www.people-press.org/2005/04/06/the-dean-activists-their-profile-and-prospects/, 3.

88 "An In-Depth Look: The Dean Activists; Their Profile and Prospects," Pew Research Center, April 6, 2005, 26.

Afghanistan to rout al-Qaeda and the Taliban in the wake of the attacks. But as the United States moved closer to war with Iraq, the latent antiwar segment of the Democratic Party began to stir.

The Lie that "Bush Lied"

Elected Democrats running for president, such as John Kerry and John Edwards, could have stood their ground, defended their votes, and defended the Iraq War in the face of Howard Dean's surging popularity. They could have advocated a different strategy to defeat the Iraqi insurgency and pacify Iraq. They could have reprised their prewar support for the Iraq War and explained once again that in a post-9/11 world, the possibility of a state sponsor of terrorism actively possessing or seeking weapons of mass destruction was no longer acceptable, if it ever was.

However, the pressure on these candidates from the insurgent Dean campaign, which had tapped into the antiwar movement and given it a candidate to unite around, was intense. By late 2003, the Dean campaign had all of the momentum and energy in the Democratic primary process. The fact that the antiwar movement had propelled Howard Dean to such success demonstrated just how strong the antiwar movement was within the Democratic Party and how out of step the Democratic presidential candidates had been with their base in supporting the Iraq war.

The Democratic candidates faced a difficult dilemma. If they stood by their support of the Iraq War, they surely would have no chance at winning the Democratic nomination. (Senator Lieberman maintained his support for the Iraq War during his 2004 presidential campaign, and one reporter later described that campaign as "an embarrassing flop; he was simply out of step with a liberal electorate."[89]) If they opposed the war, they would be contradicting their previous positions and arguably admitting error in their previous Iraq positions. Therefore, finding a way to oppose the war while being

89 Howard Kurtz, "Joe Lieberman's Slow-Motion Divorce from the Democratic Party," The Daily Beast, July 18, 2012, http://www.thedailybeast.com/articles/2012/07/18/joe-lieberman-s-slow-motion-divorce-from-the-democratic-party.html.

consistent with their past positions became a political imperative for the 2004 Democratic presidential candidates.

Unable or unwilling to defend their former support for the Iraq War and unable to admit error in supporting the war, these Democrats chose a third way: blaming President Bush for hoodwinking them into supporting the war and rushing the country to war without giving them an opportunity properly to consider the issues involved. With this neat trick, the candidates and others who previously supported the war attempted to absolve themselves of responsibility for the war and provide themselves a basis for joining the antiwar camp.

The decision by Democratic candidates to seize upon the argument that the Bush administration "lied" the United States into war was driven by the need to placate the antiwar movement and maintain their political viability in the 2004 election. In this way, just as in Vietnam, the antiwar movement led, and the politicians followed. In Vietnam, the antiwar movement had been a movement in search of a presidential candidate before finding Eugene McCarthy. In Iraq, the antiwar movement went in search of a presidential candidate and found Howard Dean. But in 2004, Dean's success came early enough in the presidential campaign that the other candidates had time to make course corrections and join the antiwar camp well before the first voting in Iowa and New Hampshire.

Having made the decision to claim they supported the Iraq war based on the Bush administration's false pretenses, the Democratic candidates and the Democratic Party had to emphasize in their public statements that the Bush administration "lied" the United States into war and had to seek additional evidence, wherever possible, to undermine the Bush administration's credibility. Opponents of the Iraq War, from the presidential candidates and other politicians to the media and the antiwar movement, became deeply invested in proving the Bush administration's perfidy. In order to maintain the idea that "Bush lied," it became essential for the political opponents of the war to find as many ways as possible to demonstrate the administration's lack of credibility.

With the decision by most of the 2004 Democratic candidates to move into the antiwar camp, the idea that President Bush "lied" the United States into war, already percolating in certain quarters, entered the mainstream. It hearkened back to the Vietnam War, when American politicians and much of the antiwar American public concluded that the country had been "lied" into Vietnam with the Gulf of Tonkin Resolution and fed continued lies in the form of facts and figures released by Robert McNamara's Defense Department. As noted previously, antiwar activists cited the Gulf of Tonkin Resolution in their protests against the Iraq War before the Iraq War had even begun. "Bush lied, people died" became almost as ubiquitous as "Hey, hey, LBJ, how many kids did you kill today?"

However, the monomania that "Bush lied and people died" that gripped the antiwar movement proved deeply corrosive to the war effort. Instead of being able to strategize and fight the war, the Bush administration found itself consumed with defending itself in the court of public opinion and, later, in federal court from accusations of lying the country into war.

The "Sixteen Words" Controversy

One early controversy intended to call the Bush administration's credibility into question involved President Bush's statement in his 2003 State of the Union address that "the British government has learned that Saddam Hussein recently sought significant quantities of uranium from Africa."[90] The controversy over the "sixteen words" roiled the Bush administration. The fact was the British government had made this claim, and in the wake of the controversy, in its Butler Report, the British government stood by this claim.[91] Nevertheless, the Bush administration was forced to defend itself from relentless attack. National Security Advisor Condoleezza Rice, while expressing incredulity at the extent to which the "sixteen words" controversy had become a major

90 James Risen, "Those 16 Words Threaten the Tenure of the Long-Serving C.I.A. Chief," *New York Times*, July 27, 2003, http://www.nytimes.com/2003/07/27/us/those-16-words-threaten-the-tenure-of-the-long-serving-cia-chief.html.

91 Lauren Johnston, "New Fight over Iraq Nuke Claim," CBS News, June 25, 2003, http://www.cbsnews.com/news/new-fight-over-iraq-nuke-claim/.

story, nevertheless conceded that the words should not have been included in the State of the Union speech.[92] This concession damaged the administration's credibility and ultimately proved to be unnecessary. Throughout the controversy, the British government and Prime Minister Blair stood by British intelligence reports that Iraq had attempted to obtain yellowcake uranium from Niger.[93] Nearly one year later, a *Washington Post* editorial quietly noted that the sixteen words may have been justified after all.[94]

As US troops consolidated control of Iraq, it became clearer that they would not find large-scale WMD stocks or manufacturing facilities. The failure to find WMD stocks led to accusations that the Bush administration had been dead set on invading Iraq and had "politicized" or "cherry-picked" intelligence to support its rationale for the war.[95] The evidence for this claim was scant; as noted previously, members of Congress who had been in Congress not only for the Bush presidency but also the Clinton presidency—and who had seen the same intelligence Presidents Clinton and Bush had—had made some of the strongest statements in support of the war. In 1998, the Clinton administration had launched Operation Desert Fox to destroy what the United States believed to be WMD infrastructure in Iraq. The idea that Iraq had the capacity to develop and, in fact, had developed and continued to develop WMD was not a ruse made out of whole cloth by the Bush administration. George Tenet, Bush's CIA director—who had been appointed by Clinton and retained by Bush—declared the WMD case against Iraq a "slam dunk."

Despite these facts, the "sixteen words" controversy began the process of undermining the legitimacy of the Iraq War and credibility of the Bush administration in the same fashion that Vietnam protesters undermined the

92 "Rice: 16 Words Dispute 'Enormously Overblown,'" CNN, July 14, 2003, http://www.cnn.com/2003/ALLPOLITICS/07/13/cnna.wolf.rice/.

93 "Blair: WMD Reports 'Accurate,'" CNN, December 25, 2003, http://www.cnn.com/2003/ALLPOLITICS/07/09/sprj.irq.uranium.uk/.

94 Editorial, "The Sixteen Words, Again," *Washington Post*, July 21, 2004, http://www.washingtonpost.com/wp-dyn/articles/A482-2004Jul20.html.

95 For example, see Walter Pincus, "Ex-CIA Official Faults Use of Data on Iraq," *Washington Post*, February 10, 2006, http://www.washingtonpost.com/wp-dyn/content/article/2006/02/09/AR2006020902418.html; "Cherry-picked Intelligence," The Nation, February 16, 2006, https://www.thenation.com/article/cherry-picked-intelligence/.

legitimacy of the Vietnam War. Once again, a political administration stood accused of lying and falsifying information in order to wage a war.

The "sixteen words" controversy led to and was a warm-up act for the second major controversy that took the "Bush lied" theme to a higher level and plagued the Bush administration throughout the course of the Iraq War: the Valerie Plame case.

The Next Antiwar Club: The Plame Affair

On July 6, 2003, former foreign-service officer and ambassador Joseph Wilson published an opinion piece in the *New York Times*.[96] In "What I Didn't Find in Africa," Wilson described how the CIA sent him to Niger in 2002 to investigate reports that Saddam Hussein sought yellowcake uranium in Niger. Ambassador Wilson further claimed that the CIA undertook this mission because of questions Vice President Dick Cheney raised about an intelligence report on Iraq seeking yellowcake uranium in Niger. Ambassador Wilson stated that he concluded that it was "highly doubtful" Iraq had sought uranium in Niger.

In explaining the importance of his conclusion, Wilson stated,

> The question now is how that answer was or was not used by our political leadership. If my information was deemed inaccurate, I understand (though I would be very interested to know why). If, however, the information was ignored because it did not fit certain preconceptions about Iraq, then a legitimate argument can be made that we went to war under false pretenses. (It's worth remembering that in his March "Meet the Press" appearance, Mr. Cheney said that Saddam Hussein was "trying once again to produce nuclear weapons.") At a minimum, Congress, which authorized the use of military force at the president's behest, should want to know if the assertions about Iraq were warranted.[97]

---

96 Joseph C. Wilson IV, "What I Didn't Find in Africa," July 6, 2003, http://www.nytimes.com/2003/07/06/opinion/what-i-didn-t-find-in-africa.html.

97 Ibid.

With this statement, Wilson effectively insinuated that the administration, particularly Vice President Cheney, had lied to Congress and the American people in describing the WMD threat Saddam Hussein posed. The article renewed and further inflamed the "sixteen words" controversy about whether Iraq truly had sought uranium in Niger.

On July 14, 2003, Robert Novak, writer and columnist for the *Washington Post*, wrote a story about Wilson's trip to Niger, stating it was the type of trip routinely made at a low level.[98] Fatefully, Novak included the following paragraph in the article: "Wilson never worked for the CIA, but his wife, Valerie Plame, is an agency operative on weapons of mass destruction. Two senior administration officials told me that Wilson's wife suggested sending him to Niger to investigate the Italian report. The CIA says its counterproliferation officials selected Wilson and asked his wife to contact him. 'I will not answer any question about my wife,' Wilson told me."[99]

This paragraph, and its mention of Joseph Wilson's wife, Valerie Plame, set off a massive firestorm. Questions arose about whether the release of Plame's name and CIA employment violated the Espionage Act and other laws protecting CIA officers. The Bush administration stood accused of having blown the cover of a CIA official as a vindictive act designed to strike back at Wilson for his accusations that the White House lied about Iraq's seeking uranium in Niger.

In response to the controversy, the Justice Department appointed a special prosecutor, Patrick Fitzgerald, who investigated the case for years. The US government convicted no one for the allegedly illegal release of Valerie Plame's identity. The only conviction Fitzgerald secured was that of I. Lewis "Scooter" Libby, Vice President Cheney's chief of staff, on perjury charges, for allegedly having told false statements to the grand jury. Revelations in a 2015 book by Judith Miller, a former *New York Times* reporter at the center of the controversy who spent time in jail during the Fitzgerald investigation for refusing

98 Robert D. Novak, "Mission to Niger," *Washington Post*, July 14, 2003, http://www.washingtonpost.com/wp-dyn/content/article/2005/10/20/AR2005102000874.html.

99 Ibid.

to reveal her sources, cast significant doubt on Libby's conviction as well as Fitzgerald's tactics in obtaining it.[100]

The Plame case raises a number of important questions of legal ethics, the role of a special prosecutor, and the ability of the media to shield its sources. However, most important to the thesis of this book is that the Plame case represented a major escalation by the antiwar movement and antiwar politicians to delegitimize the Iraq War. The entire controversy, from Wilson's article to the criminal case surrounding the release of Plame's identity, provided further ammunition for those who wanted to claim that Bush "lied" the United States into war. Those who might have previously supported the war could now say that they were misled into supporting the war based on false information that the Bush administration provided. All of the Democrats' prewar support and their denunciations of Saddam Hussein's WMD efforts that dated back to the Clinton administration could now be waved away by saying that their support was based on false evidence that the Bush administration had presented them.

The Plame controversy enhanced this argument by elevating it, literally, to a federal criminal case. In effect, the antiwar movement and its Democratic supporters could claim that the administration committed federal crimes in order to win support for the Iraq War. The claims that the Bush administration deliberately misled the United States into war thus went from being mere lies to criminal acts. Implicit in this argument was the notion that politicians who had supported the war could not be held responsible for their support if it required criminal acts by the president to win their support.

Wilson went on to join the presidential campaign of John Kerry in February 2004.[101] In so doing, he furthered Kerry's ability to move toward the antiwar position without seeming to have reversed his position on the war. Kerry could instead say that he, like everyone else, supported the war based on the president's lies, lies that may have been crimes. As Kerry's press secretary said at the time Wilson joined the campaign, "I think his support speaks

100 Peter Berkowitz, "Judith Miller Recants: Where's the Media?," *Real Clear Politics*, April 18, 2015, http://www.realclearpolitics.com/articles/2015/04/18/judith_miller_recants_wheres_the_media_126289.html.

101 "Spouse of Outed CIA Official Signs On with Kerry," *Washington Times*, February 14, 2004, http://www.washingtontimes.com/news/2004/feb/14/20040214-120835-4661r/?page=all.

volumes about this administration's blustering foreign policy as well as about the breach of trust they've had with the American people."[102]

Just before the 2004 Democratic presidential primary, Wilson spoke to hundreds of students at a foreign policy forum at the University of Washington. He stated, "We went to war under false pretenses and that is becoming abundantly clear to the American people. I don't care who you vote for, but get out there and caucus. Don't leave it to the neoconservatives and evangelical Christians."[103] He referred to Vice President Cheney as "a lying son of a bitch" in Iowa in December 2004.[104] With comments like these, Wilson revealed himself to be an ardent opponent of the Bush administration's Iraq policies. However, his comments continued to erode the Bush administration's credibility.

The antiwar movement did not leave the accusations that the Bush administration lied the United States into war to Wilson alone. The antiwar movement turned the Wilsons into martyrs and victims. In some sense, the antiwar movement turned the Wilsons into the Iraq War version of Daniel Ellsburg, who released the Pentagon Papers to the *New York Times* in 1971 and whose psychiatrist was the victim of a break-in believed to be the work of Nixon administration operatives seeking to discredit Ellsburg. John Dean, former White House counsel in the Nixon White House, wrote in the *New York Times* that Wilson was the victim of "the most vicious hatchet job inside the Beltway since my colleague in Richard Nixon's White House, the dirty trickster Charles W. Colson, copped a plea for defaming Daniel Ellsberg and his lawyer."[105]

The Wilsons became celebrities. *Vanity Fair* published a fawning profile of the couple in January 2004, complete with photos of them driving through

---

102 Ibid.

103 Ibid.

104 Ibid.

105 John W. Dean, "Don't Tread on Joseph Wilson," review of *The Politics of Truth*, by Joseph Wilson, *New York Times*, May 23, 2004, http://www.nytimes.com/2004/05/23/books/don-t-tread-on-joseph-wilson.html,

Washington, DC, dressed as glamorous spies.[106] Hollywood made a movie about them, released in 2010 and starring Sean Penn, called *Fair Game*. The MSNBC network ran with this story for years; it regularly led MSNBC broadcasts. From 2004 through 2007, one could not watch an MSNBC program without some coverage, often breathless and indignant, of the Plame case.

Wilson himself became a leading celebrity of the antiwar movement. He stated at an August 2003 forum sponsored by antiwar Congressman Jay Inslee (D-WA) that "at the end of the day, it's of keen interest to me to see whether or not we can get Karl Rove frog-marched out of the White House in handcuffs."[107] In an interview with CNN in 2005, he stated, "I think that Karl Rove should be fired. I think that this idea that you can, with impunity, call journalists and leak national security information is repugnant."[108] In fact, it is now well known that Deputy Secretary of State Richard Armitage, not Rove, leaked Plame's name to Robert Novak. Nevertheless, the fact that Wilson impugned Rove and claimed he should be an explicit target of the special prosecutor's investigation further undermined the credibility of the Bush White House.

In the CNN interview, when asked if he would do it all over again, Wilson said,

> I would have written the article as I did because I believe—I believe firmly—that it is a civic responsibility to hold your government to account in a strong democracy.
>
> And I can't think of much I would have changed. I suspect that, given the two-year character assassination campaign which was really designed to divert attention from the two key issues—the 16 words in the State of the Union address and who leaked Valerie's name—that

106 Vicky Ward, "Double Exposure," *Vanity Fair*, January 2004, http://www.vanityfair.com/news/2004/01/plame200401.

107 Timothy Noah, "Did Rove Blow a Spook's Cover?," *Slate*, September 16, 2003, http://constantcontact.com/.

108 "Joseph Wilson: 'Karl Rove Should Be Fired,'" CNN, November 1, 2005, http://edition.cnn.com/2005/US/10/31/wilson.interview/.

> there may have been some things I might have done differently, such as perhaps not getting engaged in a political campaign.
>
> Although I will say this about that, and that is that I resent deeply the idea that others would try and deny me my right to participate fully in the selection of this country's leaders.[109]

Wilson characterized his treatment as a character assassination campaign designed to divert attention from what he perceived to be Bush administration lies. The antiwar movement ran with this characterization for the entirety of the Bush administration.

The effect of the Plame controversy was to make it even more difficult for the Bush administration to prosecute the Iraq War. By eroding the administration's credibility, the antiwar movement ensured that every effort to alter the war strategy and to pacify Iraq would be met with deep skepticism. It hamstrung the Bush administration's ability to consider and pursue different strategies on the ground. In addition, it gave politicians—mostly Democrats—cover to turn on the war in a superficially responsible way by saying that they, like the country, were misled into supporting the war by the Bush administration's deliberately and criminally false misrepresentations.

Reprising 1972, the Democrats Fully Embrace the Antiwar Position

The "Bush lied" theme continued throughout the second term of the Bush presidency. Although John Kerry narrowly lost the 2004 presidential election, by the end of that election, the Democrats had transformed themselves fully into an antiwar party committed to the principle that Bush "lied" the United States into Iraq. Democratic politicians—particularly those running for president in 2008—needed to toe the antiwar line or risk the fate of Sen. Joe Lieberman, who lost his Democratic primary to first-time candidate Ned Lamont in the Democratic Senate primary in 2006. (Lieberman went on to win the general election running as an "Independent Democrat.")

109 Ibid.

Lieberman's 2006 primary provided ample evidence that the antiwar movement had taken over the Democratic Party just as it had between the 1968 and 1972 presidential elections. Observers saw the primary as a referendum on the Iraq War and, particularly, Lieberman's support for it.[110] Lamont, Lieberman's challenger, ran as an antiwar Democrat and made the Iraq War a centerpiece of his campaign. Indeed, *Slate* referred to Lamont as "less a fleshed-out alternative to Lieberman than a stand-in for an anti-war, anti-Bush movement" whose "campaign was made plausible by Web-based 'Net roots' activists who cared principally about the war in Iraq."[111] Lamont's primary victory was additional evidence of just how powerful the antiwar movement had become and how much it had changed a Democratic Party that just six years earlier had nominated Lieberman for vice president.

In his primary victory speech, Lamont said that the time had come to fix "George Bush's failed foreign policy" and that he would push to withdraw US forces from Iraq. He went on to say, "It's high time to bring them home to a hero's welcome." The assembled crowd chanted, "Bring them home, bring them home."[112] Six years after he was the Democratic Party's vice presidential nominee, the Democratic Party dumped Lieberman solely because of his support for the Iraq War.

Meanwhile, Iraq was shaken by ethnic and sectarian violence that rapidly escalated in the wake of the terrorist bombing of Iraq's Golden Mosque in Samarra in December 2006. In response to the growing violence, the United States launched the surge. By June 2007, all of the surge troops had reached Iraq.[113] These troops began a number of offensive activities "to expand the gains achieved in the preceding months in Anbar Province; clear Baqubah,

---

110 Dan Balz and Shailagh Murray, "Lieberman Defeated in Democratic Primary," *Washington Post*, August 9, 2006, http://www.washingtonpost.com/wp-dyn/content/article/2006/08/08/AR2006080800596.html.

111 Jacob Weisberg, "Dead with Ned: Why Lamont's Victory Spells Democratic Disaster," *Slate*, August 9, 2006, http://www.slate.com/articles/news_and_politics/the_big_idea/2006/08/dead_with_ned.html.

112 Balz and Murray, "Lieberman Defeated in Democratic Primary."

113 Gen. David H. Petraeus, "Report to Congress on the Situation in Iraq," September 10–11, 2007, 2.

several key Baghdad neighborhoods, the remaining sanctuaries in Anbar Province, and important areas in the so-called 'belts' around Baghdad; and pursuing Al Qaeda in the Diyala River Valley and several other areas."[114]

In September 2007, General David Petraeus, commander of the Multinational Forces in Iraq, testified before the Senate regarding the progress that had been made as a result of the surge. Armed with charts and a bevy of statistics, Petraeus testified that the surge and the Anbar Awakening had made significant progress in the fight against al-Qaeda in Iraq and other extremists. He presented the following indicators of this success to the Senate:

- The level of security incidents had decreased significantly since the start of the surge of offensive operations in mid-June 2006, declining in 8 of the 12 weeks preceding Gen. Petraeus's testimony, with the level of incidents in the two weeks preceding Gen. Petraeus's testimony the lowest since June 2006 and with the number of attacks this in the week preceding Gen. Petraeus's testimony the lowest since April 2006.
- Civilian deaths (other than by natural causes) had declined by over 45% Iraq-wide since the height of the sectarian violence in December 2006.
- Civilian deaths (other than by natural causes) had declined by 70% in Baghdad since December 2006.
- The number of ethno-sectarian deaths dropped by over 55% since December 2006, and by 80% in Baghdad.
- From January through September 2007, US forces had found and cleared over 4,400 weapons caches, nearly 1,700 more than we discovered in all of 2006.
- IED attacks had declined by about one-third between June and September 2007.
- Monthly attack levels in Anbar had declined from 1,350 in October 2006 to a bit over 200 in August 2007.[115]

114 Ibid., 2.

115 Ibid., 3–4.

In response to this cautious report of progress, Sen. Hillary Clinton said that Petraeus's report required a "willing suspension of disbelief."[116] Without saying so explicitly, she effectively accused General Petraeus of being a liar. Then-senator Obama accused Petraeus of "changing the definition of success to stay the course."[117] Just as in Vietnam, the antiwar movement and its political supporters sought to discredit evidence of success.

Worse, to the extent the antiwar senators acknowledged improvements in conditions in Iraq, they were loath to give the surge strategy and the US forces executing it credit for its success. Contradicting General Petraeus's testimony, then-senator Obama stated, "I'm not sure that the success in Anbar has anything to do with the surge. You yourself said it was political."[118] Senator Clinton said that "although the charts [that General Petraeus presented in his testimony] tell part of the story, I don't think they tell the whole story." Rather, she asserted that the reports of "bottom-up" political reconciliation in Iraq were "anecdotal" and that the success in Anbar Province began before the surge.[119] Rather than acknowledging the evident success of the surge in stabilizing Iraq, leading Democrats such as Clinton and Obama took a lawyerly approach, trying to find reasons other than the surge to account for the decrease in violence in Iraq over the course of 2007. They sought to poke holes in General Petraeus's testimony in the same way a defense lawyer looks for openings and vulnerabilities in witness testimony to undermine the jury's acceptance of that testimony and to create reasonable doubt and confusion in the public's mind about the source of the newfound success in pacifying Iraq.

Several Democrats on the Foreign Relations Committee before which General Petraeus testified, including Clinton and Sen. Chris Dodd of Connecticut, called for a firm date of withdrawal of US troops from Iraq. Then-senator Obama stated that "the time to end the surge and to start bringing our troops home is now, not six months from now."[120] Each of these

116 Eli Lake, "Clinton Spars with Petraeus on Credibility," New York *Sun*, September 12, 2007, http://www.nysun.com/national/clinton-spars-with-petraeus-on-credibility/62426/.

117 Ibid.

118 Ibid.

119 Ibid.

120 Lake, "Clinton Spars with Petraeus on Credibility."

Democratic senators was running for the 2008 Democratic presidential nomination at the time of the hearing. Each clearly felt that he or she needed to project an antiwar position and advocate withdrawal. General Petraeus's statistics showing progress and a path to success impeded their efforts to win favor with the antiwar movement controlling the Democratic Party.

Clinton was not the only antiwar outlet alleging Petraeus was a liar. On the day of the hearing, the left-wing group MoveOn.org ran a full-page ad in the *New York Times* that asked the question, "General Petraeus or General Betray Us?"[121] The ad read as follows:

> General Petraeus or General Betray Us?
>
> Cooking the Books for the White House
>
> General Petraeus is a military man constantly at war with the facts. In 2004, just before the election, he said there was "tangible progress" in Iraq and that "Iraqi leaders are stepping forward." And last week Petraeus, the architect of the escalation of troops in Iraq, said, "We say we have achieved progress, and we are obviously going to do everything we can to build on that progress."
>
> Every independent report on the ground situation in Iraq shows that the surge strategy has failed. Yet the General claims a reduction in violence. That's because, according to the *New York Times*, the Pentagon has adopted a bizarre formula for keeping tabs on violence. For example, deaths by car bombs don't count. The *Washington Post* reported that assassinations only count if you're shot in the back of the head—not the front. According to the Associated Press, there have been more civilian deaths and more American soldier deaths in the past three months than in any other summer we've been there. We'll hear of neighborhoods where violence has decreased. But we won't hear that those neighborhoods have been ethnically cleansed.
>
> Most importantly, General Petraeus will not admit what everyone knows: Iraq is mired in an unwinnable religious civil war. We may

121 Jake Tapper, "MoveOn.org Ad Takes Aim at Petraeus," ABC News, September 10, 2007, http://abcnews.go.com/Politics/Decision2008/story?id=3581727.

> hear of a plan to withdraw a few thousand American troops. But we won't hear what Americans are desperate to hear: a timetable for withdrawing all our troops. General Petraeus has actually said American troops will need to stay in Iraq for as long as ten years.
>
> Today, before Congress and before the American people, General Petraeus is likely to become General Betray Us.[122]

This infamous ad in no uncertain terms accused General Petraeus of being a liar who was "cooking the books" for President Bush. MoveOn.org's accusation that the American military was "cooking the books" for its political leadership reprises the criticisms lodged against the Pentagon during the Vietnam War. Just as the antiwar movement discredited Pentagon statistics and information about the Vietnam War effort, the Iraq War antiwar activists sought to undermine the credibility of the information the Pentagon provided about the American military's surge successes in Iraq. MoveOn.org sought to perpetuate the myth of the Bush administration and the American military as liars who misled the United States into the Iraq War and now were lying about the surge. In fact, the information and statistics General Petraeus provided were true. But by continuing efforts to undermine the credibility of the Bush administration and American military, the antiwar movement attempted to make the Iraq War this generation's version of the Vietnam War and turn the American public against the war or keep it from believing that the United States had turned the tide with its new strategy.

The intended effect of the antiwar movement's claims that the surge statistics could not be believed was to create the impression that the supposed successes of the surge were a mirage and the United States could not achieve victory and success in Iraq. This effect would be similar to the effect of the antiwar movement on America's Vietnam strategy. In Vietnam, America installed a new commander, Creighton Abrams, and a new strategy, but the successes of these new efforts were undermined by the antiwar movement's successful efforts to end political support for the war. The arguments of the

122 MoveOn.org advertisement in *New York Times*, September 10, 2007, http://media.washingtonpost.com/wp-srv/politics/documents/moveon_Petraeus_NYTad.pdf.

Iraq War antiwar movement were intended to undermine the surge strategy in the same way—to continue to diminish political support for the war effort at the very moment the tide of war turned in America's favor.

The defeatism did not stop with Congress. The media also made efforts to find the dark cloud in the silver lining of the surge's success. The Anbar Awakening was the aligning of Sunni tribes in Anbar Province with United States and coalition forces to fight al-Qaeda in Iraq that coincided with and was a successful part of the surge strategy. Yet the *New York Times* wrote a piece titled "In a Force for Iraqi Calm, Seeds of Conflict."[123] The article focused on the rifts among different groups aligned with the awakening, including Sunni-Shia rifts and continuing rifts between the awakening groups and the central government. Although the surge and the Anbar Awakening had dramatically lessened violence in Iraq in a relatively short period of time, the *New York Times* sought and found a way to sound a pessimistic, negative note. As will be seen later in greater detail, overall coverage of the war diminished as the surge succeeded, yet the *Times* still managed to find negative stories to produce on the surge.

History has shown that the surge did, in fact, succeed in defeating al-Qaeda in Iraq and the other sectarian extremist groups operating to destabilize Iraq and foment sectarian strife. By the end of 2008, when George Bush left office, Iraq was largely stable—so much so that, in February 2010, Vice President Joe Biden told Larry King on CNN the following:

> I am very optimistic about—about Iraq. I mean, this could be one of the great achievements of this administration. You're going to see 90,000 American troops come marching home by the end of the summer. You're going to see a stable government in Iraq that is actually moving toward a representative government.
>
> I spent—I've been there [Iraq] 17 times now. I go about every two months—three months. I know every one of the major players in all

123 Alissa J. Rubin and Damien Cave, "In a Force for Iraqi Calm, Seeds of Conflict," *New York Times*, December 23, 2007, http://www.nytimes.com/2007/12/23/world/middleeast/23awakening.html?pagewanted=all.

> of the segments of that society. It's impressed me. I've been impressed how they have been deciding to use the political process rather than guns to settle their differences.[124]

But what is unmistakable about the MoveOn.org ad, in addition to its inaccuracy, is the startling level of defeatism it exudes. The ad explicitly states that "Iraq is mired in an unwinnable religious war" and that "every independent report on the ground situation in Iraq shows that the surge strategy has failed." The surge had achieved its full troop strength only in June 2007, and antiwar activists proclaimed the surge a failure by September 2007. Antiwar activists wrote off any signs of the surge's success by claiming the successes either started before the surge or were due to factors other than the surge.

The parallels with Vietnam are apparent. The antiwar movement seized on the alleged lies the US government told regarding the war (for example, the Gulf of Tonkin Resolution and the various statistics of the Defense Department) as undermining the entire rationale for the war. The Bush administration, if anything, was much more transparent and open about the Iraq War than the Johnson administration was about Vietnam. The Bush administration consulted with other allied intelligence services prior to going to war. The administration allowed reporters to embed themselves with military units on the front lines of the war. And when the United States failed to find WMD in Iraq after the invasion, the Bush administration publicly acknowledged this fact and launched investigations into why the prewar intelligence may have been inaccurate.

In addition, the idea that the United States was mired in an unwinnable religious war hearkened back to the argument against the Vietnam War that the United States was intervening in the middle of someone else's civil war. Just as the antiwar movement and politicians claimed that Vietnam was a civil war with no wider Cold War implications, antiwar activists claimed that the Iraq War was a local religious and ethnic conflict in which the United States had no interest and would be unable to achieve military success.

---

124 Transcript of CNN Interview with Vice President Joe Biden, February 10, 2010, http://transcripts.cnn.com/TRANSCRIPTS/1002/10/lkl.01.html.

Nevertheless, the antiwar movement's efforts to erode the credibility of the Bush administration took their toll on the United States' ability to prosecute the Iraq War, just as the efforts to revise the war's strategy took shape. Despite tremendous unpopularity, the Bush administration launched the surge of troops in 2006 and 2007, which, with the help of the local population and its leaders, routed al-Qaeda and successfully pacified Iraq. The Anbar Awakening, in which the United States won the support of local (primarily Sunni) leaders and tribes in Anbar Province, turned the Sunnis away from their support of al-Qaeda against the central government in Baghdad. By 2008, Iraq had achieved a fragile stability, and al-Qaeda in Iraq was defeated.

Tying It All Back to Vietnam, Again

In a 2004 article in the *New Yorker*, Howard Dean made explicit the connection between the lies he believed the US government told during the Vietnam War and the lies he believed the Bush administration was telling about the Iraq War. He said,

> One professor who made a big impression was Wolfgang Leonhard, who taught Russian history. He'd been a Party official in East Germany and had defected. A fantastic lecturer. He once told us, "*Pravda* lies in such a way that not even the opposite is so." That really hit home. I felt he wasn't just referring to the Soviet government but to our own at the time. You knew it from some of the things Nixon talked about—denying the bombing of Cambodia—or from Kissinger's "Peace is at hand" statement, when clearly peace wasn't at hand. They said these things just to get reelected. I think there are some similarities between George Bush's Administration and Richard Nixon's Administration: a tremendous cynicism about the future of the country; a lack of ability to instill hope in the American people; a war which doesn't have clear principles behind it; and a group of

> people around the President whose main allegiance is to each other and their ideology rather than to the United States.[125]

The quotation drives home the fact that opponents of the Iraq War saw the war directly through the lens of Vietnam. Moreover, they saw it through the lens of the Vietnam War they believed occurred—Richard Nixon's (Republican) war, not a war the United States began in the Kennedy administration and dramatically escalated under President Johnson.

Just as in Vietnam, the political party that ultimately came to stand for opposition to the war—the Democratic Party—supported the initial US engagement. Only two Democrats opposed the Gulf of Tonkin Resolution, and both Presidents Kennedy and Johnson supported and escalated the effort. Their political descendants in the Democratic Party made regime change in Iraq the formal policy of the United States in the 1990s and strongly and publicly supported the Iraq War at first. As time passed and the country began to oppose the Vietnam War, Democrats, first in a trickle and then in a flood, opposed the war. By 1972, the Democratic Party firmly opposed the war and nominated an unabashed, outspoken opponent of the war, George McGovern, for president in 1972. Similarly, by 2004, the antiwar movement had captured the party, so much so that John Kerry, who in 2002 said the United States could not "afford to ignore the possibility that Saddam Hussein might provide weapons of destruction to some terrorist group bent on destroying the United States," even if the threat was not "imminent," said in 2004 that he was an antiwar candidate.[126]

Recall the unequivocal statements about Saddam Hussein's WMD programs that Democratic candidates and leaders prior to the Iraq War recounted in an earlier chapter. The arguments that these Democrats made as they moved into opposition to the war represented a stark 180-degree turn from their prewar support. That these Democratic candidates and leaders so

125 Mark Singer, "Running on Instinct," *The New Yorker*, January 12, 2004, http://www.newyorker.com/magazine/2004/01/12/running-on-instinct.

126 "Hardball in a Political Ad," NBC News, August 17, 2004, http://www.nbcnews.com/id/5727982/ns/msnbc-hardball_with_chris_matthews/t/hardball-political-ad/#.Vd7p8bWjxvk.

quickly changed their positions (with some admirable exceptions, such as Sen. Joe Lieberman of Connecticut) demonstrated the power of the antiwar movement and bodes ill for the United States' ability to prosecute and win future wars and conflicts.

If the Democratic candidates and leaders in 2003 and 2004 truly believed what they said in 2002 and early 2003 leading up to the Iraq War about Saddam Hussein's possession of WMD, the antiwar movement's influence within the Democratic Party is so strong that whenever the United States enters a serious conflict involving the long-term commitment of ground troops, there exists a strong risk that Democratic politicians, even those initially supportive of the use of force, ultimately will be pulled to the antiwar position and eventually oppose the conflict. Official opposition of one of the two political parties to any prolonged combat mission is likely to undermine the mission by limiting the freedom of action of the political and military leadership of the United States as well as commanders on the ground. The United States' enemies in conflict, taking this into account, recognize that they need only wait for opposition to a war to tie the hands of the US government sufficiently that the enemy can win the war. That is, the enemy can simply wait for the inevitable opposition to the war to arise and then achieve its objectives.

If the Democratic candidates and leaders in 2003 and 2004 already were sympathetic to the antiwar movement's position on Iraq but feared the political consequences of opposing the war after September 11, the antiwar movement's influence within the Democratic Party is complete and total. This possibility raises the concern that politicians ostensibly supportive of a military action will go into full-throated opposition at the first sight of an opportunity to do so without political consequences. Such a position might pose even greater danger to the United States' ability to defend its interests around the world, because one of America's two political parties essentially would oppose any prolonged use of force to obtain national security objectives. Moreover, such posturing allows American political leadership to commit US troops to combat believing it has the support of the American people, only to discover once combat has begun that such support did not really exist. The United States then would find itself committed to combat with a loud, vocal opposition that would grow especially loud when inevitable setbacks in the war occurred.

It is important to note that the Iraq War was the longest and hottest conventional military conflict involving significant ground forces since Vietnam. Most of the military conflicts in between Vietnam and Iraq were shorter campaigns, such as Grenada and Panama, or conflicts that involved primarily air strikes, such as Kosovo and Bosnia. The Gulf War in 1991 lasted less than one hundred days, and ground troops did not invade and attempt to pacify enemy territory in Iraq. And in Afghanistan in 2001, the United States and the Northern Alliance quickly toppled the Taliban and did not face as intense an insurgency as the United States faced in Iraq. The first time the United States faced a long and difficult war with large numbers of US troops deployed for an extended period—the Iraq War—the antiwar movement came to life and relentlessly attacked the US government and the war effort.

An important takeaway of this chapter is that the first few years of the Iraq War, the 2003 through 2006 period, show that there remains an irrepressible antiwar movement. This antiwar movement is largely, though not exclusively, aligned with the Democratic Party. As long as there is a candidate within the Democratic Party that is willing to be unabashedly antiwar and a movement willing to malign the decision to use force as based on warmongering, profiteering, and lying to the American public, the country is very likely to fracture over wars and other military actions. Only military action that lasts a short period of time, before the antiwar movement gains momentum, will be able to succeed. This fact is particularly true for Republican presidents, on whom the antiwar Left and Democratic politicians will turn quickly when wars face unexpected obstacles—that is, when the enemy casts its vote.

A second key takeaway is that just as with the Vietnam and Iraq Wars, the antiwar movement likely will systematically attempt to undermine the credibility and legitimacy of the war if it is not won quickly. When American forces began to experience setbacks after completing the initial phase of combat, the antiwar movement began to reprise its Vietnam role of claiming that the Bush administration deliberately misrepresented Iraq's WMD capabilities to take the United States to war. Antiwar political candidates came to their antiwar position based on the claim that the president and his administration "lied" the United States into war to absolve themselves of responsibility for it. Yet many them had publicly stated that they had seen with their own eyes intelligence reports indicating that, as John Kerry said, "all US intelligence experts agree that Iraq is seeking nuclear weapons" and that "there is little question that Saddam Hussein wants to develop nuclear weapons."

A corollary of this second takeaway is that an antiwar movement's assaults on the credibility of an administration, if allowed to take root and not firmly refuted, will badly hamstring future foreign policy actions. The assaults on the Bush administration's credibility had lasting effects beyond the Iraq theater. The protests and the charges against the Bush administration of deliberately misleading the United States into war neutered the United States' ability to respond to other foreign crises. The Bush administration spent all of its political capital in executing the successful surge in Iraq in 2006 and 2007. It simply had no more political juice available to deal with other crises.

When the United States began raising concerns about the Iranian nuclear program, the antiwar movement and antiwar politicians accused the Bush administration of wanting another Middle Eastern war. A chastened Bush administration could not develop a muscular response, backed with force, which the Iranian nuclear issue required. The vacuum created by the neutered United States gave Iran space and oxygen to develop its nuclear program without threat of military attack. Similarly, when the Israeli government presented the United States evidence that Syria was constructing a nuclear reactor at al-Kidar with North Korean assistance, the Bush administration refused to take military action. In September 2007, the Israelis took their own military action with a bombing raid that destroyed the reactor.

A third key takeaway is that by assaulting the Bush administration's credibility by repeatedly stating that Iraq was not an imminent threat, antiwar activists and politicians effectively raised the burden of proof substantially for the United States' going to war or otherwise deploying force. Antiwar politicians regularly asserted that Saddam Hussein's Iraq was not an "imminent" threat. Antiwar activists and politicians regularly denigrated the Bush doctrine of "preemption." In effect, antiwar activists and politicians created a new standard of proof for military action, one to which the United States adheres today. In order to take military action in response to the threat of WMD in the hands of a rogue regime, the United States now must have near-certain proof that a rogue regime has or is actively developing WMD and evidence the rogue regime is an "imminent" threat to the United States. The consequences of this new burden of proof are dramatic. Countries that effectively conceal their WMD programs can be confident that they will not face a US military strike. Rather than demanding absolute transparency from rogue states regarding WMD, the United States now feels obligated to negotiate and sign up to inspection regimes that time and again have been circumvented by rogue regimes while offering the United States a false sense of security.

The United States has forgotten that rogue states are highly capable of concealing illicit weapons programs. The United States was taken by surprise at the extent of Gaddafi's WMD program when he unilaterally revealed it to the West in the wake of the Iraq War and agreed to dismantle the program. One Bush administration official stated that Libya's nuclear program was much further advanced than US intelligence believed, with completed centrifuges, thousands of centrifuge parts, and a uranium-enrichment program.[127] (It is frightening to contemplate the consequences of Libya's nuclear program being intact and more fully developed when Gaddafi fell in 2011 and jihadists, ISIS, and others emerged in Libya.) In fact, Iraqi units fighting in the Iraq War carried chemical weapons protection suits with them. US troops who captured a military base in Nassiriya in March 2003 found three thousand chemical weapons protection suits and a chest full of the chemical weapons antidote atropine.[128] British troops found numerous chemical weapons protection suits and respirators, all in working order, when they captured an Iraqi military headquarters building in southern Iraq in March 2003.[129] If Saddam

127 "Bush Official: Libya's Nuclear Program a Surprise," CNN, December 19, 2003, http://www.cnn.com/2003/WORLD/africa/12/19/libya.nuclear/index.html.

128 Julian Borger, "Discovery of Chemical Suits at Iraqi Base Raises Fears of Gas Attack," *The Guardian*, March 25, 2003, http://www.theguardian.com/world/2003/mar/26/iraq.julianborger.

129 "UK: Chemical Suits Found in Iraq," CNN, March 27, 2003, http://www.cnn.com/2003/WORLD/meast/03/27/sprj.irq.iraq.chemical.suits/index.html?iref=mpstoryview.

Hussein was bluffing and in fact did not have WMD or the capacity to make WMD, he fooled even his own troops.

With the benefit of hindsight, it is possible that Saddam Hussein's Iraq no longer maintained WMD capacity and infrastructure. (Of course, it is also possible, as some in Israel reported, that he spirited his WMD arsenal to Syria before the war began.[130]) Even if Saddam Hussein did not have a WMD program, he acted in a manner suggesting he wanted the world to think he might have WMD. If the neighbors of a hostile rogue state believe that the rogue state has nuclear, chemical, or biological weapons, they will want WMD capability as well to counter the threat. This chain of events is playing out in relation to the Iranian nuclear threat, as countries like Saudi Arabia and Egypt openly consider whether to launch nuclear programs of their own to counter Iran.

130 Ira Stoll, "Saddam's WMD Moved to Syria, an Israeli Says," *New York Sun*, December 15, 2005, http://www.nysun.com/foreign/saddams-wmd-moved-to-syria-an-israeli-says/24480/.

CHAPTER 5

Fetishizing Multilateralism

ANOTHER PERNICIOUS FALSEHOOD THAT ANTIWAR politicians used to ex post rationalize and explain away their votes in favor of the Iraq War was to insist that the Bush administration decided to "go it alone," that it was acting "unilaterally," that it led a "rush to war," and that it was alienating the world. Howard Dean said in a speech at Drake University on February 17, 2003 that "reckless bluster with our allies over Iraq has caused what could be lasting friction in important relationships and has injured our standing in the world community."[131] In that same speech, Dean said, "And yet, 18 months [after the September 11 attacks], a lot of that international support is gone. Surveys tell us that majorities in Europe see the United States as a major threat to world peace. Surveys tell us that regard for the United States has declined in every country and on every continent. In countries that have long been our allies, leaders are getting elected because of the fervor of their anti-America message." Dean went on to say that "this Administration squandered the world's good will toward us." As noted previously, in a major address to the Democratic National Committee, Howard Dean rhetorically asked, "What I want to know is why in the world the Democratic Party leadership is supporting the President's *unilateral* attack on Iraq."[132]

131 Gov. Howard Dean, "Defending American Values—Protecting America's Interests," foreign policy address at Drake University, February 17, 2003, http://www.gwu.edu/~action/2004/dean/dean021703sp.html.

132 Singer, "Running on Instinct" (emphasis added).

Dean was not the only Democrat to claim that America had lost friends and allies because of the Iraq War. In a speech on May 26, 2004, former vice president Al Gore said that President Bush "decided not to honor the Geneva Convention. Just as he would not honor the United Nations, international treaties, the opinions of our allies, the role of Congress and the courts, or what Jefferson described as 'a decent respect for the opinion of mankind.'"[133]

This second line of attack, that the United States acted unilaterally, further undermined the credibility of the war. It provided the impression of an American colossus rampaging all over the world without any legitimacy or any concern for the opinions of other nations. This effort to undermine the legitimacy of the Iraq War dovetailed with the effort to undermine the credibility of the Bush administration described previously. The antiwar movement sought to make the Iraq War illegitimate not only because it was supposedly based on lies but also because it supposedly lacked international support.

With this second line of attack on the Bush administration, the antiwar movement and its political supporters established a second pernicious principle that imperils the United States' ability to project power: the principle that the United States can only act when it has the support of the world community.

First, the notion that the United States went to war in Iraq unilaterally or without allies is simply and indisputably false. Politically, the United States' greatest allies on Iraq included the United Kingdom and Spain. UK Prime Minister Tony Blair was outspoken in his support of the Iraq War. In a speech to the British House of Commons on March 18, 2003, Prime Minister Blair strongly supported the Iraq War on the grounds that Iraq maintained a robust WMD program and that, in the wake of the terror attacks of September 11 and elsewhere in the world, the world had to take on "the two begetters of chaos: tyrannical regimes with WMD and extreme terrorist groups who profess a perverted and false view of Islam."[134] Other political supporters abroad

133 "Al Gore Links Abu Ghraib Prison Abuses to Deep Flaws in Bush Policy," May 26, 2004, http://www.prnewswire.com/news-releases/al-gore-links-abu-ghraib-prison-abuses-to-deep-flaws-in-bush-policy-74232392.html.

134 "Full Text: Tony Blair's Speech," *The Guardian*, March 18, 2003, http://www.theguardian.com/politics/2003/mar/18/foreignpolicy.iraq1.

included Spain's prime minister, José María Aznar, and Australia's prime minister, John Howard.

Many nations provided the United States much more than political support for the Iraq War. The United States also received tangible, practical military assistance—troops, equipment, and financial support—from a host of countries. In fact, thirty-seven countries supplied 150,000 troops from the initial invasion through July 2009.[135] This "coalition of the willing" included close allies such as the United Kingdom, Spain, and Australia. The UK and Australian navies and special forces each played important combat roles in the early combat of the war.[136] Poland also joined the coalition, with Polish commandos participating in the fight to take Baghdad.[137] The coalition included many other countries not ordinarily thought of as US military partners. Twenty countries deployed troops to Iraq after May 2003: Azerbaijan, Bulgaria, Estonia, Georgia, Honduras, Hungary, Italy, Kazakhstan, Latvia, Lithuania, Macedonia, Moldova, the Netherlands, New Zealand, Nicaragua, Norway, Philippines, Romania, Slovakia, and Thailand.[138] Some of these countries were not even independent states as of the first Gulf War in 1991, and several others had suffered under the yoke of Soviet domination.

After the successful invasion of Iraq, the coalition created the Multi-National Force—Iraq (MNF-I) to control regions of Iraq. The United States took the lead in several regions. However, the Poles had lead responsibility for the MNF-I Center-South force (covering a region south of Baghdad), the British had lead responsibility for the MNF-I Southeast force (covering the southeast portion of Iraq, including Basra and Iraq's outlet to the Persian Gulf), and South Korea had lead responsibility for the MNF-I Northeast force (covering a portion of Iraqi Kurdistan).[139]

The greatest and most outspoken hostility to US action in Iraq came from European countries such as France and Germany as well as Turkey, which

135 Stephen A. Carney, *Allied Participation in Operation Iraqi Freedom* (Center of Military History, United States Army), vii.

136 Ibid., 9.

137 Ibid., 9

138 Ibid., 13.

139 Ibid., 22–23.

ultimately refused to let the United States open a northern front in the Iraq War from Turkey.[140] (Recall the US ships left bobbing off the Turkish coast with supplies waiting for permission to land—permission that never came.[141] The United States' inability to open a northern front in the Iraq War may have impaired its ability to consolidate control over all of Iraq quickly and may have given insurgents space to regroup.)

It was primarily the public hostility of France and Germany to the Iraq War that gave fuel to the antiwar movement's contention that the United States was somehow "going it alone" in Iraq. European countries by no means had a common position on the war. Eight European countries wrote the public "Letter of Eight" in January 2003, expressing support for the US position on Iraq and opposition to France and Germany's effort to develop a common European antiwar position. The letter was signed by the leaders of Spain, Portugal, Italy, the United Kingdom, the Czech Republic, Hungary, Poland, and Denmark.[142] (The Czech Republic's signatory was Vaclav Havel.) On February 5, 2003, a group of countries known as the Vilnius Ten released a similar letter expressing support for the United States' stance on Iraq.[143] The Vilnius Ten comprised Albania, Bulgaria, Croatia, Estonia, Latvia, Lithuania, Macedonia, Romania, Slovakia, and Slovenia.

Both the Letter of Eight and the letter of the Vilnius Ten were viewed as a rebuke to France and Germany. France lashed out at the authors of the letters and the challenge they represented to France's conception of itself as the leader

---

140 Carol Migdalovitz, "Iraq: Turkey, the Deployment of US Forces, and Related Issues," Congressional Research Service, May 2, 2003, http://congressionalresearch.com/RL31794/document.php?study=Iraq+Turkey+the+Deployment+of+US+Forces+and+Related+Issues; https://file.wikileaks.org/file/crs/RL31794.pdf.

141 Yochi J. Dreazen, "Some US Soldiers Train and Watch—and Wait," *Wall Street Journal*, March 20, 2003, http://www.wsj.com/articles/SB104811627135338200.

142 "Leaders' Statement on Iraq: Full Text," BBC News, January 30, 2003, accessed October 24, 2015, http://news.bbc.co.uk/2/hi/europe/2708877.stm; Mark Champion, "Eight European Leaders Voice Their Support for US on Iraq," *Wall Street Journal*, January 30, 2003, http://www.wsj.com/articles/SB1043875470158445104.

143 "Statement of the Vilnius Group Countries," Sofia News Agency, February 5, 2003, http://www.novinite.com/articles/19022/Statement+of+the+Vilnius+Group+Countries.

of European foreign policy.[144] Although France demanded a multilateral approach to Iraq, France's parochial interests in leading the antiwar bloc became apparent when Chirac responded to European nations inclined to support the US invasion of Iraq by saying, "These countries have been not very well behaved and rather reckless of the danger of aligning themselves too rapidly with the American position…It is not really responsible behavior. It is not well brought-up behavior. They missed a good opportunity to keep quiet."[145] Chirac lambasted these countries as being immature, reckless, and disloyal.[146]

France views the European Union in part as a counterweight to the American "hyperpower" and an alternative pole in France's desired multipolar world. In keeping with this philosophy, France effectively wanted to unify Europe in opposition to the Iraq War and was unwilling to accept differing points of view from other European nations.

The antiwar movement and its candidates did not consider the possibility that the countries opposing the Iraq War might have parochial motivations. For example, France had significant oil interests in Saddam's Iraq, and Iraq was an important trading partner for Germany. The French government at the time was led by the unpopular prime minister Jacques Chirac and foreign minister Dominique de Villepin. Both men found playing to anti-American crowds enhanced their popularity. As one reporter wrote in February 2003, "A year into his second presidential term, the conservative Gaullist president is enjoying soaring popularity at home, which has eluded him for much of his political career."[147] Chirac even made the short list for the Nobel Peace Prize in 2003.[148]

---

144 Adrian Hyde-Pierce, *European Security in the 21st Century: The Challenge of Multipolarity* (London and New York: Routledge), 25; Janusz Bugajski and Ilona Teleki, *Atlantic Bridges: America's New European Allies*, (Lanham: Rowman & Littlefield Publishers), 139.

145 "Chirac Lashes Out at 'New Europe,'" CNN, February 18, 2003, http://www.cnn.com/2003/WORLD/europe/02/18/sprj.irq.chirac/.

146 Bugajski and Teleki, *Atlantic Bridges: America's New European Allies*, 66.

147 Elizabeth Bryant, "France Says 'Oui' to Chirac's 'Non' on Iraq / Opposition to US Makes Him Popular," *SFGate*, February 22, 2003, http://www.sfgate.com/politics/article/France-says-oui-to-Chirac-s-non-on-Iraq-war-2668876.php.

148 Ibid.

American antiwar politicians also ignored the fact that France had never been a stout US ally and always had a vein of anti-American feeling.[149] History is replete with examples of France acting counter to American interests. France left NATO's military structure in 1962 and had always attempted to chart a foreign policy course more independent of the United States and United Kingdom. The French refused to allow US aircraft to cross French airspace when the United States bombed Libya in 1986 in retaliation for a terrorist attack on a discotheque in Berlin that killed American servicemen. France and Chirac regularly referred to their vision of a "multipolar" world.[150] The Iraq War presented France an opportunity to cement its position at the head of a European foreign policy that represented an alternative—and frequently outright opposition—to the United States.[151]

France's commitment to multilateral diplomacy and a multipolar world represents an effort to punch above its weight in foreign affairs. There is nothing inherently unexpected in France's seeking to maximize its influence in foreign affairs; countries do what they need to do to assert their interests as they see them. However, it is important to see efforts like France's and the United Nations' for what they are: efforts by a nation (or group of nations) to assert its own interests. Multilateralism should not be seen as conveying a special legitimacy on diplomatic or military action, and actions taken by a

---

149 Robert Novak, "France's American Problem," December 2, 2004, http://www.cnn.com/2004/ALLPOLITICS/12/02/france.problem/index.html?_s=PM:ALLPOLITICS.

150 Jean-Marc Coicaud, with Helene Gandois and Lysette Rutgers, "Explaining France's Opposition to the War against Iraq," in *The Iraq Crisis and World Order*, eds. Ramesh Thakur and Waheguru Pal Singh Sidhu (Tokyo: United Nations University Press, 2006), 241, Google Books edition, https://books.google.com/books?id=e8prnhxUutkC&pg=PA234&lpg=PA234&dq=Explaining+France%E2%80%99s+Opposition+to+the+War+in+Iraq+by+Jean-Marc+Coicaud,+with+Helene+Gandois+and+Lysette+Rutgers&source=bl&ots=0hODFgBzTX&sig=jADHlIWZxjm4vC2i95ce5nJwiLc&hl=en&sa=X&ved=0CCIQ6AEwAWoVChMIp8_RyPbbyAIVRRo-Ch3P0QSt#v=onepage&q=Explaining%20France%E2%80%99s%20Opposition%20to%20the%20War%20in%20Iraq%20by%20Jean-Marc%20Coicaud%2C%20with%20Helene%20Gandois%20and%20Lysette%20Rutgers&f=false.

151 John O'Sullivan, "Blair vs. Chirac," *National Review Online*, March 24, 2003, accessed October 24, 2015, http://www.nationalreview.com/article/206299/blair-vs-chirac-john-osullivan.

nation unilaterally should not, ipso facto, be viewed as illegitimate. Nations come together in coalitions and alliances based on their national interests. If multilateralism is in a country's national interest, that country will support multilateralism; if not, it probably will not support multilateralism. It has ever been thus, and to read more into France's opposition to the Iraq War—that somehow the United States lost friends and allies as a result of the war—gives France, the United Nations, and the concept of multilateralism credit they do not deserve.

Moreover, as a number of articles have observed, France had many reasons based on its own parochial, national interests for opposing the Iraq War.[152] France had close economic relations with Iraq dating back to the 1970s.[153] French oil companies such as Total had significant interests in Iraqi oil fields.[154] France proposed and was a driving force behind the United Nations' Oil for Food program, which investigators later discovered to be thoroughly corrupt.[155] France also believed it might be in line for additional oil concessions should the UN sanctions regime on Iraq be weakened.[156] France's vision of a multipolar world, with France at the center of the European pole and limiting US freedom of action in international venues such as the United Nations, played a role in France's Iraq War opposition.[157] Finally, France simply may have had a different conception of the threat of terrorism, not having experienced anything on the scale of September 11.[158]

The canard that the United States had invaded Iraq unilaterally was a powerful one and came to define the antiwar movement and the Democratic Party in both the 2004 and 2008 elections. The same Pew survey cited earlier found that 78 percent of 2004 Dean primary voters believed that the United

---

152 Jae-Seung Lee, "Defending the National Interests?: Rethinking France and the Iraq War," *Korean Journal of International Relations*, vol. 46, no. 5 (2006).

153 Coicaud et al., "Explaining France's Opposition to the War in Iraq," 240; Lee, "Defending the National Interests?: Rethinking France and the Iraq War," 83–85.

154 Ibid., 83.

155 Ibid., 84.

156 Ibid., 241.

157 Ibid.

158 Ibid., 242–43.

States should strongly take into account the interests of its allies.[159] Dean supporters far outpaced other voters in this belief; Pew found that even among Democrats only 49 percent held this view, while 38 percent believed the US foreign policy should focus mainly on US interests.[160] Moreover, a whopping 96 percent of Dean voters said they believed "effective diplomacy" rather than "military strength" was "the best way to ensure peace."[161] Dean's voters were the harbinger of things to come, as the idea of "effective diplomacy" replacing military force became a dominant theme of the Obama administration's foreign policy.

Having internalized the antiwar movement's elevation of diplomacy and its attacks on the Bush administration supposed diplomatic failures, John Kerry in 2004 and Barack Obama in 2008 both ran on the importance of having the support of the world when undertaking any military action. In the second 2004 presidential debate against George Bush, John Kerry enunciated a "global test" for the use of American force.[162] Barack Obama repeatedly cited how the Bush administration's foreign policy had left the United States alone and isolated in the world and called for the use of "smart power" to achieve America's aims in the world. The terminology *smart power* clearly implied that the United States had been exercising the opposite under President Bush.

Obama's unflinching belief in diplomacy came through in various points of the campaign. In a 2008 primary debate, when asked if he would sit down to negotiate with enemies of the United States without preconditions, he stated, "I would."[163] At the time, columnist Charles Krauthammer referred to this statement as a "metastatic gaffe," arguing that the statement in the debate was a gaffe but, rather than walking it back or adding caveats to it, the Obama

159 "An In-Depth Look: The Dean Activists: Their Profile and Prospects," Pew Research Center, 4.

160 Ibid., 4.

161 Ibid., 27.

162 "John Kerry: 'Global Test,'" March 18, 2003, http://www.c-span.org/video/?c4390391/john-kerry-global-test; "Kerry Dismisses Criticism of 'Global Test' Remark as 'Pathetic,'" CNN, October 5, 2005, http://www.cnn.com/2004/ALLPOLITICS/10/04/kerry.global/.

163 "YouTube Debate: Would You Meet With Syria/Iran/North Korea?," PoliticsTV.com, https://www.youtube.com/watch?v=x1dSPrb5w_k.

campaign elevated it to a policy centerpiece.[164] In fact, Obama's statement in the debate neatly reflected the antiwar movement's approach to foreign policy in the wake of the Iraq War and the elevation of diplomacy and multilateralism as the only legitimate means of resolving international disputes. The point may have been metastatic, but it was not a gaffe. It was the embodiment of a new approach to foreign policy that the antiwar movement and the antiwar Democratic Party elevated to prominence as a direct result of the Iraq War well before Obama's debate response.

In July 2008, as a presidential candidate, Barack Obama gave a speech on the situation in Iraq and Afghanistan. In it, he stated,

> But the depth of this tragedy also drew out the decency and determination of our nation. At blood banks and vigils; in schools and in the United States Congress, Americans were united—more united, even, than we were at the dawn of the Cold War. The world, too, was united against the perpetrators of this evil act, as old allies, new friends, and even long-time adversaries stood by our side. It was time—once again—for America's might and moral suasion to be harnessed; it was time to once again shape a new security strategy for an ever-changing world.
>
> Imagine, for a moment, what we could have done in those days, and months, and years after 9/11.
>
> We could have deployed the full force of American power to hunt down and destroy Osama bin Laden, al Qaeda, the Taliban, and all of the terrorists responsible for 9/11, while supporting real security in Afghanistan.
>
> We could have secured loose nuclear materials around the world, and updated a 20th century non-proliferation framework to meet the challenges of the 21st.

---

164 Charles Krauthammer, "Obama's Metastatic Gaffe," *Washington Post*, May 23, 2008, http://www.washingtonpost.com/wp-dyn/content/article/2008/05/22/AR2008052203016.html.

> We could have invested hundreds of billions of dollars in alternative sources of energy to grow our economy, save our planet, and end the tyranny of oil.
>
> We could have strengthened old alliances, formed new partnerships, and renewed international institutions to advance peace and prosperity.
>
> We could have called on a new generation to step into the strong currents of history, and to serve their country as troops and teachers, Peace Corps volunteers and police officers.
>
> We could have secured our homeland—investing in sophisticated new protection for our ports, our trains and our power plants.
>
> We could have rebuilt our roads and bridges, laid down new rail and broadband and electricity systems, and made college affordable for every American to strengthen our ability to compete.
>
> We could have done that...
>
> This must be the moment when we answer the call of history. For eight years, we have paid the price for a foreign policy that lectures without listening; that divides us from one another—and from the world—instead of calling us to a common purpose; that focuses on our tactics in fighting a war without end in Iraq instead of forging a new strategy to face down the true threats that we face. We cannot afford four more years of a strategy that is out of balance and out of step with this defining moment.[165]

Although this is couched in reasonable-sounding language, the Democrats actually were enunciating a radical new requirement—highly influenced by the antiwar movement—that the world support a US foreign policy goal before the United States takes action to achieve it. Never in world history has a world power suggested this level of solicitousness of world opinion to achieve its national security and foreign policy aims. By saying that the United States pursued a foreign policy under the Bush administration that divided "us from the

---

165 "Obama's Remarks on Afghanistan," *New York Times*, July 15, 2008, http://www.nytimes.com/2008/07/15/us/politics/15text-obama.html?pagewanted=all&_r=0.

world," Obama effectively enunciated the principle that the only legitimate American military action is one that is supported by the world. The argument over the Bush administration's "unilateralism" in Iraq that the antiwar movement used to discredit the war and challenge its legitimacy proved so strong that it moved the Democrats to adopt it as fundamental policy.

Moreover, Obama and the Democrats made the idea of "strengthen[ing] alliances, form[ing] new partnerships, and renew[ing] international institutions" not a means to an end but an end itself. That is, if the United States unites the world behind it, that unity in and of itself represents success, regardless of whether the US has achieved the foreign policy objective for which it sought the world's unity in the first place.

What the antiwar movement and its political supporters failed to consider in enunciating the radical new "global test" of US foreign policy is that other countries continue to make decisions based on calculations of their own national interests or other parochial concerns (such as the political considerations of Chirac, de Villepin, and Schroeder). One of my father's undergraduate professors at Johns Hopkins University once said that there are no real international laws, just international interests, and it is these interests that govern how a country interacts with the world. The situation in Ukraine in 2014 and 2015 is instructive in this regard. While President Obama and the US State Department sonorously intoned against Russian violations of "international norms" and "twentieth-century behavior in the twenty-first century," Russia gobbled up more and more Ukrainian territory.

The antiwar movement's fetishizing the importance of world support for US foreign policy and military action, of having allies at all costs, and of playing by international norms grew directly out of the criticisms of the Iraq War. The antiwar movement, and the Democratic Party it captured, elevated a critique of the Iraq War—that the war did not have universal world support—into a guiding principle of their foreign policy. John Kerry's "global test"—considered a gaffe in the 2004 debates—is now a fundamental tenet of Democratic foreign policy.

The Pew poll results that showed 96 percent of Dean voters believed more strongly in "effective diplomacy" than "military strength" to ensure peace is mirrored almost perfectly by the Obama administration's foreign policy statements. From the first, the Obama administration sought to distinguish its foreign policy from President Bush's. The president-elect website for the Obama administration included the following foreign policy imperatives:

> *Renew our Alliances:* Obama and Biden will rebuild our alliances to meet the common challenges of the 21st century. America is strongest when we act alongside strong partners. Now is the time for a new era of international cooperation that strengthens old partnerships and builds new ones to confront the common challenges of the 21st century—terrorism and nuclear weapons; climate change and poverty; genocide and disease.
>
> *Talk to our Foes and Friends:* Obama and Biden will pursue tough, direct diplomacy without preconditions with all nations, friend and foe. They will do the careful preparation necessary, but will signal that America is ready to come to the table and is willing to lead. And if America is willing to come to the table, the world will be more willing to rally behind American leadership to deal with challenges like confronting terrorism and Iran and North Korea's nuclear programs.[166]

These policies were designed to sound like a direct response to and rebuke of the Bush administration's diplomacy on Iraq and the supposed diminishing of US alliances that resulted from the diplomatic maneuverings before and during the Iraq War. The language used to describe America's approach to the Iranian nuclear issue neatly reflects this world view in its emphasis on being willing to come to the table, working in cooperation with international partners and achieving "international cooperation," and achieving diplomatic solutions at all costs without any real threat of military force should diplomacy fail. In effect, the policy simply does not allow for diplomacy to fail.

As events have unfolded in the Middle East, Ukraine, Asia, and elsewhere, this policy demonstrably is untenable. As Russia, China, Iran, and

166 "Agenda—Foreign Policy," Change.gov, Office of the President-Elect, accessed October 24, 2015, http://change.gov/agenda/foreign_policy_agenda/.

others demonstrate with painful regularity, other world powers—particularly those that seek to do the most harm to US national interests and the US homeland itself—do not employ a "global test" in taking action. These countries understand the language of power, and worse, they understand that the United States' overemphasis on global approval and support leaves the United States fighting with one hand tied behind its back.

One additional point: the United States had the world's goodwill after the September 11 attacks because it was the victim of the most heinous single terrorist attack on civilians in history. The United States was wounded, injured, and suffering. Yet the antiwar movement and the Democratic Party it captured look to the immediate post–September 11 period as a halcyon period for US relations with the rest of the world. It is when the United States is in a weakened condition that the world sympathizes with it and supports it. That is, in order for the United States to have the support of the world, it must be wounded, bleeding, and humbled. When the United States projects power to defend what it perceives as its national security interests, this world consensus suddenly is shattered. According to the antiwar movement and the Democratic candidates it captured during the 2004 campaign, shattering that consensus was unacceptable.

Much of the antiwar movement's critique about the need to unite the world behind US military action and their adoption of the "global test" for the use of military force can be traced to the run-up to the Iraq War. The fact that the Iraq War appeared to divide countries and lose allies for the United States can be traced to the outspoken opposition of France and Germany to the Iraq War. And much of the French and German opposition to the Iraq War can be traced to the political ambitions and popularity seeking of Jacques Chirac, Dominique de Villepin, and Gerhard Schroeder. So a fundamental plank of current Democratic foreign policy thinking ultimately can be traced back to the craven political needs of unpopular (and in the case at least of Chirac, corrupt) French and German politicians.

Ironically, the same international community that so berated the United States' "unilateral" war in Iraq when George W. Bush was president now wishes for greater US involvement in world affairs. Many of the same people who decried US action in Iraq now decry US inaction in Syria. The *Economist* featured a cover story on "why America must not abandon the [Middle East]" in its June 6, 2015, issue. The lead article referenced America's supposedly "dangerous modesty" and concluded that, by taking an active role in the upheaval in the Middle East, the United States might help transition the region to better governance or at least avoid some of the worst possible outcomes. Moreover, when the United States does disengage, other countries are forced to try to deal with crises. In the case of the Middle East, no country in the region—not Turkey, not Saudi Arabia, not even Israel—truly is capable of projecting the level of force likely to defeat ISIS or resist Iran's efforts to become the regional hegemon. Moreover, these countries' disparate interests make coordinated action to achieve common ends unlikely. Turkey, for example, entered the war against ISIS only in the summer of 2015 but used that combat as cover for a relentless assault on the Kurds, who are one of the few effective anti-ISIS forces. Painful experience is once again leading to the conclusion that only the United States has the combination of power and ideals necessary to create an acceptable outcome. No one is looking to the Russians or the Chinese to solve the conflict; even though the United States has deliberately stayed removed from the Syrian conflict, expressly stating that it will not embark on another Iraq-style involvement, only the United States is seen as the country both capable of brokering and likely to broker the most palatable outcome to the most parties.

The upshot of all of these events and the world's reaction to US involvement in them is that the United States will never please the world when it comes to involvement in world affairs. Overly aggressive US intervention leads to condemnation of the "cowboy" United States; too little intervention or a hands-off approach leads to chaos and ultimately, as in Syria, pleas for deeper US involvement. In short, the United States is damned if it does and damned if it doesn't. Knowing that, the United States simply should assert its own interests when it concludes action is necessary. In the immortal words of Rick Nelson, "You can't please everyone, so you've got to please yourself."

CHAPTER 6

The Beginning of the Iraq Occupation and Abu Ghraib: Renewed Antiwar Sentiment and Finding Iraq's My Lai

THE ANTIWAR OPPOSITION HAD BEGUN to stir and take steps to discredit the war even in the earliest moments of the victory over Saddam, as looters ransacked museums and the artistic community held the US military responsible for not protecting museums adequately in the aftermath of the fall of Saddam. Three members of the President's Advisory Committee on Cultural Property resigned in protest of the looting of museums in Baghdad and Mosul.[167] One of the resigning members, Martin Sullivan, who had been the chairman of the committee, snidely remarked that "in a pre-emptive war that's the kind of thing you should have planned for."[168] One almost can hear the disdain and derision in Mr. Sullivan's voice as he invokes the term "preemptive war" to suggest that the Bush administration, in planning for everything else about the war, should have also anticipated the looting of museums. Mr. Sullivan and his two colleagues likely did not support the Iraq War or the doctrine of preemption and used the admittedly unfortunate looting of the museums to discredit the Bush administration and the larger war effort. For these antiwar activists, the looting of a museum outweighed the obvious delight of Iraqis

167 "US Experts Resign over Iraq Looting," BBC News, April 18, 2003, http://news.bbc.co.uk/2/hi/entertainment/2958009.stm.

168 Ibid.

celebrating the fall of the hated Saddam Hussein, one of the most murderous tyrants of the second half of the twentieth century.

As will be described in more detail later in this book, the press also fed the notion that the war was unsuccessful and destined to failure. As if to reprise the role of Walter Cronkite in his opposition to the Vietnam War, which he concluded was unwinnable after the Tet Offensive, network news channels regularly reported every grim milestone of the war—2,000th casualty, 2,500th casualty, 3,000th casualty, and so on.[169] The *Washington Post* had a feature displaying the "Faces of the Fallen," though it displayed only the faces of the fallen and not their stories—who they were and why they chose to serve.[170] Each such milestone was accompanied by defeatist media coverage. An office building on K Street in Washington, DC, featured a sign listing the number of casualties in the war.

The Events at Abu Ghraib Prison

The next major event that the antiwar movement seized upon to discredit the Iraq War was the prison abuse scandal at Abu Ghraib. In the fall of 2003, US soldiers responsible for managing detainees in prisons in Iraq committed a series of prisoner abuses. Some resulted in prisoner deaths; in some cases, US soldiers photographed the abuse.

In January 2004, Army Specialist Joseph Darby discovered photographs showing detainee abuse in Iraq and turned them in to his supervisors. The Army launched an investigation of the 800th Military Police Brigade, which was responsible for the operation of Abu Ghraib prison. The investigation, led by Maj. Gen. Antonio Taguba, produced the Taguba Report, which Lt. Gen. Ricardo Sanchez, commander of US forces in Iraq, received in April 2004.[171] The Taguba Report found numerous instances of misconduct within

169 "US Deaths in Iraq Reach 2,500," *USA Today*, June 15, 2006, http://usatoday30.usatoday.com/news/world/iraq/2006-06-15-iraq-deaths_x.htm.

170 "Faces of the Fallen," *Washington Post*, http://apps.washingtonpost.com/national/fallen/.

171 "Iraq Prison Abuse Fast Facts," CNN, http://www.cnn.com/2013/10/30/world/meast/iraq-prison-abuse-scandal-fast-facts/; "Final Report of the Independent Panel to Review DoD Detention Operations" (hereinafter, "Schlesinger Report"), August 2004, 39.

the 800th Military Police Brigade. The Taguba Report found a number of "egregious acts and grave breaches of international law" at Abu Ghraib and attributed them to poor leadership, inadequate training, poor communications, and a desire to obtain intelligence from detainees.[172]

Lieutenant General Sanchez commissioned a second investigation under the leadership of Maj. Gen. George Fay. The investigation focused on the involvement of military intelligence in the abuses at Abu Ghraib. The Fay Report concluded that the "primary causes [of the prisoner abuses] are misconduct (ranging from inhumane to sadistic) by a small group of morally corrupt soldiers and civilians, a lack of discipline on the part of the leaders and Soldiers of the 205th MI BDE and a failure or lack of leadership by multiple echelons within CJTF-7. Contributing factors can be traced to issues affecting Command and Control, Doctrine, Training, and the experience of the Soldiers we asked to perform this vital mission."[173] In the cases of the most egregious sadistic and sexual abuse, the Fay Report found that "soldiers knew they were violating the approved [interrogation] techniques and procedures."[174] The Fay Report also found numerous failures of commanders to supervise soldiers properly but that "neither Department of Defense nor Army doctrine caused any abuses."[175] Nevertheless, the Fay Report recommended that the Army refine and update guidance on performing interrogations.[176]

The Department of Defense also commissioned an investigation into the prisoner abuse allegations. The Department of Defense investigation panel was chaired by former defense and energy secretary James Schlesinger and also included former defense secretary Harold Brown, who served President Jimmy Carter, and former congresswoman Tillie Fowler (D-FL). The Schlesinger panel released its report to Defense Secretary Rumsfeld on August 26, 2004. With regard to the abuses at Abu Ghraib's Cell Block 1, the famous photos

---

172 AR 15-6 Investigation of the 800th Military Police Brigade (hereinafter, "Taguba Report"), 15–21, 50.

173 Investigation of Intelligence Activities at Abu Ghraib (hereinafter, "Fay Report"), Executive Summary, 2.

174 Fay Report, 3.

175 Ibid.

176 Ibid.

of which CBS's *60 Minutes* released in an April 2004 story about the Abu Ghraib abuses, the Schlesinger panel concluded that "the aberrant behavior that occurred on the night shift in Cell Block 1 would have been avoided with proper training, leadership, and oversight. Though acts of abuse occurred at a number of locations, those in Cell Block 1 have a unique nature fostered by the predilections of the noncommissioned officers in charge. Had these noncommissioned officers behaved more like those on the day shift, these acts, which one participant described as 'just for the fun of it,' would not have taken place."[177] The Schlesinger Report generally concurred with the findings of the Taguba and Fay Reports, including with regard to leadership and command problems and confusion about which interrogation techniques had been authorized for use in Iraq. In particular, the report found that command officers and their staffs at various levels failed in their duties and staff officers provided poor advice regarding detention and interrogation.[178] The report also noted that the various military police and intelligence organizations were underresourced, particularly as it became clearer that a longer counterinsurgency campaign was likely.[179]

The Schlesinger Report also described a complicated, detailed process in which Secretary Rumsfeld sought to develop stronger interrogation techniques to "counter tenacious resistance from detainees" at the prison facility at Guantánamo Bay, Cuba.[180] Secretary Rumsfeld had established a working group to develop interrogation policies for Guantánamo Bay, which produced a list of techniques approved for use at Guantánamo.[181] However, the Schlesinger Report found that some of these policies migrated to Iraq and became more problematic when used outside Guantánamo's carefully controlled conditions.[182]

177 Schlesinger Report, 13.

178 Ibid., 43.

179 Ibid., 15.

180 Ibid., 6.

181 Ibid., 8.

182 Ibid., 9.

The Schlesinger Report also provided evidence that detainee abuse was not widespread. The report noted that, from the beginning of hostilities in Afghanistan and Iraq to mid-August 2004, US forces had apprehended approximately fifty thousand individuals. As of mid-August 2004, the military faced approximately 300 allegations of abuse in Afghanistan, Iraq, and the prison at Guantánamo Bay, Cuba. Of these approximately 300 allegations, the military had investigated 155 of them and found 66 substantiated cases.[183] The report stated that about one-third of the allegations of abuse stemmed from the moments of capture or at the tactical collection point and not after settlement within a prison facility.[184]

Overall, a few threads are apparent from the various reports commissioned by the Army and Department of Defense. First, the most heinous, egregious, sadistic abuses had been perpetrated by individual soldiers personally predisposed to such acts, and those individual soldiers had indisputably violated the rules and regulations governing their conduct. A variety of command and control issues led to inadequate supervision and oversight of military police and intelligence personnel. Finally, the military police and intelligence were overstretched because of poor planning resulting from the failure to anticipate a prolonged counterinsurgency and the infiltration of al-Qaeda elements into Iraq.

The investigations of Abu Ghraib found substantial fault throughout the military chain, from the military police and intelligence personnel serving at Abu Ghraib for their egregious misconduct, to their commanders, who failed to impose adequate supervision and oversight, to the political leadership of the Pentagon and at the White House, which failed to plan to have sufficient resources available for a prolonged insurgency. These investigations did not whitewash responsibility. Moreover, the Schlesinger panel was bipartisan, comprised of former senior defense and elected officials from both the Republican and Democratic parties.

The Schlesinger Report's finding of only sixty-six substantiated cases of abuse resulting from the detention of nearly fifty thousand individuals

---

183 Ibid., 5.

184 Ibid.

demonstrated that the abuse was not widespread, systemic, or ordered or encouraged by the highest levels of American government. There was no smoking gun order from the White House or Pentagon stating, "Thou shalt abuse prisoners in violation of international law." The Schlesinger Report found that "the vast majority of detainees in Guantánamo, Afghanistan, and Iraq were treated appropriately, and the great bulk of detention operations were conducted in compliance with US policy and directives."[185]

When one reviews the reports, it becomes apparent that the US military has the most developed military justice system of any major world power and that the investigations went to a depth unfathomable in any other world military except perhaps Israel. It is unthinkable that the Russians, for example, would conduct three detailed investigations of military misconduct and acknowledge failures in the midst of an ongoing conflict. To this day Russia denies it supplied the missiles that shot Malaysian Airlines Flight 17 out of the sky in eastern Ukraine.[186] The Chinese military would not engage in such soul-searching. And for countries like Iran, Syria, Venezuela, and North Korea, let alone ISIS, brutal atrocities are a regular part of the military's arsenal.

Abu Ghraib Becomes This Generation's My Lai

However, the antiwar movement and its followers in the political arena used Abu Ghraib to continue their efforts to discredit the entire war effort and to spread the belief that the war was illegitimate. To do this, the antiwar movement had to extend the conclusions of the investigative reports beyond their scope to impugn the motives of the highest officials of the Bush administration. Sen. Ted Kennedy in May 2004 said that "on March 19, 2004, President Bush asked, 'Who would prefer that Saddam's torture chambers still be open?'...Shamefully, we now learn that Saddam's torture chambers reopened

185 Ibid., 18.

186 Nicola Clark and Andrew E. Kramer, "Malaysia Airlines Flight 17 Most Likely Hit by Russian-Made Missile, Inquiry Says," *New York Times*, October 13, 2015, http://www.nytimes.com/2015/10/14/world/europe/mh17-malaysia-airlines-dutch-report.html?_r=0.

under new management: US management."[187] The idea that the United States simply "reopened" Saddam Hussein's torture chambers undermined the notion that the United States removed Saddam Hussein because of the threat he posed to his own people. Despite the vicious nature of this attack against US servicemen and servicewomen—calling them the equivalent of Saddam's torturers—the Democratic Party stood silently by and said nothing. *Boston Globe* columnist Jeff Jacoby wrote that "Kennedy's vile calumny should have triggered outrage. Here was the most prominent liberal politician in America accusing his own government of the very savagery it said it had gone to war to uproot. It was the worst kind of anti-American poison, and it was coming not from a crackpot with no following but from one of the most powerful Democrats in Congress. It should have unleashed an uproar. It unleashed nothing."[188]

By equating the actions of some US troops with the terror apparatus of the Iraqi state of Saddam Hussein, the antiwar movement intimated that the Iraq War had no purpose, no legitimacy, and no moral foundation. By implying that the United States had simply replaced one cruel dictatorial regime with another, the antiwar movement soured the American public on the war.

Former vice president Al Gore went even further, stating that prison abuses were the direct result of the Bush administration's approach to the war on terror. In a May 26, 2004, speech, Gore said,

> What happened at the prison, it is now clear, was not the result of random acts by "a few bad apples," it was the natural consequence of

---

187 Congressional Record—Senate, June 4, 2004, at 11548, Google Books edition, https://books.google.com/books?id=ZMdG0AlVQZoC&pg=PA11548&lpg=PA11548&dq=Shamefully,+we+now+learn+that+Saddam%E2%80%99s+torture+chambers+reopened+under+new+management:+US+management&source=bl&ots=H9q-BfYcru&sig=g73gQ0ORiM82-fSSK3_ZtZ0wJ8o&hl=en&sa=X&ved=0CB8Q6AEwAGoVChMItpHC0PfdyAIVxnE-Ch2vwgZX#v=onepage&q=Shamefully%2C%20we%20now%20learn%20that%20Saddam%E2%80%99s%20torture%20chambers%20reopened%20under%20new%20management%3A%20US%20management&f=false.

188 Jeff Jacoby, "Ted Kennedy's Anti-American Slander," *Boston Globe*, May 25, 2004, http://www.boston.com/news/globe/editorial_opinion/oped/articles/2004/05/25/ted_kennedys_anti_american_slander?pg=full.

> the Bush Administration policy that has dismantled those wise constraints and has made war on America's checks and balances.
>
> The abuse of the prisoners at Abu Ghraib flowed directly from the abuse of the truth that characterized the Administration's march to war and the abuse of the trust that had been placed in President Bush by the American people in the aftermath of September 11th…
>
> Private Lynndie England did not make the decision that the United States would not observe the Geneva Convention. Specialist Charles Graner was not the one who approved a policy of establishing an American Gulag of dark rooms with naked prisoners to be "stressed" and even—we must use the word—tortured—to force them to say things that legal procedures might not induce them to say…
>
> Nor did these abuses spring from a few twisted minds at the lowest ranks of our military enlisted personnel. No, it came from twisted values and atrocious policies at the highest levels of our government. This was done in our name, by our leaders…
>
> These horrors were the predictable consequence of policy choices that flowed directly from this administration's contempt for the rule of law. And the dominance they have been seeking is truly not simply unworthy of America—it is also an illusory goal in its own right.[189]

Gore was not the only one to use Abu Ghraib to discredit the war effort and the Bush administration. John Kerry, the 2004 Democratic presidential nominee at the time the Abu Ghraib scandal broke, called on Secretary of Defense Donald Rumsfeld to resign in the wake of the scandal. Kerry claimed that Rumsfeld had "set the climate in which these kinds of abuses were able to take place."[190]

These statements stood in stark contrast to the findings of the Taguba, Fay, and Schlesinger Reports. In effect, Al Gore, the former vice president of

---

189 Remarks by Al Gore, May 26, 2004, http://pol.moveon.org/goreremarks052604.html.

190 "Kerry Reiterates Call for Rumsfeld to Resign," CNN, August 25, 2004, http://www.cnn.com/2004/ALLPOLITICS/08/25/kerry.rumsfeld/.

the United States, and John Kerry, the would-be president, accused the current president of the United States and his administration of implementing policies that condoned and demanded that military interrogators and prison guards torture and commit sadistic acts against detainees. This accusation ignored the reams of evidence that the Bush administration neither ordered nor condoned such behavior. The detainee violations were reported by another soldier at Abu Ghraib and the US military and Department of Defense investigated the accusations and released the investigative reports publicly. The military prosecuted the perpetrators of the scandalous acts at Abu Ghraib.

Nevertheless, Gore's complaint fit snugly with the rest of the antiwar movement's attempts to undermine the credibility of the Bush administration. Gore cavalierly and without evidence connected the abuse at Abu Ghraib with "the abuse of the truth that characterized the Administration's march to war." Gore cited no specific abuses of the truth, though presumably he was referring to the failure to find large stocks of WMD or an active WMD program in Iraq. Gore left unspoken why a worldwide intelligence failure should bear any relationship to a prison scandal. However, by connecting the failure to find WMD with the Abu Ghraib prison scandal in the service of the theory that "Bush lied," the antiwar movement continued the Vietnam-esque effort to delegitimize the war and American political leadership.

The antiwar movement's drawing parallels between Abu Ghraib and the depravity of Saddam Hussein's regime was also an effort to draw moral equivalence between American actions in Iraq and Saddam's former regime. In effect—and Senator Kennedy essentially said it explicitly—the United States was no better than its enemies. This type of moral equivalence often is trotted out by the antiwar movement to oppose American intervention. Recall the moral equivalence expressed by the authors of the Not in Our Name "statement of conscience" described previously. After 9/11, rather than wanting to take the war to the terrorists who attacked the United States, antiwar activists in the United States engaged in a bout of "why-do-they-hate-us" handwringing. Making the case that America is no better than its enemies undermined the war effort by saying, in effect, that American intervention to rid Iraq of Saddam was hypocritical.

The antiwar movement and media also moved to expressly link Abu Ghraib to Vietnam and, in particular, the My Lai massacre. The *Los Angeles Times* published an opinion piece by Andrew Bacevich on August 31, 2004, one week after the release of the Schlesinger Report, titled "Military Must Squarely Face New My Lai."[191] In the article, Bacevich claimed that the Defense Department's response to Abu Ghraib and My Lai were similar in that "first came denial and then damage control. In passing off Abu Ghraib as the work of a few bad apples, Defense Department officials in 2004 behaved very much as had their predecessors in 1969. Then as now the hunt for expendable scapegoats began almost immediately, with Lt. William Calley the precursor of today's Pfc. Lynndie England."[192] The media placed great emphasis on the story; a dissertation written by Ramune Braziunaite found that coverage of prisoner abuses accounted for 23 percent of the *New York Times'* Iraq coverage and 25 percent of the *Washington Post*'s Iraq coverage during the period from April 29, 2004 (the day after the *60 Minutes* report on the Abu Ghraib abuses) through May 14, 2004.[193]

In fact, the Schlesinger Report, and the Fay and Taguba Reports before it, did not "hunt for expendable scapegoats"; the Schlesinger Report laid blame throughout the chain of command and noted that the political leadership's postwar planning was inadequate. None of these reports claimed that the scandal was merely the result of "a few bad apples." Yet the antiwar movement and the media quickly compared Abu Ghraib to My Lai. Given the perception of Vietnam as an immoral and failed war, comparing Iraq to Vietnam moved public opinion toward the conclusion that Iraq was an immoral, failed, unwinnable war.

Seymour Hersh, the *New Yorker* reporter who broke the My Lai story, ran a piece in the May 10, 2004, issue of the *New Yorker* titled "Torture in Abu Ghraib." The lede was, "American soldiers brutalized Iraqis. How far up

---

191 Andrew Bacevich, "Military Must Face New 'My Lai,'" *Los Angeles Times*, August 31, 2004, http://articles.latimes.com/2004/aug/31/opinion/oe-bacevich31.

192 Ibid.

193 Ramune Braziunaite, "Isolated Incidents or Deliberate Policy? Media Framing of US Abu Ghraib and British Detainee Abuse Scandals during the Iraq War" (PhD diss., Bowling Green State University, 2011), 104, 127.

does the responsibility go?"[194] This lede insinuated the possibility that the responsibility for the prisoner abuses reached the political leadership within the Pentagon and White House. The article quoted extensively from the Taguba Report. However, unlike the Taguba Report, Hersh hinted at the possibility of political leadership within the Bush administration being responsible for the abuses. Hersh wrote, "As the international furor grew, senior military officers, and President Bush, insisted that the actions of a few did not reflect the conduct of the military as a whole. Taguba's report, however, amounts to an unsparing study of collective wrongdoing and the failure of Army leadership at the highest levels."[195] However, the Taguba Report did not implicate the "highest levels" of Army leadership—the secretary of defense, secretary of the army, army chief of staff, and so on. Rather, it laid blame on "senior leaders in both the 800th MP Brigade and the 205th MI Brigade."

Hersh's series of articles on Abu Ghraib in 2004 became part of the narrative linking Iraq to Vietnam. As the *New York Times* put it, Hersh's *New Yorker* articles "helped set the political agenda by reporting that once again American soldiers in the midst of a war where the enemy is elusive and the cause is complicated had committed atrocious acts."[196] The media thus expressly linked Vietnam and Iraq as similar wars—an "elusive enemy" and a cause that was "complicated" resulting in similar war crimes by American soldiers.

Bacevich went on to say that "in a war that is ultimately about values, as the war on terror surely is, the erosion of soldierly standards in the US armed forces, if left unchecked, could well mean the difference between our victory and defeat."[197] This sentiment once again reveals the antiwar movement's use of a belief that the war on terror is a war about "values" and that if the United States somehow fails to live up to its values in every instance, it will lose

194 Seymour M. Hersh, "Torture at Abu Ghraib," *The New Yorker*, May 10, 2004, http://www.newyorker.com/magazine/2004/05/10/torture-at-abu-ghraib.

195 Ibid.

196 David Carr, "Dogged Reporter's Impact, from My Lai to Abu Ghraib," *New York Times*, May 20, 2004, http://www.nytimes.com/2004/05/20/arts/dogged-reporter-s-impact-from-my-lai-to-abu-ghraib.html.

197 Bacevich, "Military Must Squarely Face New 'My Lai.'"

the war. It is the same logic that the antiwar movement frequently deploys, without evidence, to claim the United States is creating terrorists by maintaining the prison at Guantánamo.

The fact is that victory in Iraq did not depend on the United States being viewed as having better "values." The Islamic State of Iraq and Syria (ISIS), the terrorist group which took control of significant portions of western Iraq and eastern Syria in 2014 and 2015, has claimed many victories, held a huge swath of territory at the end of 2015, and is not equipped with a JAG Corps. Torture, sex slavery, and terrorism are official ISIS policies. Claiming responsibility for the attacks of November 2015 it perpetrated in Paris, ISIS referred to the attacks as "blessed." In fact, the Iraqis may well have been shocked that the United States investigated the activities at Abu Ghraib and prosecuted and punished the perpetrators. When opponents of the war claim that particular incidents are undermining the war on terror because the incidents undermine American values, they are effectively advocating not engaging in conflict under any circumstances. And when they argue that the United States is just as bad as its enemies, they are making the case that American intervention under any circumstances would be hypocritical and unjustified.

CHAPTER 7

Vietnam Envy in Full: The Antiwar Movement's Vietnam Pantomime Reaches Full Flower

---

As the Iraq War continued past the 2004 election, into the difficult years of 2005–2007 before the surge, the antiwar movement was emboldened as setbacks in Iraq continued. But as the protests and political opposition turned even stronger and more strident, it became more apparent that the antiwar movement didn't just believe the Iraq War was becoming another Vietnam. In some ways, they *wanted* it to become another Vietnam. They craved another Vietnam. For the younger generation, Iraq provided it its own opportunity to protest in the streets, to speak truth to power, and to experience the frisson of campus activism for which the 1960s have become legendary. For veterans of the Vietnam antiwar movement, Iraq represented a chance to relive old glories, to shut down the streets while carrying American flags with peace symbols. For general antiwar and anti-Western protesters, it represented another opportunity to embarrass and humiliate the global capitalist hegemon. During the 2005–2007 period, when opportunities to mimic Vietnam War opposition and protests presented themselves, the antiwar movement quickly seized them.

The Public Antiwar Movement Reaches Its Peak

The setbacks in the United States' occupation of Iraq injected new life into the antiwar movement, which had flagged to some degree after the quick overthrow of Saddam Hussein's regime. By 2005, as the occupation continued to suffer at the hands of al-Qaeda in Iraq and contend with the threats of Iranian-backed Shia militias, the antiwar movement added further challenges to the United States' ability to fight and win in Iraq.

On September 25, 2005, a massive rally took place in Washington, DC, as a crowd of between one hundred thousand and two hundred thousand protesters came to the National Mall to protest the Iraq War.[198] Protests also took place in San Francisco, London, and elsewhere. Once again, one of the organizers of the protest was ANSWER, an anticapitalist group operated by the Workers World Party that journalist David Corn once said "is run by WWP activists to such an extent that it seems fair to dub it a WWP front."[199] In other words, the antiwar protests in September 2005 that supposedly demonstrated the public turning against the war were organized by outfits that are opposed to the United States, capitalism, and the West generally. In fact, ANSWER was formed three days after the September 11, 2001, attacks. The timing of its formation suggests its intent was to restrain any US response to the attacks.

The protest had all of the trappings of the typical antiwar protest: peace symbols, preprinted International ANSWER placards, placards saying that Bush was "making a killing" with dollar signs in his eyes, and the American flag with peace symbols instead of stars.[200] Other protesters brandished signs saying "Bush lied, thousands died" and "End the occupation."[201] The canard that Bush had somehow "lied" the United States into Iraq was alive and well and formed the foundation of the protest. The loaded term *end the occupation* was a not-so-subtle allusion to the idea that the United States was an imperialist, occupying power rather than a country trying to midwife a free, stable, and

198 Gwyneth K. Shaw, "Tens of Thousands Protest Iraq War," *Baltimore Sun*, September 25, 2005, http://articles.baltimoresun.com/2005-09-25/news/0509250018_1_iraq-war-washington-bush.

199 David Corn, "Behind the Placards," *LA Weekly*, October 30, 2002, http://www.laweekly.com/news/behind-the-placards-2135513.

200 Eugene Taylor, "Anti-War Protest Washington, D.C.," YouTube video, September 24, 2005, https://www.youtube.com/watch?v=WB3t0WmUNIo.

201 Miranda S. Spivack and Petula Dvorak, "Antiwar Protests Commence in Washington," *Washington Post*, September 24, 2005, http://www.washingtonpost.com/wp-dyn/content/article/2005/09/24/AR2005092400852.html.

independent Iraq. The *Washington Post* said that, within the protest, which included a march past the White House, "riffs on Vietnam-era protests were plentiful, with messages declaring, 'Make Levees, Not War' [referencing the levees that failed during Hurricane Katrina in New Orleans in August 2005], 'I never thought I'd miss Nixon' and 'Iraq is Arabic for Vietnam.' Many in the crowd had protested in the 1960s; others weren't even born during those tumultuous years."[202]

There were other signs and banners that made an appearance—signs that said, "If you want real peace make friends of enemies," "From New Orleans to Iraq: stop the war on the poor," and "No more blood for oil"; signs with the flags of Palestine and Venezuela; a few signs from Socialist Alternative; signs that said, "Free quality healthcare," "Israel's apartheid democracy," and "These colors don't run the world"; and a sign with a pigtailed, sad-eyed girl that said, "Stop the war in Iraq."[203] Another sign, hearkening back to the 1960s, read, "Our leaders are incompetent, reckless, arrogant so we must again question authority." There were large groups of university students with signs with the peace sign. Demonstrators set up a large faux cemetery on the National Mall with crosses for gravestones and pictures of soldiers killed in action.

In these signs, one can identify the Obama administration's foreign policy in embryo—the need for a humbler United States not "running the world"; the importance of "nation building" at home rather than abroad ("free quality healthcare"); the sympathy with the Palestinians and Venezuela (recall Obama's "bro shake" with Hugo Chávez early in the Obama presidency); and, perhaps most ominously, the need to speak to enemies without preconditions ("If you want real peace, make friends of enemies").

Celebrities and politicians turned out to excoriate the Bush administration. Rep. Maxine Waters demanded George Bush stop sending CIA agents overseas to undermine governments and said that "there are other Hugo Chavez's in the world who will stop you from undermining their country,"

---

202 Petula Dvorak, "Antiwar Fervor Fills the Streets," *Washington Post*, September 25, 2005, http://www.washingtonpost.com/wp-dyn/content/article/2005/09/24/AR2005092401701.html.
203 Eugene Taylor, "Anti-War Protest Washington, D.C."

demonstrating obvious solidarity with the Venezuelan dictator.[204] Actress Jessica Lange also spoke at the protest, continuing to press the lie that the Bush administration intended to colonize Iraq and the Middle East: "They say there is no way to withdraw now. The truth is, they never intend to withdraw. What they planned was a continuing military presence in the Middle East, control over the region, control over the oil. They had their eyes on the prize, the master plan."[205] The ubiquitous Joan Baez made another appearance to sing the antiwar ballad "Where Have All the Flowers Gone?" Before she took the stage, she was introduced as someone who was "still fighting the power."

All told, the protest combined the traditional hallmarks of 1960s protest—somewhere, Jake Elwood was enjoying the band getting back together—with trendier causes of the modern-day antiwar, anti-Western left. A protester in her late fifties told a reporter, "I was marching in '68, and I'm back today."[206]

Nevertheless, the public began to sympathize with the antiwar movement. In a *USA Today*/Gallup poll taken the weekend before the September 2005 protests, a 55 percent majority said the United States should intensify efforts to withdraw from Iraq—which had risen from 37 percent in August 2004.[207] Asked about this turn of public opinion against the Iraq War, historian Robert Dallek, a biographer of Presidents Kennedy and Johnson, stated that he believed Bush suffered the same "credibility gap" Johnson suffered over Vietnam and that the United States' efforts to build a successful democracy in Iraq resemble Johnson's efforts in Vietnam.[208] Dallek even said he believed the Iraqi insurgency looked like an updated version of the Viet Cong.[209]

---

204 Ibid.

205 "Actor Jessica Lange Speaks Out at Antiwar Protest in DC," *Democracy Now!*, September 26, 2005, http://www.democracynow.org/2005/9/26/actor_jessica_lange_speaks_out_at.

206 Spivack and Dvorak, "Antiwar Protests Commence in Washington."

207 John Ritter, "Anti-War Protesters Pick Up Steam and Take Cause to D.C.," *USA Today*, September 22, 2005, http://usatoday30.usatoday.com/news/washington/2005-09-22-protest-dc_x.htm.

208 Ibid.

209 Ibid.

Therefore, it is apparent that the protests had their intended effect—to cause the American public to sour on the war and, worse, to see the war through the lens of Vietnam. Perhaps more detailed, public reporting on the organizers of the protests might have affected the public reaction to them.

The Cindy Sheehan Episode

Perhaps the greatest throwback to the Vietnam-era protest movement was the rise and promotion of Cindy Sheehan. Sheehan was the mother of Army Specialist Casey Sheehan, who was killed in action in Iraq in April 2004.[210] Sheehan became a media celebrity and a celebrity of the antiwar movement when she camped out near President Bush's Crawford, Texas, ranch beginning on August 6, 2005, hoping to see the president while he was vacationing there.[211] Her story quickly became major news, and by August 12—one week later—Sheehan was working with a political consultant and a team of public relations professionals and starring in a television advertisement.[212]

The antiwar movement quickly sprung to life to champion its newest hero. The *Washington Post* noted that "her cause has also been aided by political organizers who swiftly mobilized around her—recognizing an opportunity to cause acute discomfort for a vacationing president and put a powerful emotional frame around the antiwar movement."[213] The *Post* stated that cable news was "dominated by coverage of Sheehan's crusade."[214] An antiwar group led by Ben Cohen (of Ben & Jerry's Ice Cream) hired a public relations firm to promote Sheehan, obtain media coverage, and host press conferences.[215]

---

210 "Honor the Fallen," *Military Times*, http://thefallen.militarytimes.com/army-spc-casey-sheehan/257123; "Mother of Fallen Soldier Protests at Bush Ranch," August 7, 2005, http://www.washingtonpost.com/wp-dyn/content/article/2005/08/06/AR2005080601337.html.

211 "Soldier's Mom Digs In Near Bush Ranch," CNN.com, August 7, 2005, http://www.cnn.com/2005/POLITICS/08/07/mom.protest/.

212 Michael A. Fletcher, "Cindy Sheehan's Pitched Battle," *Washington Post*, August 13, 2005, http://www.washingtonpost.com/wp-dyn/content/article/2005/08/12/AR2005081201816.html.

213 Ibid.

214 Ibid.

215 Ibid.

Howard Dean's 2004 campaign consultant, Joe Trippi, held a conference call with Sheehan for Internet bloggers to further promote the story.[216]

Salon said that Sheehan "launched an antiwar movement" and that her demand to meet with the president for him to explain why her son died "has immense power in a country that's beginning to understand it was lied to about the reasons for the Iraq war, at a time when the carnage seems not only endless but futile."[217] The echoes of Vietnam are apparent in *Salon*'s description of the Iraq War as one of "endless and futile" carnage based on presidential lies. Sheehan, like her predecessors in the Vietnam antiwar movement, served as the symbol and leader of protests against a pointless war based on lies. The author of the *Salon* piece, Joan Walsh, wrote, "I'm just old enough to remember grim footage from Vietnam on the nightly news, and it's starting to look familiar—maps of the latest attacks, the dead and wounded soldiers, the grieving families and, now, Cindy Sheehan and antiwar protesters. "[218] Exalting her heroic status, ABC News referred to Sheehan as an "antiwar icon."[219] Senator Barbara Boxer said that "What you're seeing with [Sheehan] trying to meet with President Bush is echoes of Vietnam. Because no one is seeing the light at the end of the tunnel."[220]

Sheehan also launched a TV ad in the local Waco market. In the ad, Sheehan restated the antiwar argument that the Bush administration deliberately misled the United States into war, saying, "You lied to us. And because of your lies, my son died."[221] She went on to ask, "How many more of our loved ones need to die in this senseless war?" In her comments, we once again hear

216 Ibid.

217 Joan Walsh, "The Mother of All Battles," *Salon*, August 16, 2005, http://www.salon.com/2005/08/16/mother_8/.

218 Ibid.

219 Eric Noe, "Cindy Sheehan: Antiwar Icon," ABC News, August 18, 2005, http://abcnews.go.com/GMA/story?id=1045556.

220 "Soldier's Mom Digs In Near Bush Ranch," CNN.com.

221 "Cindy Sheehan's Protest," *PBS NewsHour*, August 16, 2005, http://www.pbs.org/newshour/bb/military-july-dec05-sheehan_8-16/.

the echoes of John Kerry's famous question in his Senate testimony, "How do you ask a man to be the last man to die for a mistake?"[222]

Antiwar pundits seized the opportunity to attack the Bush administration. Maureen Dowd, columnist for the *New York Times*, famously claimed that Cindy Sheehan's "moral authority" was "absolute" as a mother who lost a son in Iraq.[223] When President Bush's staff pointed out the unhelpful fact that Sheehan previously had met the president and described the meeting warmly, Dowd accused Bush of simply trying to discredit her and, referring to the Plame affair, suggested that if Sheehan's husband was a CIA operative, "the Bushies could out him."[224]

By the end of August 2005, Sheehan and her "Camp Casey" was a media sensation. Folk singer Joan Baez came to the site and held concerts. Less than one month after Sheehan began her protest, a CBS News political analyst said that Sheehan had "become a logo…for the leftist anti-war movement which does seem to be growing."[225]

Sheehan spoke in front of the Capitol in Washington on September 21, a few days before the September 24, 2005, antiwar rally on the National Mall, having arrived as part of her Bring Them Home Now Tour.[226] Byron York, then a writer for the *National Review*, observed after Sheehan spoke that many of the protest organizers were protest veterans—of the protests against globalism, the World Bank, and the IMF in 2000 and elsewhere. York overheard a cameraman saying, "I've seen a lot of these people before." Pointing to a woman a few feet away, he said, "That one was at the World Bank thing. They're

---

222 "Vietnam Veterans against the War Statement by John Kerry to the Senate Committee on Foreign Relations," the Sixties Project, University of Virginia, accessed October 25, 2015, http://www2.iath.virginia.edu/sixties/HTML_docs/Resources/Primary/Manifestos/VVAW_Kerry_Senate.html.

223 Maureen Dowd, "Why No Tea and Sympathy?," *New York Times*, August 10, 2005, http://www.nytimes.com/2005/08/10/opinion/why-no-tea-and-sympathy.html.

224 Ibid.

225 Sean Alfano, "Joan Baez Joins Peace Mom's Cause," CBS News, August 22, 2005, http://www.cbsnews.com/news/joan-baez-joins-peace-moms-cause/.

226 Nicholas Ehrenberg, "The Cindy Sheehan Peace Train," CBS News, September 22, 2005, http://www.cbsnews.com/news/the-cindy-sheehan-peace-train/.

professional protesters."[227] When they drove to the White House to present a letter to the president, they sang, "All We Are Saying Is Give Peace a Chance," and an external sound system played *The Very Best of Peter, Paul and Mary.*[228]

2006–2007: Continued Vietnam-Style Protest

The protests against the Iraq War continued into 2006 and 2007 and continued to replay the Vietnam protest script. On September 26, 2006, police arrested seventy-one people in the US Capitol complex at a protest that featured prayer services, sit-ins, and sing-alongs.[229] In the atrium of the Hart Senate Office Building, "the demonstrations were reminiscent of the Vietnam era, with protesters strumming guitars, singing peace songs, holding flowers and wearing hats made of balloons."[230] A protest in New York City in April 2006 featured tens of thousands of marchers, including Cindy Sheehan and Rev. Al Sharpton.[231] United for Peace and Justice, the Rainbow/PUSH Coalition, and the National Organization for Women—another collection of professional protesters—organized and led the New York protest. One protester—a fifty-six-year-old musician and environmental educator—said, "Someone asked me if I did it for love. I'm from the 60's, I'm one of those guys. I'm doing it out of habit. But it's a good habit."[232]

In admitting he was protesting "out of habit," this protester effectively gave the game away. The protesters were not looking at Iraq qua Iraq; they looked at American military intervention and reflexively said, "American intervention bad," especially in a non-Western country. The events of 9/11, the increased threats of WMD, and the overall changed circumstances since the

---

227 Ehrenberg, "The Cindy Sheehan Peace Train."

228 Ibid.

229 Lisa Goddard, "Peaceful Iraq Protests Prompt 71 Arrests," CNN, September 26, 2005, http://www.cnn.com/2006/US/09/26/dc.protests/.

230 Ibid.

231 Nicholas Confessore, "Tens of Thousands in New York March against Iraq War," *New York Times*, April 30, 2006, http://www.nytimes.com/2006/04/30/nyregion/30protest.html?_r=0.

232 Ibid.

1960s—none of that mattered to the protesters. America acted militarily, and, "out of habit," the protesters came out of the woodwork. These same protesters never marched and held signs with sad-eyed Iraqi girls whose parents were murdered by Saddam's regime, though there is no doubt Saddam, al-Qaeda, and Shiite militias murdered more people in Iraq (and more innocent civilians, by orders of magnitude) than American forces may have killed in the Iraq War. These signs only appeared when America was at war.

At this same New York City protest, held not long after the United States began ratcheting up rhetoric against Iran, protesters also held signs opposing military intervention against Iran.[233] The stirrings of protest against possible intervention against the Iranian nuclear program were a harbinger of things to come. In addition to affecting the United States' ability to succeed in Iraq, these protests now began to tie the United States' hands in other foreign policy areas, particularly regarding the Iranian nuclear threat.

The year 2006 featured protests throughout the world as well. Coordinated protests on the third anniversary of the beginning of the Iraq War took place in March 2006 in the United States, the United Kingdom, and elsewhere. At the UK protest, the convener of the Stop the War Coalition, Lindsey German, said, "We believe that a peaceful solution to the chaos caused by the illegal war in Iraq will only be possible when the occupying foreign armies have all been removed so that the Iraqi people will be free to decide on their own political future."[234] Events, of course, proved otherwise, raising questions about the supposedly superior wisdom and strategy of the antiwar coalition.

The March 2006 UK protest also included protests against possible intervention in Iran. Kate Hudson, the chairwoman of CND, one of the protest organizers, said there was "grave concern" about the threat of an attack against Iran. She went on to say that "the US is making charges about a covert nuclear weapons programme in Iran without presenting any credible evidence" and that "these charges are strikingly similar to the false accusations raised to

---

233 Ibid.

234 "Thousands Join Anti-War Protest," BBC News, March 18, 2006, http://news.bbc.co.uk/2/hi/uk_news/england/london/4818952.stm.

justify the invasion of Iraq three years ago."[235] The limiting effect of the Iraq War on the United States' and the world's ability to respond to the growing threat of Iran's nuclear program was already apparent by 2006.

Protests continued into 2007. January 2007 saw the swearing in of the newly elected Democratic Congress and a further invigorated protest movement. On January 21, 2007, tens of thousands gathered on the National Mall for another Iraq War protest. The crowd featured many of the same antiwar celebrities that had been vocal up to that point, including Sean Penn, Danny Glover, Tim Robbins, and Susan Sarandon.[236] A twelve-year-old from Massachusetts read a petition, saying, "Now we know our leaders either lied to us or hid the truth. Because of our actions, the rest of the world sees us as a bully and a liar." The statement encapsulated the two canards of the antiwar movement—that Bush deliberately misled the American public and that the United States went to war unilaterally—and showed just how deeply these falsehoods had sunk into the American public's consciousness.[237]

The antiwar movement's defeatism—the notion that the Bush administration's policy in Iraq had failed and the United States ought to leave Iraq—was on display. Interviewed during the rally, Robbins said that it was irresponsible of American elected officials "to ask very brave young men and women to sacrifice their lives for a failed policy."[238] At that time, acknowledging the problems with its Iraq strategy, the Bush administration was considering revisions to its Iraq policy—namely, the troop surge to stabilize Iraq.

But perhaps the most newsworthy celebrity to come out to denounce the Iraq War at the January 2007 antiwar protest was Jane Fonda, who infamously visited North Vietnam in July 1972 in opposition to the Vietnam War. At the 2007 rally, Fonda said, "Silence is no longer an option," and she expressly connected the Vietnam War to the Iraq War in saying that both

235 Ibid.

236 "War Protesters Demand US Troop Withdrawal," NBC News, January 27, 2007, http://www.nbcnews.com/id/16841070/ns/world_news-mideast_n_africa/t/war-protesters-demand-us-troop-withdrawal/#.VYAEt1LF5vk.

237 Ibid.

238 "Iraq War Protest—Jan. 27, 2007," PoliticsTV.com, https://www.youtube.com/watch?v=oEYELcLoU0s.

involved "blindness to realities on the ground, hubris…thoughtlessness in our approach to rebuilding a country we've destroyed."[239] With the appearance of the woman who to this day is derisively referred to as "Hanoi Jane," the anti–Iraq War protest movement came full circle with its Vietnam War predecessor. Rep. John Conyers also hearkened back to the Vietnam War, telling protesters, "It's not only in our power to stop Bush, it is our obligation to stop Bush. We stopped the war in Vietnam, didn't we?"[240]

The January 2007 protest once again featured the signs saying "Bush lied, thousands died" and "Impeach Bush for war crimes."[241] American flags with the peace symbol replacing the stars that were staples of Vietnam-era protests could be seen.[242] The "War is not the answer" signs with a dove of peace that first popped up in the 1960s appeared again.[243] One sign described President Bush as "the crowning achievement of a country that eats too much and thinks too little."[244] Protesters also held signs opposing the planned troop surge in Iraq. The preprinted signs of the United for Peace and Justice organization dotted the protest.[245] Pictures with George Bush in a Nazi swastika appeared.[246] Reprising John Kerry's famous quotation in his 1971 testimony against the Vietnam War, one sign read, "How do you ask a soldier to be the last person to die for a lie?"[247] The protests featured street theater, with people in Bush costumes, some with blood dripping from their hands.[248] Also of particular interest, the protest included signs reading,

---

239 "War Protesters Demand US Troop Withdrawal," NBC News.

240 Deborah Barfield Berry and John Yaukey, "Anti-War Protesters Press Congress to Bring Troops Home," *USA Today*, January 27, 2007, http://usatoday30.usatoday.com/news/nation/2007-01-27-dc-iraq-protest_x.htm.

241 J. A. Pentz, "Anti War Protest in Washington, D.C.,—January 27, 2007," http://www.dailymotion.com/video/x2qr5op.

242 Ibid.

243 Ibid.

244 Ibid.

245 Ibid.

246 Ibid.

247 Ibid.

248 "March on the Capitol—Anti-War Protest—Washington, DC, March 27, 2007," https://www.youtube.com/watch?v=dRSWugBHZgQ.

"Stop war on Iran."[249] The antiwar movement was starting to leverage the unpopularity of the war in Iraq to prevent military action against Iran's nuclear program.

Antiwar activists were quoted reiterating another antiwar movement canard, that "the war has benefitted no one except Bush's friends and cronies."[250] Rep. Jerrold Nadler trotted out a Santayana quote, identifying Bush's proposed surge as the actions of a fanatic, "one who redoubles his effort when he has forgotten his purpose."[251] However, Nadler did not state what he believed Bush's purpose to be. Nadler went on to state that every reason given for the war was "a lie."[252] One protester talked about how people felt "safer" to speak out.[253] Another young protester said that "obviously the troop surge is pretty ridiculous at this point," even though the surge had not been implemented yet. She said, "At least the Democrats are in office now in the Congress and we can get things done with raising minimum wage and helping the economy with blue collar workers losing all their jobs."[254] This type of comment, the many signs regarding issues other than Iraq, and the presence of United for Peace and Justice suggest that the protesters had more on their minds than Iraq—namely a broad-based opposition to the Bush administration and its policies generally.

In March 2007, on the fourth anniversary of the beginning of the Iraq War, antiwar protesters once again descended on Washington to protest the Iraq War. Continuing the theme of hearkening back to the days of Vietnam protest, the protest also commemorated the fortieth anniversary of the 1967 march on the Pentagon.[255] The *Washington Post* also explicitly made the connection between the 2007 protest and its 1967 predecessor with this descrip-

249 "Iraq War Protest—Jan. 27, 2007," PoliticsTV.com; "Iraq Anti-War Protest—Washington, DC—January 27, 2007."

250 "Iraq War Protest—Jan. 27, 2007," PoliticsTV.com.

251 Ibid.

252 Ibid.

253 Ibid.

254 "March on the Capitol—Anti-War Protest—Washington, DC, March 27, 2007."

255 Steve Vogel and Michael Alison Chandler, "4 Years after Start of War, Anger Reigns," *Washington Post*, March 18, 2007, http://www.washingtonpost.com/wp-dyn/content/article/2007/03/17/AR2007031700539.html; Steve Vogel, "Once More to the Pentagon," *Washington Post*, March 16, 2007, http://www.washingtonpost.com/wp-dyn/content/article/2007/03/15/AR2007031502206.html.

tion of the 2007 protest: "At times, verbal clashes during the cold and blustery day demonstrated that the bitter divisions of four decades ago sparked by Vietnam are very much alive in the debate over Iraq."[256] Statements by protesters demonstrated just how deeply the notion that Bush "lied" the United States into Iraq had taken hold over time. One protester, a marine veteran of the Korean War, stated, "I was like everybody else. I trusted the people who ran the country, and I'm tired of being lied to…I feel so bad for the young Marines who are getting their legs blown off and losing their lives."[257]

In September 2007, another ANSWER-sponsored rally in Washington included a "die-in" at the Capitol and a protest consisting of approximately ten thousand protestors in Lafayette Park in front of the White House.[258] This protest, like so many preceding it, covered a number of other causes, including Palestinian rights, health care, and, incongruously, vegan lifestyles.[259] Former US attorney general Ramsey Clark spoke of Iraqi refugees the United States created by starting the war.

All told, the various street protests overtly and expressly tied themselves to the Vietnam antiwar movement, reviving the same symbols, slogans, and participants used forty years prior by the antiwar movement against Vietnam. Additionally, protesters used the antiwar protests to promote opposition to other Bush administration policies, demonstrating that the protesters had a variety of ulterior motives.

Reprising Vietnam's Veterans against the War

The antiwar movement also incorporated another element that gained particular prominence in the Vietnam War: the antiwar veteran. In 2004, antiwar

256 Ibid.

257 Ibid.

258 Michelle Boorstein, V. Dion Hayes, and Allison Klein, "Thousands March to Capitol to Protest Iraq War," *Washington Post*, September 16, 2007, http://www.washingtonpost.com/wp-dyn/content/article/2007/09/16/AR2007091600602.html.

259 Ibid.

veterans of the Iraq and Afghanistan conflicts formed the Iraq Veterans Against the War (IVAW). Its self-described goal was "to mobilize the military community to withdraw its support for the war and occupation in Iraq."[260] A number of the IVAW members participated in Cindy Sheehan's Camp Casey protest and in her subsequent protest activities. In April 2008, IVAW held an event outside Washington, DC, called "Winter Soldier Iraq and Afghanistan" featuring fifty-five veterans of the Iraq and Afghanistan Wars telling the stories and experiences of their combat.[261] The name deliberately hearkened back to the Winter Soldier Investigation and public testimony event held by the Vietnam Veterans Against the War in 1971. Thus, in yet another way, Vietnam provided the inspiration for the antiwar protests against the Iraq War.

The 2008 Winter Soldier testimonies included a number of different panels—panels on racism and dehumanization of the enemy, "corporate pillaging," breakdowns in the military, and the cost of the war at home.[262] One speaker on the "corporate pillaging" panel, Antonia Juhasz, stated that the war was being fought for oil.[263] She contended that the United States failed to provide basic services to Iraq while rewriting the economic laws of Iraq.[264] Another speaker discussed corruption within the Iraqi government, noting that 30 to 50 percent of soldiers on the Iraqi army's payroll were "ghosts" who did not exist.[265] The issue of corruption was a real one and an issue to be dealt with; the inspector general for Iraq regularly reported on corruption issues

---

260 "Founding of IVAW," Iraq Veterans Against the War, http://www.ivaw.org/founding-ivaw.

261 Gerald Nicosia, "Veterans' Testimonies Heard at 'Winter Soldier Iraq and Afghanistan,'" *SFGate*, April 4, 2008, http://www.sfgate.com/opinion/article/Veterans-testimonies-heard-at-Winter-Soldier-3288604.php.

262 "Winter Soldier," Iraq Veterans Against the War, http://www.ivaw.org/wintersoldier.

263 "Antonia Juhasz," Iraq Veterans Against the War, http://www.ivaw.org/blog/corporate-pillaging/antonia-juhasz.

264 Ibid.

265 "Luis Montalvan," Iraq Veterans Against the War,. http://www.ivaw.org/blog/corporate-pillaging/luis-montalvan.

within the Iraq occupation.[266] However, the purpose of the IVAW's Winter Soldier testimonies and investigation was not to develop suggestions to better fight the war; IVAW was Iraq Veterans *Against* the War, not "Iraq Veterans Advocating a More Effective Strategy to Win the War." IVAW's purpose in presenting the testimonies of antiwar veterans was to discredit and ultimately end the war.

Just as with its predecessor, the Vietnam Winter Soldier Investigation, IVAW's testimony again attempted to discredit the war as a corrupt war (for oil, in the case of Iraq) in which US soldiers regularly committed atrocities. The goal was to undermine the US effort in Iraq and the Bush administration's effort to manage the occupation.

Artists Hop on the Antiwar Bandwagon

A graduate student this author worked with once said artists need times of social ferment to create truly great art. The graduate student compared the 1960s and the music, movies, and art created during that decade with the art and music of the 1970s, 1980s, and 1990s. Predictably, artists saw the antiwar movement as the 1960s-esque social ferment of their day and flocked to the opportunity to join the antiwar movement and create antiwar art, literature, and music.

In music, the Rolling Stones in 2005 released a song called "Sweet Neo-Con." The lyrics include the following:

---

266 For example, see statement of Stuart W. Bowen Jr., special inspector general for Iraq reconstruction, before the Unites States Senate Judiciary Committee, SIGIR investigations on Iraq, March 20, 2007, https://books.google.com/books?id=YwTqaXJmmKIC&pg=PA83&dq=the+Inspector+General+for+Iraq+regularly+reported+on+corruption+issues+within+the+Iraq+occupation&hl=en&sa=X&ved=0CB0Q6AEwAGoVChMIsoeUkfjdyAIVw1k-Ch0aOgPb#v=onepage&q=the%20Inspector%20General%20for%20Iraq%20regularly%20reported%20on%20corruption%20issues%20within%20the%20Iraq%20occupation&f=false; House Oversight and Government Reform Committee, statement of Stuart W. Bowen Jr., special inspector general for Iraq reconstruction, before the United States House of Representatives Committee on Government Reform, September 23, 2010, accessed October 25, 2015, https://oversight.house.gov/wp-content/uploads/2012/01/20100923Bowen.pdf.

> You call yourself a Christian
> I think that you're a hypocrite
> You say you are a patriot
> I think that you're a crock of shit
> And listen now, the gasoline
> I drink it every day
> But it's getting very pricey
> And who is going to pay
> How come you're so wrong
> My sweet neo con…Yeah
> It's liberty for all
> 'Cause democracy's our style
> Unless you are against us
> Then it's prison without trial
> But one thing that is certain
> Life is good at Halliburton
> If you're really so astute
> You should invest at Brown & Root…
> We must have lots more bases
> To protect us from our foes
> Who needs these foolish friendships
> We're going it alone.[267]

The banal leftist criticism of the Iraq War was on full display in these lyrics. The idea that the Iraq War was some form of latter-day Crusades (with the reference to Christianity), the recoiling at the idea that prisoners of war might be held without trial, the notion that the United States went to war unilaterally and without allies, and the idea that the United States went to war for oil and Halliburton—all of these were standard antiwar fare by 2006. One can imagine the outcry had a religion other than Christianity been chosen for these lyrics. The claim that the United States went to war for Halliburton,

---

267 "Sweet Neo Con Lyrics," MetroLyrics, http://www.metrolyrics.com/sweet-neo-con-lyrics-rolling-stones.html.

Brown & Root, or any other oil industry company is fanciful. The Iraqi government permitted companies from any country to bid on Iraqi oil contracts. As described previously, the idea the United States was "going it alone" in Iraq was simply false; the United States had a number of other countries supporting it in Iraq, including providing troops. And the dismissing of the Bush administration's patriotism, after years of indignant complaints about the Bush administration's supposedly impugning its opponents' patriotism, was jarringly hypocritical.

The Rolling Stones had plenty of company in creating antiwar art. Bruce Springsteen released "Bring Them Home," a remake of the old Pete Seeger song.[268] In 2006, Neil Young released an album, *Living with War*, described as a "fierce, comprehensive indictment of the Bush Administration and all its failures."[269] The album included a song called "Let's Impeach the President."[270] Somewhat unsubtly presaging the future, Young's song "Looking for a Leader" was "an unvarnished call for a new authority figure who can right the wrong, clear out the corruption, and make the nation's symbols feel pure again" with the lyrics "Someone walks among us, and I hope he hears the call…Maybe it's a woman, or a black man after all."[271]

The Pet Shop Boys released "I'm With Stupid," a "valentine from Tony Blair to Bush."[272] Sheryl Crow's "God Bless This Mess," from her 2008 *Detours* album, included the following lyrics:

> Heard about the day
> That two skyscrapers came down
> Firemen, policemen

268 Edna Gundersen, "Anti-War Tunes Are Getting a Hearing," *USA Today*, June 30, 2006, http://usatoday30.usatoday.com/life/music/news/2006-06-29-iraq-music_x.htm.

269 Robert Everett-Green, "Neil Young Lets Loose a War Cry," *Toronto Globe and Mail*, April 26, 2006, http://www.theglobeandmail.com/arts/neil-young-lets-loose-a-war-cry/article1098729/.

270 Oliver Burkeman, "Neil Young Joins the Hate Bush Bandwagon," *The Guardian*, April 28, 2006, http://www.theguardian.com/world/2006/apr/28/usa.arts.

271 Everett-Green, "Neil Young Lets Loose a War Cry."

272 Gundersen, "Anti-War Tunes Are Getting a Hearing."

And people came from all around
The smoke covered the city
And the body count arise
The president spoke words of comfort
With tears in his eyes
Then he led us as a nation
Into a war all based on lies.[273]

P. F. Sloan rerecorded his 1960s anti–Vietnam War ballad "Eve of Destruction" and released it in 2006.[274] An American band called Blow Up Hollywood released an album called *The Diaries of Private Henry Hill*, based on the diaries of a fallen soldier.[275] Blow Up Hollywood described the album as a "concept album [that] narrates a first-hand account of the transformation of a real man from citizen to soldier to killer to martyr."[276] A host of other experimental musicians released ballads opposing the Iraq War and the Bush administration's foreign policy.[277]

As the public mood on the war shifted, Hollywood became more involved in creating films implicitly critical of the Iraq War. Movies like *Lions for Lambs*, *In the Valley of Elah*, *Rendition*, and *Stop Loss* came out in 2007.[278] In November 2007, *Lions for Lambs* was released, a movie about two students who, challenged by their professor to do something with their lives, enlist and fight in Afghanistan. It also features a right-wing senator with a new strategy for the war in Afghanistan and a left-wing journalist skeptical of the plan. The movie features some of the most bankable stars of Hollywood,

273 "Sheryl Crow Lyrics 'G-d Bless This Mess,'" AZ Lyrics, http://www.azlyrics.com/lyrics/sherylcrow/godblessthismess.html.

274 Gundersen, "Anti-War Tunes Are Getting a Hearing."

275 Ibid.

276 Blow Up Hollywood, "Diaries of Private Henry Hill," http://www.blowuphollywood.com/diaries-private-henry-hill/.

277 Gundersen, "Anti-War Tunes Are Getting a Hearing."

278 Ewen MacAskill, "Hollywood Tears Up Script to Make Anti-War Films while Conflicts Rage," *The Guardian*, August 13, 2007, http://www.theguardian.com/world/2007/aug/14/iraq.film.

Tom Cruise, Robert Redford, and Meryl Streep, with "Cruise as a rightwing senator doing an interview with TV journalist Streep; [and] Redford as a college professor teaching one of his students about the importance of political engagement."[279] In teaching his students about political engagement, the professor challenges them about why they are not opposing Bush's policies in the same way he opposed the Vietnam War.[280] Once again, the specter of Vietnam raises itself in the movies critical of the Bush administration's foreign policy. The makers of the film intended for it to critique the Afghanistan war; in a question-and-answer session about the film, "Cruise and screenwriter Matthew Michael Carnahan spoke about the film's impassioned critique of the government's strategy."[281] The United Kingdom's *Daily Mail* described the movie as "a crude, anti-Republican polemic."[282] In a press conference at the Rome Film Festival, Redford himself stated, "Our country has hit a point where we have lost so much. We have lost lives, we've lost sacred freedoms, we've lost financial stability; we've lost our position of respect on the world stage."[283]

Stop Loss chronicles the story of a soldier who survives a horrific ambush and, suffering from posttraumatic stress disorder after returning from Iraq, is kept in the Army and ordered to return to Iraq under the Army's stop-loss regulation. Instead, refusing to return, the soldier goes AWOL.[284] One critic described *Stop Loss* as "hammered-in, blatant Bush-bashing" that "left me feeling as though I'd just walked out of a fanatic-filled political rally, not

---

279 Dade Hayes, "Cruise Rolls Out 'Lions for Lambs,'" *Variety*, October 21, 2007, http://variety.com/2007/film/markets-festivals/cruise-rolls-out-lions-for-lambs-1117974448/.

280 Christopher Tookey, "Redford's Anti-War Lecture Lions for Lambs Is Missing in Action," *The Daily Mail*, November 13, 2007, http://www.dailymail.co.uk/tvshowbiz/reviews/article-492601/Redfords-anti-war-lecture-Lions-For-Lambs-missing-action.html.

281 Hayes, "Cruise Rolls Out 'Lions for Lambs.'"

282 Tookey, "Redford's Anti-War Lecture Lions for Lambs Is Missing in Action."

283 Nick Vivarelli, "'Lions' Star Roars at Rome," Variety, October 23, 2007, http://variety.com/2007/film/markets-festivals/lions-star-roars-at-rome-1117974560/.

284 Peter Travers, "Stop-Loss," review of the film *Stop-Loss*, *Rolling Stone*, March 28, 2008, http://www.rollingstone.com/movies/reviews/stop-loss-20080328; A.O. Scott, "Back from Iraq, on a Road Going Nowhere," review of the film *Stop*-Loss, *New York Times*, March 28, 2008, http://www.nytimes.com/2008/03/28/movies/28stop.html?_r=0.

a change-your-world-view cinematic experience."[285] The film *Rendition* describes the capture and extraordinary rendition of an Egyptian-born American chemical engineer from a United States–bound flight from South Africa by the CIA.[286] The engineer is tortured to obtain information about possible terrorist activities based on telephone calls supposedly made by a terrorist to the engineer's cell phone.

Many of the Iraq War movies that criticized the war or the Bush administration's policy in Iraq and the war on terror did not fare well with the moviegoing public. Despite all-star casts and heavy press coverage, the films by and large flopped at the box office.[287] Nevertheless, Hollywood's steady drumbeat of negative, critical takes on the Iraq War and the Bush administration continued to undermine confidence in the administration and the prosecution of the wars. The relentless negativity further demoralized an already weary public.

All of these various forms of protest—the antiwar artists, the protest throngs, and the 1960s throwbacks—all further eroded the American public's confidence in and support of the Iraq action. Even if the protests were small and the movies not terribly popular, the volume of the protests and antiwar songs and art combined with their disproportionate coverage by a sympathetic media led Americans to sour further on the Iraq War. They led Americans to a sense of unraveling, of chaos, and of the need for new leadership. In addition, they perpetrated the myths of the Iraq War—that it was based on lies and a deliberate misleading of the American people, that it was a war for oil, and that President Bush was a unilateralist cowboy. The cumulative effect of the repetitive efforts of artists and protesters took their toll on American public opinion, demonstrating the axiom that if one says something often enough, people believe it to be true. It also wore down the American psyche and reinforced the notion that Iraq was an unwinnable failure.

---

285 Scott Gwin, "Movie Review: Stop-Loss," review of the film *Stop-Loss*, CinemaBlend, http://www.cinemablend.com/reviews/Stop-Loss-3046.htmls.

286 Roger Ebert, "Rendition," RogerEbert.com, October 18, 2007, http://www.rogerebert.com/reviews/rendition-2007.

287 Paul Farhi, "The Iraq War, in Hollywood's Theater," *Washington Post*, March 25, 2008, http://www.washingtonpost.com/wp-dyn/content/article/2008/03/24/AR2008032403254.html.

Combined with the setbacks in Iraq and the need for a new strategy there, by 2006 and 2007, the public had turned against the Iraq War.

Politicians Turn Iraq into Vietnam

For elected opponents of the war, the difficulties of the occupation of Iraq provided an opportunity to climb upon a moral pedestal and play the role of "conscience of the nation," abasing themselves as they confessed America's sins in Iraq. In June 2005, Senator Dick Durbin took to the floor of the US Senate and notoriously compared American interrogators of Iraqi prisoners to the enforcers of Pol Pot's hideous Cambodian regime, the Nazis, and the Soviet gulags.[288]

Factually speaking, this attempt at historical analogy was grossly inaccurate. Durbin was comparing the tactics allegedly used by American interrogators to obtain intelligence from enemy soldiers in the Iraq War with the treatment of civilian Jews in Nazi concentration camps, political prisoners in the Soviet Union, and innocent, nonpolitical Cambodian civilians. Moreover, the extent of this calumny may have been lost on Senator Durbin and those who cheered him on. Pol Pot's and the Khmer Rouge's Cambodian Communist nightmare is estimated to have slaughtered one to three million people in order to create a new Communist, agrarian-based society. Upon taking power, the Khmer Rouge forced everyone out of Cambodian cities and into the countryside, where many died of disease, starvation, and exhaustion. Khmer Rouge enforcers would kill babies by smashing them against trees. When the Vietnamese invaded Cambodia in 1979 and finally put an end to the Khmer Rouge's madness, they found depressions throughout the countryside that upon investigation were revealed to be mass graves. It was to these Khmer Rouge monsters that Senator Durbin compared US troops. Yet Senator Durbin paid no political price for this outrageous attack on US troops. Durbin issued an apology, stating, "Some may believe that my remarks

288 "Durbin Apologizes for Nazi, Gulag, Pol Pot Remarks," FoxNews.com, June 22, 2005, http://www.foxnews.com/story/2005/06/22/durbin-apologizes-for-nazi-gulag-pol-pot-remarks.html.

crossed the line. To them, I extend my heartfelt apologies."[289] After that apology, Durbin's comments were forgotten.

However, alleging that war had turned US personnel into monsters has been a tried-and-true tactic of the antiwar left to undermine the justification for war and the morale of the American public. With his indiscriminate slander of US troops, Senator Durbin reprised the role of John Kerry, who in 1971 testified that US troops were committing atrocities in the manner of Genghis Khan. In testimony before the US Senate in 1971, Kerry stated that American soldiers "had personally raped, cut off ears, cut off heads, taped wires from portable telephones to human genitals and turned up the power, cut off limbs, blown up bodies, randomly shot at civilians, razed villages in fashion reminiscent of Genghis Khan, shot cattle and dogs for fun, poisoned food stocks, and generally ravaged the countryside of South Vietnam in addition to the normal ravage of war, and the normal and very particular ravaging which is done by the applied bombing power of this country."[290] These accusations likely were false and in any event were hearsay; Kerry had not witnessed the events himself and had no personal knowledge of whether what he was saying was true.

Nevertheless, the picture of the ugly American, rampaging through countries in pursuit of selfish, imperialist American interests, became part of the antiwar movement's Vietnam lore. This is the image the antiwar movement always sees when the United States goes to war, regardless of where or when or the rationale for the war. Abu Ghraib provided the antiwar movement with a fresh opportunity to deploy this criticism against a new generation of American soldiers in a new American war. Rarely did the American media present the good works American troops undertook in Iraq.

In 2007, as the United States prepared to implement the now-famous surge of troops, Senate Majority Leader Harry Reid declared, "This war is

289 Shailagh Murray, "Durbin Apologizes for Remarks on Abuse," June 22, 2005, http://www.washingtonpost.com/wp-dyn/content/article/2005/06/21/AR2005062101654.html.

290 "Vietnam War Veteran John Kerry's Testimony before the Senate Foreign Relations Committee," History 398: The Vietnam Experience, ed. Professor Ernest Bolt, University of Virginia, https://facultystaff.richmond.edu/~ebolt/history398/JohnKerryTestimony.html.

lost."[291] Secretary of Defense Robert Gates called Reid's statement "one of the most disgraceful things I have heard a politician say."[292] According to Reid, he privately told President Bush that he did not want Bush to follow the path of President Lyndon B. Johnson, who "did not want a war loss on his watch."[293] What Reid advocated, essentially, was more US self-abasement—admitting defeat, acknowledging error, and withdrawing, tail between its legs. In other words, another Vietnam. For the antiwar movement, the Iraq War was another case of the United States once again getting its comeuppance at the hands of indigenous fighters wanting to rid their country of foreign invaders and influence. Reid said he told President Bush he believed the Iraq War could not be won through military force but that the United States could still pursue political, economic, and diplomatic means to bring peace to Iraq.[294] In effect, Reid was proposing "peace with honor"—modern-day Paris Peace Accords that inevitably would result in American withdrawal and an unstable, chaotic Iraq.

Rep. David Obey, who was chairman of the House Appropriations Committee, said he believed the United States won the war quickly, "but now they are stuck in a civil war, and the only solution is a political and diplomatic compromise…And there is no soldier who can get that done."[295] This represented another Vietnam flashback—the United States, once again mired in a civil war, where the only solution was political and diplomatic. That is, America was once again stuck in a war it could not win militarily and needed to find a way out of that did not involve military victory. The antiwar movement and its political supporters did not consider the possibility that the strategy for winning the war needed to change. They immediately jumped to

291 Jeff Zeleny, "Leading Democrat in Senate Tells Reporters, 'This War is Lost,'" *New York Times*, April 20, 2007, http://www.nytimes.com/2007/04/20/washington/20cong.html?_r=0.

292 "Gates: Harry Reid's 'War Is Lost' Comment Was 'One of the Most Disgraceful Things I've Heard,'" *RealClearPolitics*, http://www.realclearpolitics.com/video/2014/01/15/gates_harry_reids_war_is_lost_comment_was_one_of_the_most_disgraceful_things_ive_heard.html.

293 Zeleny, "Leading Democrat in Senate Tells Reporters, 'This War is Lost.'"

294 Anne Flaherty, "Reid: US Can't Win the War in Iraq," April 19, 2007, http://www.washingtonpost.com/wp-dyn/content/article/2007/04/19/AR2007041901150.html.

295 Ibid.

the conclusion that the war was unwinnable. In 2007, they sought to impose a timetable, complete with a deadline, for withdrawing American troops from Iraq.

In fact, the unrest in Iraq had a number of different sources and was not a neat "civil war" fitting the Vietnam template, as the antiwar movement would have it. The unrest was partly a religious sectarian battle between Shiite and Sunni Muslims. Two major forces from outside Iraq abetted this religious conflict, however, and were largely responsible for the conflict's escalation in violence. The first force was al-Qaeda in Iraq, a Sunni-aligned group led by Abu Musab al-Zarqawi (a Jordanian), whose goal was to foment chaos and create opportunities to develop a foothold in postwar Iraq while attacking and killing Americans. Al-Qaeda in Iraq bombed the Golden Mosque in 2006, triggering open sectarian conflict until the surge.[296] The second force was Iran, which saw an opportunity to gain power and influence in Iraq after Saddam's downfall. Iran supported numerous Shiite militias, including the Mahdi Army of cleric Moqtada al-Sadr and the Badr Brigades.[297] Left to their own devices, Iraqis might not have devolved into violence. But the malignant influences of al-Qaeda in Iraq on the one hand and Iran on the other led to the violence of 2005–2007. What took place in Iraq was not so much a civil war as opportunistic violence fomented by external bad actors seeking to achieve their own aims in Iraq and taking advantage of and exacerbating latent but previously quiescent sectarian fissures. Nevertheless, the idea of an unwinnable civil war fit neatly into the antiwar movement's effort to portray Iraq as another Vietnam.

The antiwar movement's relentless emphasis on political and diplomatic means to solve every conflict, in fact, has matters precisely backward. The real

---

296 Ellen Knickmeyer and K. I. Ibrahim, "Bombing Shatters Mosque in Iraq," *Washington Post*, February 23, 2006, http://www.washingtonpost.com/wp-dyn/content/article/2006/02/22/AR2006022200454.html.

297 Lionel Beehner, "Iraq's Militia Groups," Council on Foreign Relations, October 26, 2006, http://www.cfr.org/iraq/iraqs-militia-groups/p11824#p3; Anthony H. Cordesman and Jose Ramos, "Sadr and the Mahdi Army: Evolution, Capabilities, and a New Direction," Center for Strategic and International Studies, August 4, 2008, http://csis.org/files/media/csis/pubs/080804_jam.pdf, 26.

lesson of Vietnam and Iraq is that successful political and diplomatic efforts can take place only when the conditions on the ground are favorable. That means the United States has to create a stable security situation through military force *first*, when the United States has imposed its will and made clear it is not going anywhere. A stable security situation provides the backdrop for political and diplomatic negotiation. Negotiating first, when the security situation is unstable, is a sure signal that the United States wants to leave and forces the United States to negotiate from a position of weakness.

The Media Gives Iraq the Vietnam Treatment

Protesters were not the only segment of society reprising its Vietnam antiwar role. The broadcast media also sought to replay the role it is perceived to have played in Vietnam: that of the conscience of an antiwar nation. The broadcast media, through its words, actions, and coverage choices, attempted to once again portray a war as an unwinnable morass that the United States should abandon. Particularly as the insurgency gained strength and attacks on US troops rose in 2005 and 2006, the media emphasized grim milestones and US setbacks. The portrayal of the war as unwinnable by a media cohort that generally opposed President Bush undermined the ability of the United States to fight the war and to take the necessary steps to win.

By piling on and emphasizing the bad news from Iraq, the media—intentionally or unintentionally—made the Iraq War seem as though it was going poorly and was a failure. This perception, in turn, further sapped support for the war.

On the first anniversary of the day President Bush declared "Mission accomplished" in the Iraq War in May 2004, Ted Koppel of ABC's *Nightline* read the names of all 721 US servicemen and servicewomen killed in Iraq.[298] The *New York Times* described this episode of *Nightline* as "a conscious echo

298 Katharine Q. Seelye, "At 2,000, Iraq's Military Deaths Got the Media's Full Attention," *New York Times*, October 31, 2005, http://www.nytimes.com/2005/10/31/business/at-2000-iraqs-military-deaths-got-the-medias-full-attention.html.

of a famous, Vietnam War–era issue of *Life* magazine."[299] The executive producer of *Nightline* acknowledged that "his inspiration for the program was a June 1969 issue of Life, which presented photos of all the men killed during one week in Vietnam."[300] On January 19, 2005, the day before President Bush's second inauguration, ABC News put out a request looking for military funerals scheduled for January 20, the day of the inauguration, possibly in an effort to juxtapose reporting from the funeral with the inauguration ceremonies.[301]

As the Iraqi insurgency worsened and the United States suffered more setbacks, it became easier for the media to oppose the war. Just as with the antiwar movement, which went quiet during the early days of the war only to become reinvigorated as setbacks during the occupation occurred, it became less likely that the media opponents of the Iraq War would end up on the "wrong" side—that is, having opposed a successful war.

Media coverage began to take a decidedly negative turn as the insurgency gained steam and US casualties increased. The media gave substantial coverage to "grim milestones" and "grim statistics" in Iraq, such as the deaths of the 2,000th, 2,500th, and 3,000th US troops in the war. When the United States suffered the 2,000th casualty in the war, the media gave the event substantial coverage. The *New York Times* ran a story titled "2,000 Dead: As Iraq Tours Stretch On, a Grim Mark."[302] The story particularly focused on the fact that many of the casualties had been on their second or third tour during the war. Sen. Ted Kennedy said, "Our armed forces are serving ably in Iraq under enormously difficult circumstances, and the policy of our government must

---

299 Bill Carter, "'Nightline' to Read Off Iraqi War Dead," *New York Times*, April 28, 2004, http://www.nytimes.com/2004/04/28/business/media/28TUBE-LONG.html.

300 Ibid.

301 *Captain's Quarters Blog*, http://www.captainsquartersblog.com/mt/pubfiles/story.htm.

302 James Dao, "As Iraq Tours Stretch On, a Grim Mark," *New York Times*, October 26, 2005, http://www.nytimes.com/2005/10/26/world/middleeast/2000-dead-as-iraq-tours-stretch-on-a-grim-mark.html?_r=0.

be worthy of their sacrifice. Unfortunately, it is not, and the American people know it."[303]

The Army blasted the use of these "artificial marks on the wall" and noted that the two-thousandth casualty should not be a "milestone," as the two-thousandth casualty "is just as important as the first that died and will be just as important as the last to die in this war against terrorism and to ensure freedom for a people who have not known freedom in over two generations."[304]

The *New York Times* greeted the three-thousandth US casualty in Iraq with a long article focused on the stories of a number of American soldiers killed in action in Iraq. The article was titled "3,000 Deaths in Iraq, Countless Tears at Home."[305] The article focused heavily on the greater lethality of improvised explosive devices as well as the improved medical procedures that kept casualty rates from being higher. Only at the very end of the article did the author note that the wife of one of the soldiers killed in action, whose story the piece recounted, said, "[The war] was hard, but he felt he was making a difference. He believed truly, that if he wasn't over there, they would be trying to harm us here."[306] Many soldiers likely held such an opinion, and a story exploring deployed soldiers' commitment to and belief in the mission might have had a different effect on its readers, but the *Times* did not choose to produce such a piece.

The *New York Times* was not the only media outlet that highlighted the three thousandth casualty in Iraq. NBC reported on the three thousandth casualty in Iraq, acknowledging that the death toll was "tiny" compared with previous wars but that "even so, the steadily mounting toll underscores the relentless violence that the massive US investment in lives and money—surpassing $350 billion—has yet to tame, and may in fact still be getting

---

303 "US Military Death Toll in Iraq Hits 2,000," *USA Today*, October 25, 2005, http://usatoday30.usatoday.com/news/world/iraq/2005-10-25-military-casualties_x.htm.

304 Ibid.

305 Lizette Alvarez and Andrew Lehren, "3,000 Deaths in Iraq, Countless Tears at Home," *New York Times*, January 1, 2007, http://www.nytimes.com/2007/01/01/us/01deaths.html?pagewanted=all.

306 Ibid.

worse."[307] The NBC News article made no mention of Iranian involvement in and responsibility for the increased violence. CNN also reported on the "grim milestone" of the three thousandth US fatality in Iraq, identifying a different soldier as the three thousandth casualty than the *Times* or NBC because CNN was keeping its own count of US fatalities in Iraq.[308]

PBS NewsHour featured a report on January 1, 2007, in which anchor Ray Suarez and correspondent Spencer Michaels looked at "the loss of more than three thousand Americans in Iraq and its impact back home."[309] The report noted that a third of the approximately 2,400 American soldiers killed in hostilities had been killed by IEDs. The report did not make any mention of Iran's involvement in enhancing the IEDs used in the Iraq theater to make them more effective and deadly. Rather, the article once again focused on the families of the soldiers killed in action.

Articles also focused on the protests surrounding the "grim milestones." United for Peace and Justice—a group discussed in great detail previously—asked protesters to wear black armbands with the number "3,000" printed on them and to contact media outlets to focus Americans' attention on the three-thousandth American death in Iraq.[310] Other protest groups in the United States used the "milestone" to hold protests and perform readings of casualties in Iraq.[311]

Another element of defeatism the news reports injected into the debate was the fact that the Iraq War and the American occupation of Iraq following the end of major combat operations had lasted longer than World War II. World War II was the most cataclysmic war in human history, so articles

---

307 "US Sustains 3,000th Fatality in Iraq," NBC News, January 1, 2007, http://www.nbcnews.com/id/16418524/ns/world_news-mideast_n_africa/t/us-sustains-th-fatality-iraq/#.VZARg1LF5vk.

308 "US Troop Deaths Reach 3,000," CNN, December 31, 2006, http://www.cnn.com/2006/US/12/31/iraq.deathtoll/.

309 "US Military Death Toll in Iraq Reaches 3,000," *PBS NewsHour*, January 1, 2007, http://www.pbs.org/newshour/bb/military-jan-june07-troop_1-01/.

310 Bill Trott, "Peace Groups Rally after 3,000th Soldier Killed," Reuters, January 1, 2007, http://www.reuters.com/article/2007/01/01/us-iraq-usa-casualties-protests-idUSN3121190420070101.

311 Ibid.

saying the Iraq War had lasted longer made the Iraq War seem, in a temporal sense, worse by comparison. CNN, for example, noted in its article about the three thousandth US casualty that, by December 2006, the Iraq War had lasted longer than World War II.[312] The same *New York Times* piece on the three-thousandth American fatality in Iraq also noted that "if the conflict continues into March [2007], the Iraq war will be the third longest in American history, ranked behind the Vietnam War and the American Revolution."[313]

Noting that the Iraq War and subsequent Iraq occupation lasted longer than World War II was a wholly defeatist point, which could have only one effect on Americans: to further demoralize them about the prospect for success in Iraq. Of course, the fact that the Iraq War lasted longer in time than World War II was not an entirely relevant fact; much of the violence in Iraq was the work of al-Qaeda in Iraq (a nonstate terrorist group), Iranian influence over Shia elements in Iraq, and Sunni responses to Shia violence. Moreover, the United States did not wage "total war" in Iraq as it had in World War II. Had the full might of the United States been deployed in Iraq as it was in World War II against Japan and Germany—with the firebombing and atomic bombing of cities and the singular, nonnegotiable goal of unconditional surrender by the Axis powers—the Iraq War might have been much shorter. However, the American public, and certainly the media and antiwar activists trumpeting the fact that the Iraq War was lasting longer than World War II, would have objected to such total war on other grounds. Indeed, by making "winning hearts and minds" the sine qua non of modern warfare, the media and antiwar activists virtually guarantee longer and more protracted conflicts.

The news media noted even nonobvious "grim milestones." On September 22, 2006, CBS News reported that the casualties in the Iraq and Afghanistan Wars had passed the death toll on 9/11.[314] The article opened by stating, "Now the death toll is 9/11 times two. US military deaths from Iraq and Afghanistan now surpass those of the most devastating terrorist attack in America's history,

---

312 "US Troop Deaths Reach 3,000."

313 Alvarez and Lehren, "3,000 Deaths in Iraq, Countless Tears at Home."

314 Sean Alfano, "War Casualties Pass 9/11 Death Toll," CBS News, September 22, 2006, http://www.cbsnews.com/news/war-casualties-pass-9-11-death-toll/.

the trigger for what came next."[315] The subtext of this opening was obvious: the United States has now lost more people in fighting since the 9/11 attacks and so perhaps these conflicts are not worth fighting any further. It recalls historian George Santayana's observation that a fanatic is someone who redoubles his efforts when he has forgotten his aim. In fact, the article went on to make this point, stating, "Not for the first time, a war that was started to answer death has resulted in at least as much death for the country that was first attacked, quite apart from the higher numbers of enemy and civilians killed."[316] The article went on to note that the United States had suffered substantially more casualties, and at faster rates, in previous conflicts such as World War II and, in fact, during the December 7, 1941, Japanese attack on Pearl Harbor. Nevertheless, the article went on, "Despite a death toll that pales next to that of the great wars, one casualty milestone after another has been observed and reflected upon this time, especially in Iraq. There was the benchmark of seeing more US troops die in the occupation than in the swift and successful invasion. And the benchmarks of 1,000 dead, 2,000, 2,500. Now this [the 9/11 milestone]."[317] The article effectively acknowledges the point that the steady drumbeat of "grim milestones" is defeatist and drives defeatism among the American public. CBS went on to release another article when the number of US deaths in Iraq alone exceeded the total number of deaths on 9/11.[318]

In addition to stoking defeatist sentiments within the United States, the anniversary articles sometimes attempted to drive wedges between different classes of Americans. The articles would do this by including breakdowns of US casualties by race and class. For example, when the US death toll in Iraq reached two thousand, CBS News released an article noting, "One-quarter of the soldiers killed in Iraq and Afghanistan are from rural America, CBS News correspondent David Martin reports, according to the most recent statistics,

---

315 Ibid.

316 Ibid.

317 Ibid.

318 Sean Alfano, "US Troop Deaths in Iraq Exceed 9/11 Toll," CBS News, December 26, 2006, http://www.cbsnews.com/news/us-troop-deaths-in-iraq-exceed-9-11-toll/.

even though only one-fifth of the military-age population lives there. In other words, Martin says, small-town America is suffering more than its fair share of sacrifice."[319] *CBS Evening News* featured a piece on September 16, 2006, highlighting the fact that it believed a disproportionate number of deaths came from rural America. The piece noted that while 25 percent of those killed in action in Iraq were from rural America, only 20 percent of the military-age population was rural Americans.[320]

Similarly, on the occasion of the three-thousandth US fatality in Iraq, the *New York Times* wrote, "The service members who died during this latest period fit an unchanging profile. They were mostly white men from rural areas, soldiers so young they still held fresh memories of high school football heroics and teenage escapades."[321] The article also stressed another theme: that US armed forces were stretched to the breaking point by Iraq. The article stated, "Many men and women were in Iraq for the second or third time. Some were going on their fourth, fifth or sixth deployment."[322]

The Pew Research Center studied Iraq War coverage and released a report in December 2007. The report led off with the following statement: "Through the first 10 months of the year, the portrait of Iraq that Americans have received from the news media has in considerable measure been a grim one. Roughly half of the reporting has consisted of accounts of daily violence. And stories that explicitly assessed the direction of the war have tended toward pessimism, according to a new study of press coverage of events on the ground in Iraq from January through October of 2007."[323] The report found that from January 2007 through June 2007, Iraq stories constituted 8 percent of all stories in Pew's index of news coverage. From July 2007 through September

---

319 Joel Roberts, "US Death Toll Hits 2,000 in Iraq," CBS News, October 26, 2005, http://www.cbsnews.com/news/us-death-toll-hits-2000-in-iraq/; "Small Town Suffering," *CBS Evening News*, September 16, 2006, http://www.cbsnews.com/videos/small-town-suffering/.

320 "Small Town Suffering," *CBS Evening News.*

321 Alvarez and Lehren, "3,000 Deaths in Iraq, Countless Tears at Home."

322 Ibid.

323 Pew Research Center: Journalism & Media Staff, "The Portrait from Iraq: How the Press Has Covered Events on the Ground," Pew Research Center, December 19, 2007, http://www.journalism.org/2007/12/19/the-portrait-from-iraq-how-the-press-has-covered-events-on-the-ground/.

2007, as the surge took hold and daily attacks decreased, coverage dropped to 5 percent of the stories in the Pew index. In October, when controversies about American security contractor Blackwater's activities in Iraq became a story, coverage increased, back up to 7 percent of all news stories.[324]

Even more telling are the topics of the coverage. According to Pew, news stories about Iraqi national instability varied over the course of the summer of 2007, rising in July and August as violence decreased and Iraq began to appear more stable. However, by October, stories about Iraqi national instability practically disappeared from the news media. Stories about private contractor activities—particularly the negative portrayal of Blackwater and other security contractor firms in Iraq—shot up to 65 percent of all of the news stories regarding Iraq.[325]

Historically, the Iraq War casualty rate was lower than for other wars. The United States is estimated to have lost between twenty-five hundred and forty-five hundred soldiers on D-Day alone.[326] Even in Vietnam, the first major war of the television era, fifty-eight thousand soldiers perished, approximately sixty-four hundred per year between 1964 and 1973.[327] The reporting from Iraq failed to provide this level of context. Instead, as the *New York Times* story previously described shows, the media focused on individual stories of loss and bereavement. These stories of loss are heartrending. Some involve young families losing a parent in the war, a soldier killed near the end of a tour of duty or during a second or third tour of duty, or National Guard units called up from civilian life for duty suffering losses.[328]

---

324 Pew Research Center: Journalism & Media Staff, "The Portrait from Iraq: How the Press Has Covered Events on the Ground; Coverage over Time," Pew Research Center, December 18, 2007, http://www.journalism.org/2007/12/18/coverage-over-time-2/.

325 Ibid.

326 "Still No Exact Figure for D-Day Dead," FoxNews.com, June 4, 2004, http://www.foxnews.com/story/2004/06/04/still-no-exact-figure-for-d-day-dead.html; "Normandy," US Army, http://www.history.army.mil/brochures/normandy/nor-pam.htm.

327 Josh White and Ann Scott Tyson, "Military Has Lost 2,000 in Iraq," *Washington Post*, October 26, 2005, http://www.washingtonpost.com/wp-dyn/content/article/2005/10/25/AR2005102501185.html.

328 Dao, "As Iraq Tours Stretch On, a Grim Mark"; Alvarez and Lehren, "3,000 Deaths in Iraq, Countless Tears at Home"; White and Tyson, "Military Has Lost 2,000 in Iraq."

The repetition of milestones inevitably had a demoralizing effect. The CBS News article on the 9/11 anniversary acknowledged that after Pearl Harbor, "historians doubt anyone paid much attention to sad milestones once America threw itself into the fight."[329] By contrast, by drawing attention to each new "sad milestone" and enhancing defeatism among the American public, the news media made winning the war even more difficult.

Nevertheless, combined with the failure to discover WMD in Iraq and the success of the antiwar movement in perpetuating the myth that Bush "lied" the United States into the war (as described previously) and the notion that the war was turning US soldiers into war criminals though such incidents as Abu Ghraib, each "grim milestone" further eroded support for the war and made the losses appear to be nothing more than a waste. On the occasion of the twenty-five hundredth casualty, Brigadier General Carter Ham, at the time the deputy operations chief for the Joint Chiefs of Staff, said, "It's important to remember that there is—there is a mission and there is a greater good which sometimes necessitates tremendous sacrifice."[330] Nevertheless, the media coverage made this "greater good" seem less and less clear as the war went on.

The media also failed to cover with precision the sources of the increase in US casualties in Iraq during the 2005–2007 time period. During that time, improvised explosive devices became more lethal, more complex, and more dangerous.[331] The number of suicide car bombs also increased.[332] At least some of the enhanced sophistication of the weapons insurgents deployed against American troops was the result of Iranian assistance to the makers of the IEDs. The United States knew that Iran and its Qods Force were responsible for providing weaponry to Iraqi insurgents. In March 2006, the Pentagon publicly stated that Iranian IED components were moving into Iraq and that there was Iranian intelligence

329 Alfano, "War Casualties Pass 9/11 Death Toll."

330 "Pentagon: US Death Toll in Iraq Reaches 2,500," NBC News, June 15, 2006, http://www.nbcnews.com/id/13237981/ns/world_news-mideast_n_africa/t/pentagon-us-death-toll-iraq-reaches/#.VY_pRlLF5vk.

331 Alvarez and Lehren, "3,000 Deaths in Iraq, Countless Tears at Home."

332 Ibid.

activity throughout Iraq.[333] By February 2007, the United States concluded the Iranians supplied enhanced roadside IEDs, including explosively formed penetrators (EFPs) that had much more deadly effects on armored vehicles than previous IEDs.[334] The United States further believed that the Iranian Revolutionary Guards and its Qods Force—which report directly to the Iranian supreme leader—were behind the deadlier roadside bombs and EFPs.[335] While the media provided some coverage of the US belief that Iran was supplying weapons to the Iraq insurgency, the media rarely emphasized Iranian responsibility in its articles describing the "grim milestones" and increases in American casualties in Iraq.[336] The American people, rather than possibly rising up in righteous anger at Iranian sabotage of American efforts to pacify Iraq, instead fell into defeatism and sadness as the media reported casualties without context. Instead of revealing the new enemy in Iraq—Iran—Americans came to believe the United States merely was mired in an unwinnable Iraqi civil war.[337]

---

333 Gerry J. Gilmore, "IED Components Moving across Iraq-Iran Border, General Says," *Defense News*, March 17, 2006, https://web.archive.org/web/20120414133105/http://www.defense.gov//News/NewsArticle.aspx?ID=15137

334 Tom Vanden Brook, "US Blames Iran for New Bombs in Iraq," *USA Today*, January 31, 2007, http://usatoday30.usatoday.com/news/world/iraq/2007-01-30-ied-iran_x.htm; Steven R. Hurst, "Officials: Iran behind Advanced, Lethal IED," *Army Times*, February 11, 2007, http://archive.armytimes.com/article/20070211/NEWS/702110301/Officials-Iran-behind-advanced-lethal-IED.

335 Hurst, "Officials: Iran behind Advanced, Lethal IED."

336 Michael R. Gordon, "Deadliest Bomb in Iraq Is Made by Iran, US Says," *New York Times*, February 9, 2015, http://www.nytimes.com/2007/02/10/world/middleeast/10weapons.html?pagewanted=all.

337 For example, see Jonathan Gurwitz, "Petraeus Left Iraq a Better Place than when He Took Command," *Deseret News*, September 27, 2008, http://www.deseretnews.com/article/700262021/Petraeus-left-Iraq-a-better-place-than-when-he-took-command.html?pg=all; Mike Whitney, "Provoking a Civil War in Iraq," PalestineChronicle.com, February 13, 2007, http://www.palestinechronicle.com/mike-whitney-provoking-a-civil-war-in-iraq/?print=pdf; statement of Congresswoman Lynn Woolsey, Congressional Record—House, vol. 153, pt. 2, January 18, 2007, 1628 ("Iraq is mired in a civil war, and even though we helped ignite it, we have very little influence on its outcome."), https://books.google.com/books?id=DaFQ_F0bdnYC&pg=PA1628&lpg=PA1628&dq=US+mired+in+unwinnable+civil+war+in+iraq&source=bl&ots=e8SBmWJI0c&sig=vhS0Sh1DP2l-B6LcSDYfzuoPmbI&hl=en&sa=X&ved=-0CCgQ6AEwAjgUahUKEwjY_Lftm97IAhVGyT4KHTM5BLM#v=onepage&q=US%20mired%20in%20unwinnable%20civil%20war%20in%20iraq&f=false.

For example, when the United States suffered its three-thousandth death in Iraq, the *New York Times* reported that the continued US fatalities were due to a "dedicated and ruthless Iraqi insurgency that has exploited the power of roadside bombs to chilling effect. These bombs now cause about half of all American combat deaths and injuries in Iraq."[338] The article did not mention that the "ruthless Iraqi insurgency" received enhanced roadside bomb capabilities from Iran.

The media not only provided a steady drumbeat of bad news but also failed to highlight successes as they occurred. Nowhere was this more evident than in the media's coverage of the US troop surge in 2007. Over the course of the first half of 2007, the United States implemented the surge in Iraq, adding thirty thousand troops—five combat brigades—to its existing forces in Iraq and raising the total number of US troops in Iraq to approximately 170,000.[339] By later in the summer, with most of the surge forces in place and operating, the United States saw a steady decline in combat casualties.

This media bias toward emphasizing negative stories was apparent not only in hindsight but also in real time. The columnist Thomas Sowell noted in a March 2007 column that while many front-page and cover-page media stories about the war focused on those wounded in action, deployed reservists dealing with financial difficulties, or children saying good-bye to parents being deployed to Iraq, "remarkable acts of bravery or compassion [were] passed over in silence."[340] Similarly, Michael Barone, a commentator for Fox News, said the following on an episode of Fox's *Special Report with Brit Hume*:

> And I think part of this is the question of the press corps. I mean, I asked the question, if a World War II–era Cindy Sheehan had gone to Hyde Park and Warm Springs and camped out, demanded a meeting with President Roosevelt, would she have received coverage from the press in the World War II era? And I've studied this era. And I think

---

338 Alvarez and Lehren, "3,000 Deaths in Iraq, Countless Tears at Home."

339 "Timeline: Invasion, Surge, Withdrawal; US forces in Iraq," Reuters, December 15, 2011, http://www.reuters.com/article/2011/12/15/us-iraq-usa-pullout-idUSTRE7BE0EL20111215.

340 Sowell, "'Supporting the Troops.'"

> the answer is clearly no. She would have just been thought to have been a person who was the victim of a personal tragedy and who had gone over the bend as a result of it. And they would have mercifully given her no publicity.[341]

As daily casualties dropped in Iraq during the 2007 surge, the number of media stories about Iraq dropped, and US public opinion became more cautiously optimistic about the war. Pew noted that the decrease in stories about daily violence in Iraq coincided with more Americans believing that the United States was making progress in Iraq. The number of Americans believing the United States was making progress in Iraq jumped 13 percent, from 30 percent to 43 percent, from February 2007 to November 2007.[342] The decline in overall news stories on Iraq, from July 2007 through November 2007 and coinciding with the surge, reflected the old adage that "no news is good news."[343]

However, good news is good news as well. A decline in stories overall meant less coverage overall, including coverage reflecting the success of the surge both in reducing daily casualties and in reconstructing Iraq into a stable, pacified country. One editor interviewed for the Pew report noted that the news media found it difficult to cover good news stories because even as daily attacks went down, the threat of kidnappings and violence remained.[344] This comment begs the question, however, of why the media coverage went

---

341 Nicole Casta, Josh Kalven, and Jeremy Schulman, "Limbaugh, Coulter, Liddy, Hitchens, Barone continue attacks on Cindy Sheehan," Media Matters for America, August 18, 2005, http://mediamatters.org/research/2005/08/18/limbaugh-coulter-liddy-hitchens-barone-continue/133676.

342 Pew Research Center: Journalism & Media Staff, "The Portrait from Iraq: How the Press Has Covered Events on the Ground; Changing Public Opinion," Pew Research Center, December 18, 2007, http://www.journalism.org/2007/12/18/changing-public-opinion/.

343 Pew Research Center: Journalism & Media Staff, "The Portrait from Iraq: How the Press Has Covered Events on the Ground. A Surge for the Surge," Pew Research Center, December 18, 2007, http://www.journalism.org/2007/12/18/november-a-surge-for-the-surge/.

344 Pew Research Center: Journalism & Media Staff, "The Portrait from Iraq: How the Press Has Covered Events on the Ground. The Question of Bias," Pew Research Center, December 18, 2007, http://www.journalism.org/2007/12/18/the-question-of-bias/

down as attacks dropped. The media were more than capable of fully covering the violence in Iraq during its height, so why as attacks went down would it become *more* dangerous to cover Iraq? Moreover, US armed forces permitted journalists to embed with combat troops in Iraq during the height of combat. Surely a mechanism could have been developed to assist in covering good news stories (such as the openings of schools, playgrounds, and markets, the completion of infrastructure projects, and successful elections) that could have protected journalists while allowing them to cover the good news stories. It is difficult to understand how the risk to journalists increased at a time when attacks in Iraq decreased overall.

Media coverage of the success of the surge did not reach the levels and proportions of the media coverage of the setbacks in 2005–2007. In March 2008, more than a year after President Bush announced the surge strategy, a media writer in the *New York Times* wrote an article titled "The War Endures, but Where's the Media?"[345] The article described how coverage of the Iraq War, dominant in the first half of 2007, had fallen precipitously by March 2008. The author, Richard Perez-Pena, noted that "the drop [in media coverage] accelerated with a sharp decline in violence in Iraq that began at the end of last summer."[346] In fact, according to the Pew Research Center, coverage of Iraq dropped 50 percent from January 2007 (when Iraq dominated the news, with 20 percent of all stories related to Iraq) to March 2008.[347] The Pew Center attributed part of the drop to the rise of other stories, such as the 2008 presidential election and the economy. Nevertheless, the Pew Center noted that "another key reason why the war has virtually disappeared from the headlines and talk shows these days—and that's the situation inside Iraq itself. The reduction in violence on the ground that began late last year has coincided with a significant decrease in coverage from the war zone as well."[348]

---

345 Richard Perez-Pena, "The War Endures, but Where's the Media?," *New York Times*, March 24, 2008, http://www.nytimes.com/2008/03/24/business/media/24press.html?_r=0.

346 Ibid.

347 Mark Jurkowitz, "Why Iraq News Dropped," Pew Research Center, March 26, 2008, http://www.journalism.org/2008/03/26/why-news-iraq-dropped/.

348 Ibid.

According to Pew, journalists responded to criticism that they were not providing stories that would focus on the progress being made in Iraq and the redevelopment of civil society as violence levels decreased. Some journalists responded by saying that the situation in Baghdad and elsewhere in Iraq remained very dangerous for journalists and their staffs; Pew found 57 percent of journalists reported a member of their staffs being kidnapped or killed in the preceding year.[349] However, this argument does not explain well why the number of stories and overall coverage of Iraq were substantially greater during the period before the surge, when there was greater violence throughout Iraq. Surely it was not the case that in 2005–2007, before the surge and when sectarian violence was raging, journalists were at *less* risk than after the surge. Yet according to Pew, during the height of the violence in Iraq, journalists were able to produce 50 percent more stories before the surge than after the surge. In addition, the number of embedded reporters dropped from the early days of the war to "tens" in early 2008.[350] This decrease was the result of financial constraints at the media outlets.[351] However, part of the surge strategy was to increase the number of troops that left their bases and interacted with and defended Iraqi citizens from al-Qaeda, Shia militias, and other insurgents.[352] The opportunity existed for a reinvigorated embedding program to allow journalists to see firsthand the successes of the surge.

Finally, even after the surge ended and violence decreased in Iraq, journalists were unwilling to give the surge credit for the success. Instead, journalists searched for factors other than the surge to which they could attribute the drop in violence in Iraq. In the *Washington Post*, Bob Woodward wrote an article titled "Why Did Violence Plummet? It Wasn't Just the Surge."[353] The

349 Ibid.

350 Perez-Pena, "The War Endures, but Where's the Media?"

351 David Vaina, "The Vanishing Embedded Reporter in Iraq," Pew Research Center, October 26,2006,http://www.journalism.org/2006/10/26/the-vanishing-embedded-reporter-in-iraq/.

352 Emma Sky, "Iraq: From Surge to Sovereignty," *Foreign Affairs*, March/April 2011, https://www.foreignaffairs.com/articles/middle-east/2011-03-01/iraq-surge-sovereignty.

353 Bob Woodward, "Why Did Violence Plummet in Iraq? It Wasn't Just the Surge.", *Washington Post*, September 8, 2008,
http://www.washingtonpost.com/wp-dyn/content/article/2008/09/07/AR2008090701847.html.

article cited the Anbar Awakening, which resulted from the brutality of al-Qaeda, and the Sunni tribes' disillusionment with al-Qaeda in Iraq and their resulting willingness to work with the United States to defeat AQI. Woodward also cited the Joint Special Operations Command (JSOC), which in the late spring of 2007 used new intelligence sources, methods, and operations to target and kill top insurgency and AQI leaders. While all of this was true, none of it likely would have been possible had the United States not shown its commitment to victory by implementing the surge, showing the Iraqis the United States was there for the duration, and winning their trust. National Security Advisor Stephen Hadley released the following statement in response to Woodward's *Washington Post* article: "It was the surge that helped us convince Sadr that a ceasefire was in his best interest because his Mahdi Army could not prevail on the battlefield. It was the surge that gave the Awakening Movement the confidence to continue to stand up to Al Qaeda and take back Anbar Province. It was the surge that provided more resources and a security context to support newly developed techniques and operations. And it was the surge that allowed the Iraqi Security Forces to grow and build their capacity to fight."[354] General Raymond Odierno's political adviser, Emma Sky, stated that Iraqis began to provide better intelligence, deny insurgents sanctuary, and in the case of the Anbar Sunni tribes, turn against AQI and join the Iraqi political process because Iraqis viewed the surge as showing the United States was committed to victory.[355]

The media laid all of the blame for the Iraq War's failures and setbacks at the feet of the Bush administration—whether it was poor prewar planning, bad or ineffective leadership, or leadership that supposedly encouraged detainee abuses. However, when the United States turned the tide and began to enjoy success, journalists cited factors other than US strategy as responsible for the success. The media was willing to place unvarnished blame on the

---

354 "Statement by National Security Advisor Stephen J. Hadley," *Washington Post*, September 5, 2008, http://www.washingtonpost.com/wp-dyn/content/article/2008/09/05/AR2008090503051.html.

355 Sky, "Iraq: From Surge to Sovereignty."

Bush administration for setbacks but offer only grudging credit laden with caveats for successes.

There are lessons to be drawn from the media coverage of the Iraq War. First, it is essential for the military and political leadership to wage an all-out effort to demonstrate over and over again the rationale for the war, the successes of the war and accomplishments of US troops in the field, and how the successes fit into the overall goals and strategy of the war. The US media likely will overemphasize setbacks and highlight "grim milestones." US military and political leaders need to be better prepared in advance to respond to the milestones quickly and forcefully.

The US government should be proactive in ensuring the full story is made public, particularly when the news is good. The fact that the number of embedded reporters dropped into the "tens" during the surge meant that the good news stories resulting from the surge and, more importantly, the reasons why the surge succeeded were not being covered fully. As a result, the American public could not judge the lessons of the surge fully, and politicians and commentators could spin the surge as being incomplete or inadequate to achieve victory in Iraq. As an example, to the extent reporting organizations do not have the financial resources to serve as embedded reporters, the US government should consider ways to make it cost effective for journalists to remain embedded. If journalists are concerned for their safety and unwilling to report important stories of American military and civilian successes, the US military should find a way to make that possible, whatever the cost. The American public must receive regular reports of US forces' accomplishments from the battle theater.

However, the most important lesson may be this: just as the Iraq War media coverage was colored in many ways by the way the media covered Vietnam, how the media covered the Iraq War is likely to be how the media will cover the next war. Therefore, strategies and plans must account for media coverage of the war and, most critically, the likelihood of greater and more negative coverage at the first sign of setbacks. It is often said that battle plans never survive contact with the enemy, and the enemy gets a vote in how a war proceeds. The political leadership needs to be ready to respond to the inevitable setbacks quickly and effectively, "flooding the zone" in the same way antiwar activists surely will. Moreover, transparency—describing the good and the bad, the setbacks and the successes—as part of a comprehensive picture will enhance political credibility and enable the government to better persuade the American public. If the government cedes the conversation to activists, setbacks will be magnified and successes overlooked.

CHAPTER 8

Treating Soldiers as Victims: What the Antiwar Movement Learned from Vietnam

---

DURING VIETNAM, THE ANTIWAR MOVEMENT treated returning soldiers with contempt and disrespect. Returning troops were spat upon and denigrated as "baby killers." The Army advised soldiers returning from Vietnam not to wear uniforms in public to avoid the wrath of antiwar protesters.[356] The antiwar movement came in for opprobrium after these displays. The movement's behavior toward returning American soldiers and the military generally undermined the notion that it was patriotic and opposed the war not out of a sense of anti-Americanism but out of its patriotic duty to "speak truth to power" and "question authority."

One lesson the antiwar movement learned well from the treatment of American soldiers returning from Vietnam was that treating soldiers disrespectfully did not engender support for their cause from the wider American population. Especially today, when the armed forces are an all-volunteer force, mistreating soldiers to make a political statement generally backfires. From this realization was born a new means for supporting US troops while opposing their deployment: the idea that soldiers are "victims" of US foreign policy and the best way to "support the troops" is to bring them home. James Jay Carafano, a veteran and scholar at the Heritage Foundation, said that "during Vietnam, the perception was that atrocities were everywhere—the

---

356 Rebecca Carroll, "Vietnam Vets View Anti-War Protests through Unique Eyes," *Deseret News*, April 10, 2003, http://www.deseretnews.com/article/975800/Vietnam-vets-view-anti-war-protests-through-unique-eyes.html?pg=all.

military was looked down on. There is a serious effort now not to stigmatize the military—a conscious effort to say, 'This is not a bunch of baby-killers.'"[357]

Numerous antiwar rallies featured speakers exhorting the United States to support the troops by bringing them home and protecting their safety.[358] Other antiwar protesters bootstrapped other leftist priorities, such as the need to provide quality health care and jobs for US troops and other Americans, onto their antiwar protests.[359] An Internet movement called "An Appeal for Redress from the War in Iraq" invited active-duty soldiers to send this message to their congressional leaders: "I respectfully urge my political leaders in Congress to support the prompt withdrawal of all American military forces and bases from Iraq. Staying in Iraq will not work and is not worth the price. It is time for US troops to come home."[360] The organizers of the initiative believed it was the first antiwar movement among active-duty troops since the Vietnam War.[361]

Howard Zinn, the revisionist American historian, stated in a 2005 editorial, "The first step is to support our troops in the only way that word support can have real meaning—by saving their lives, their limbs, their sanity. By bringing them home."[362] In a 2007 column for *Time* magazine, Michael

---

357 David Crary, "Iraq and Vietnam: Contrasting Protests," *Boston Globe*, March 20, 2007, http://www.boston.com/news/education/higher/articles/2007/03/20/iraq_and_vietnam_contrasting_protests/?page=full.

358 Debbie Hummel, "Thousands Protest Bush, Iraq War; Vow Support for Troops, Their Families," *Deseret News*, August 22, 2005, http://www.deseretnews.com/article/600157811/Thousands-protest-Bush-Iraq-war-vow-support-for-troops-their-families.html?pg=all; Charisse Jones, "Soldiers' Families to Hold Anti-War Rally at Ft. Bragg," *USA Today*, March 17, 2005, http://usatoday30.usatoday.com/news/nation/2005-03-17-bragg--rally_x.htm.

359 "Weekend Anti-War Demonstrations Continue," NBC News, March 18, 2007, http://www.nbcnews.com/id/17655224/ns/us_news-life/t/weekend-anti-war-demonstrations-continue/#.Vi0fIG6Btvk; Jennifer C. Kerr, "Protesters' Mantra: Bring Troops Home," *Deseret News*, October 26, 2003, http://www.deseretnews.com/article/520033791/Protesters-mantra-bring-troops-home.html?pg=all.

360 Mike Gudgell, "Soldiers Say Support the Troops by Bringing Them Home," ABC News, October 27, 2006, http://abcnews.go.com/Politics/IraqCoverage/story?id=2609936&page=1.

361 Ibid.

362 Howard Zinn, "Support Our Troops: Bring Them Home," *Information Clearing House*, January 22, 2005, http://www.informationclearinghouse.info/article7795.htm.

Kinsley noted that opponents of the war "were supporting the troops in the best possible way: by bringing them home to safety and their families."[363] He noted that then-senator Barack Obama stated that "over three thousand lives of the bravest young Americans" had been "wasted" in the Iraq War. Kinsley explicitly made the connection to Vietnam, noting that the use of the term "wasted" to describe war casualties came into vogue during Vietnam.[364] Kinsley went on to state, "The war was a horrible mistake. And as everyone comes to realize it was a mistake, continuing it becomes something much worse than a mistake." This statement, consciously or unconsciously, once again echoed the famous question John Kerry posed in his congressional testimony about Vietnam in 1971: "How do you ask a man to be the last man to die for a mistake?"[365]

A notorious article published in the *New Republic* in July 2007 by the magazine's Baghdad Diarist demonstrated the antiwar movement's investment in the "soldier as victim" narrative. The article, titled "Shock Troops," was written by an American soldier in Iraq. He described numerous incidents that made him and his fellow soldiers appear to be monsters. For example, he opened his piece by describing seeing a female soldier in his mess hall badly scarred and disfigured from an IED blast. The conversation went as follows:

> I saw her nearly every time I went to dinner in the chow hall at my base in Iraq. She wore an unrecognizable tan uniform, so I couldn't really tell whether she was a soldier or a civilian contractor. The thing that stood out about her, though, wasn't her strange uniform but the fact that nearly half her face was severely scarred. Or, rather, it had more or less melted, along with all the hair on that side of her head. She was always alone, and I never saw her talk to anyone. Members of my platoon had seen her before but had never really acknowledged

363 "*Time*: Support the Troops—Bring Them Home," *Sweetness & Lightness Blog*, http://sweetness-light.com/archive/time-mag-support-the-troops-bring-them-home.

364 Ibid.

365 "Vietnam War Veteran John Kerry's Testimony before the Senate Foreign Relations Committee," History 398: The Vietnam Experience, ed. Professor Ernest Bolt, University of Virginia.

> her. Then, on one especially crowded day in the chow hall, she sat down next to us.
>
> We were already halfway through our meals when she arrived. After a minute or two of eating in silence, one of my friends stabbed his spoon violently into his pile of mashed potatoes and left it there.
>
> "Man, I can't eat like this," he said.
>
> "Like what?" I said. "Chow hall food getting to you?"
>
> "No—with that fucking freak behind us!" he exclaimed, loud enough for not only her to hear us, but everyone at the surrounding tables. I looked over at the woman, and she was intently staring into each forkful of food before it entered her half-melted mouth.
>
> "Are you kidding? I think she's fucking hot!" I blurted out.
>
> "What?" said my friend, half-smiling.
>
> "Yeah man," I continued. "I love chicks that have been intimate--with IEDs. It really turns me on—melted skin, missing limbs, plastic noses..."
>
> "You're crazy, man!" my friend said, doubling over with laughter. I took it as my cue to continue.
>
> "In fact, I was thinking of getting some girls together and doing a photo shoot. Maybe for a calendar? 'IED Babes.' We could have them pose in thongs and bikinis on top of the hoods of their blown-up vehicles."
>
> My friend was practically falling out of his chair laughing. The disfigured woman slammed her cup down and ran out of the chow hall, her half-finished tray of food nearly falling to the ground.[366]

This story—like much of the piece—suffered from a fatal flaw: the supposed conversation never happened. It was false. Soldiers stationed at the same base as the author of the article did not recall ever seeing a woman disfigured by an IED in their mess hall.

---

366 Scott Thomas, "Shock Troops," The New Republic, July 23, 2007, http://www.newrepublic.com/article/baghdad-diarist-shock-troops.

The purpose of the story was obvious: it was intended to show how the Iraq War had taken normal young Americans and turned them into moral monsters. The Baghdad Diarist himself, writing under the pseudonym Scott Thomas, talked about how he once worked in a camp for children with developmental disabilities and was "shocked" by his cruelty in describing the IED victim. His obvious intent was to make himself sound like a victim of the war, having been made a monster from the trauma of battle.

Scott Thomas, who later identified himself as Scott Thomas Beauchamp, went on to describe other scenes: an American soldier wearing on his head the skull of a child he found in a Saddam-era mass grave and a soldier who enjoyed running down dogs in his Bradley Fighting Vehicle. As he described how other soldiers found the soldier's wearing the child's skull amusing, he noted, "That is how war works: it degrades every part of you."

A number of writers quickly questioned the truth and accuracy of the Baghdad Diarist's stories. After a review of the articles and the publication process, the *New Republic*'s editor, Franklin Foer, acknowledged that the magazine could not stand by Beauchamp's stories in Foer's own piece, "Fog of War," retracting Beauchamp's stories.[367] In "Fog of War," Foer partially attempts to defend the magazine's fact-checking process, finding that some details in Beauchamp's stories were true while others were not.[368] The story of the IED victim apparently was similar to a story that Beauchamp told on his blog in 2006, but that story occurred in Kuwait, not Iraq, before Beauchamp even arrived in the Iraq theater.[369] Therefore, the whole notion that the Iraq War had dehumanized Beauchamp to the point that he was openly mocking IED victims and coming up with the idea of a calendar featuring IED victims could not have been true. But the elements of the stories that the *New Republic* could not corroborate or that it acknowledged were erroneous—the deliberate crushing of dogs by Bradley drivers, the occurrence in the mess hall—were the very elements that made these vignettes fit the thesis of the story: that the Iraq War

367 Franklin Foer, "The Fog of War," *New Republic*, December 10, 2007, http://www.newrepublic.com/article/fog-war.

368 Ibid.

369 Foer, "The Fog of War"; "Picking Up the Pieces," *Armed Forces Journal*, September 1, 2007, http://www.armedforcesjournal.com/picking-up-the-pieces/.

had turned American soldiers into monsters. Worse, the *New Republic* admitted that one of the primary fact checkers of the story was Beauchamp's wife.[370]

The willingness of the *New Republic* to publish these stories despite limited corroborating evidence demonstrated the media's willingness to believe the worst about American soldiers and report it. The story of normal young American men and women going to war and coming back with permanent moral scars—the same narrative that played out in Vietnam—fit the antiwar movement's criticism of the war, as it showed that the antiwar movement was sensitive to what the war was doing to young soldiers without blaming them for it. That is, it showed soldiers as victims. In addition, it painted with a broad brush all American soldiers as monsters rather than considering the alternative possibility: that it reflected issues specific to the individual author. And so, despite deeply flawed fact checking, the *New Republic* ran Beauchamp's stories.

Antiwar politicians also used the "support the troops—bring them home" position to oppose the war without appearing to undermine the troops. Rep. Lynn Woolsey responded to the Americans Support Your Freedom walk on the fourth anniversary of the 9/11 attacks by stating on the House floor, "If we want to support the troops, the best thing we can do, the only thing we can do, is to bring them home, out of Iraq, where their very presence is animating the insurgency and giving rise to more intense anti-Americanism than ever."[371] In October 2005, Rep. Dennis Kucinich took to the floor of the House upon the two thousandth US casualty in Iraq to state, "Now more than ever, we need to support the troops. Support the troops by bringing them home."[372] In January 2007, Rep.

370 Foer, "The Fog of War."

371 Congressional Record—House, vol. 151, pt. 15, September 13, 2005, Google Books edition, https://books.google.com/books?id=mdE7EEbYPvAC&pg=PA6&lpg=PA6&dq=support+the+troops+bring+them+home+2005&source=bl&ots=Ke8-yFfZ5G&sig=JMJP-w8W_QA4GBC1d9--qIz8Muas&hl=en&sa=X&ved=0CCMQ6AEwATgUahUKEwiYhOHvnLbHAhVG0IAKHXjVD-E#v=onepage&q=support%20the%20troops%20bring%20them%20home%202005&f=false.

372 Congressional Record—House, vol. 151, pt. 17, October 26, 2005, accessed October 25, 2015, Google Books edition, https://books.google.com/books?id=74brGsoymBoC&pg=RA1-PA325&lpg=RA1-PA325&dq=support+the+troops+bring+them+home+2005&source=bl&ots=6Njn7_0yGR&sig=vgdj8bzVAl2_Sr5y_aKEZH3hoOw&hl=en&sa=X&ved=0CCwQ6AEwBDgUahUKEwiYhOHvnLbHAhVG0IAKHXjVD-E#v=onepage&q=support%20the%20troops%20bring%20them%20home%202005&f=false.

Jerrold Nadler, an antiwar member of the new Democratic majority in Congress, introduced a bill called the Protect the Troops and Bring Them Home Act of 2007, which would limit funds for the Iraq War to being used to withdraw US troops from Iraq and protect US troops in Iraq pending their withdrawal.[373] Thus the antiwar opposition equated supporting the troops with bringing them home. They viewed the troops not as needing a new strategy to allow them to succeed but as victims needing protection from the president's foreign policy. In February 2007, Congresswoman Lynn Woolsey sent a letter to President Bush urging him to "truly support the troops" by "bringing them home now."[374]

In February 2007, the newly elected Democratic-majority Congress passed a concurrent resolution that opposed the proposed surge, stating, "(1) Congress and the American people will continue to support and protect the members of the United States Armed Forces who are serving or who have served bravely and honorably in Iraq; and (2) Congress disapproves of the decision of President George W. Bush announced on January 10, 2007, to deploy more than 20,000 additional United States combat troops to Iraq."[375] The antiwar movement took pains to demonstrate that it supported the troops, even as it undermined the president's new strategy designed to allow the troops to succeed in their mission. Thus did the antiwar movement and its political supporters attempt to avoid recreating their post-Vietnam mistake of harassing soldiers returning from the war and denigrating their service.

A former Army psychiatrist, Elspeth Ritchie, wrote a piece in *Time* magazine shortly after her retirement from the Army in 2011 in which she recognized the impulse to see American soldiers as victims. She noted that one commonly expressed view of soldiers in the wave of military-related media stories around Memorial Day in 2011 was the soldier as victim. These stories, she noted, portrayed the American soldier as "misguided, misled, and

373 Protect the Troops and Bring Them Home Act of 2007, H.R. 455, GovTrack, https://www.govtrack.us/congress/bills/110/hr455/text.

374 Spencer Ackerman, "The Bitter End," *Washington Monthly*, June 2007, http://www.washingtonmonthly.com/features/2007/0706.ackerman.html.

375 House Concurrent Resolution 63, GovTrack, https://www.govtrack.us/congress/bills/110/hconres63/text.

helpless—'a sad sack.'"[376] She noted "some unvoiced sentiment that we troops have somehow been duped into making a bad decision."[377] She stated that she "[did] not buy that one bit" and noted, "The US has had an all-volunteer Army for decades, and our Soldiers have enlisted with a near-certainty that they will be going to war. Indeed, in my experience most *want* to go to war."[378]

The idea that soldiers are victims allows antiwar activists to pose as being more supportive of US troops than those who are deploying them into combat. But, of course, this is an argument for never deploying American force under any conditions, because, by the antiwar movement's own definition, one could not be supporting the troops by deploying them into combat. However, as an all-volunteer military, those who join the US armed forces do so of their own free will and desire to protect the United States from all enemies. They have accepted the possibility of being deployed; indeed, they joined the armed forces to protect the United States, in combat if necessary.

In fact, those who visited Iraq found that the surge increased the morale of American troops in Iraq. Spencer Ackerman, writing in the *Washington Monthly* in 2007, described how he had visited troops in Baghdad and found that "for many troops in Baghdad, the surge had brought a significant boost in morale." Ackerman also cited polling of the military that found that a plurality of the military in 2007 believed the war needed more troops, not less.[379] In short, Ackerman found that the troops on the ground "continue[d] to have faith in the mission."[380] American troops in Iraq, far from needing "protection" through withdrawal, had guarded optimism about their mission and believed it could be achieved. They did not view themselves as victims needing to be protected by pulling the plug on the mission.

Perhaps the most infamous example of soldiers being viewed as victims came from Sen. John Kerry, who in October 2006 told a group of college students,

---

376 Elspeth C. Ritchie, "Memorial Day in the Rear View Mirror: Soldiers as Heroes, and Victims," *Time*, June 5, 2011, http://nation.time.com/2011/06/05/memorial-day-in-the-rearview-mirror-soldiers-as-heroes-and-victims/.

377 Ibid.

378 Ibid.

379 Ackerman, "The Bitter End."

380 Ibid.

"We're here to talk about education but I want say something before, you know, education, if you make the most of it, you study hard, you do your homework, and you make an effort to be smart, you can do well; if you don't, you get stuck in Iraq."[381] Kerry's vision of American soldiers in Iraq was of individuals who had been victimized by their own supposedly limited intellect or poor academic performance into fighting in Iraq. The remark dripped with condescension and suggested that soldiers had joined the military because their academic performance or skill set left them no other career options. The remark ignored the fact that the US military was an all-volunteer force whose members joined of their own volition. But this unwillingness to ascribe any agency to American servicemen and servicewomen also betrayed a belief that those serving in Iraq were not there because they believed in their mission or desired to serve their country but because they were unwitting victims of a militaristic foreign policy.

Kerry's statement hearkened back to his 1971 testimony before the Senate regarding Vietnam in which he portrayed US soldiers as agents of the inhumane policies of their commanders and political leaders. Kerry told the Senate, "We are also here to ask, and we are here to ask vehemently, where are the leaders of our country? Where is the leadership? We are here to ask where are McNamara, Rostow, Bundy, Gilpatric, and so many others. Where are they now that we, the men whom they sent off to war, have returned? These are commanders who have deserted their troops, and there is no more serious crime in the law of war."[382]

Going beyond viewing all soldiers as victims, the antiwar movement and antiwar politicians and pundits also claimed that the poor and minorities represented a disproportionate number of casualties in Iraq. The idea that the poor and minorities do a disproportionate amount of the fighting and suffer disproportionate casualty rates has been a prominent antiwar criticism since the Vietnam War. The antiwar movement reprised this criticism as the United States prepared for war in Iraq and as the war progressed.

---

381 "John Kerry: Stuck in Iraq," YouTube video, https://www.youtube.com/watch?v=dRjUubkhmv4.

382 "Vietnam War Veteran John Kerry's Testimony before the Senate Foreign Relations Committee," History 398: The Vietnam Experience, ed. Professor Ernest Bolt, University of Virginia.

Rep. Charlie Rangel claimed in a December 2002 op-ed calling for reinstatement of the draft that "a disproportionate number of the poor and members of minority groups make up the enlisted ranks of the military, while the most privileged Americans are underrepresented or absent."[383] At the ANSWER rally on September 26, 2002, Jesse Jackson claimed that many of the casualties would be minorities and the poor.[384] In 2004, Jesse Jackson said, "Poor people make less and in wartime serve more. There are no rich folks' children in Iraq today. There are no CEOs' children in Iraq today. There are no congresspersons' children in Iraq today. The corporate CEOs get a tax cut, go offshore for tax avoidance, get no-bid contracts, export jobs, import guest workers and analyze how the rest of us live, suffer and die."[385] The *New York Times* columnist Bob Herbert said in a column that "if the war in Iraq is worth fighting—if it's a noble venture, as the hawks insist it is—then it's worth fighting with the children of the privileged classes. They should be added to the combat mix. If it's not worth their blood, then we should bring the other troops home."[386] In December 2002, prior to the beginning of the Iraq War, Rep. Charlie Rangel called for the reinstatement of the draft because of perceived racial and socioeconomic disparities in the military.

Rangel's claim, however, ignored the fact that while minorities served at a higher rate than their proportion of the overall population, combat troops—those at greatest casualty risk in the Iraq War—were predominately white at the time Rangel called for reinstating the draft.[387] Herbert's claim was false: studies have shown that the income distribution of military recruits closely

---

383 Charles B. Rangel, "Bring Back the Draft," *New York Times*, December 31, 2002, http://www.nytimes.com/2002/12/31/opinion/31RANG.html.

384 "Anti-War Rally," C-SPAN, October 26, 2002, http://www.c-span.org/video/?173521-1/antiwar-rally.

385 Terry M. Neal, "Bush, Blacks, and Iraq," *Washington Post*, May 20, 2004, http://www.washingtonpost.com/wp-dyn/articles/A41971-2004May20_2.html.

386 Bob Herbert, "Blood Runs Red, Not Blue," *New York Times*, August 18, 2005, http://www.nytimes.com/2005/08/18/opinion/blood-runs-red-not-blue.html?_r=0.

387 Dave Moniz and Tom Squitieri, "Front-Line Troops Disproportionately White, Not Black," *USA Today*, January 21, 2003, http://usatoday30.usatoday.com/news/washington/2003-01-20-army-usat_x.htm.

matches that of the overall population.[388] Moreover, American combat troops at the outset of the Iraq War were disproportionately white.[389] From the beginning of Iraq War combat in March 2003 through May 8, 2004, 14 percent of US casualties were African American, and African Americans made up 12.5 percent of the US population.[390]

American "victim culture" is a powerful force in American society; the examples of protests in 2015 by supposedly victimized groups on the campuses of the University of Missouri, Yale University, Claremont McKenna College, and other universities demonstrate the power of having victim status in American society. Achieving victim status can provide the power to get university presidents and administrators fired and provide speakers "absolute moral authority," in the words of columnist Maureen Dowd. By bringing American "victim culture" into the discussion of the Iraq War, the antiwar movement created an additional base of powerful opposition to the war, an opposition virtually unimpeachable in the public sphere. Opponents of the Iraq War coupled their grant of unimpeachable authority to the "victims" of the Iraq War with their attempts to silence supporters of the war by calling them "chickenhawks" who effectively had no right to advocate military intervention because they had never served in the military. These efforts bore fruit and further skewed the debate away from the national security pros and cons of the war. It also allowed the antiwar movement to oppose the war without the politically unsympathetic slandering and mistreatment of American servicemen and servicewomen that occurred after Vietnam.

---

388 Tim Kane, "Who Bears the Burden? Demographic Characteristics of US Military Recruits before and after 9/11," Heritage Foundation, November 7, 2005, accessed October 25, 2015, http://www.heritage.org/research/reports/2005/11/who-bears-the-burden-demographic-characteristics-of-us-military-recruits-before-and-after-9-11#_ftn1.

389 Moniz and Squitieri, "Front-Line Troops Disproportionately White, Not Black."

390 Neal, "Bush, Blacks, and Iraq."

CHAPTER 9

Pouring Partisan Gasoline on the Antiwar Fire: How Iraq Was Worse than Vietnam

THIS BOOK HAS EXPLORED THE many ways in which the antiwar movement resembled the antiwar movement of Vietnam consciously or unconsciously. However, in one significant way, the antiwar movement of the Iraq War differed from its Vietnam predecessor. Unlike the antiwar movement of the Vietnam War, the Iraq War's antiwar movement was deeply partisan at a much earlier stage of the war, with Republicans supporting the war and Democrats firmly turning on the war less than a year after it began and nearly unanimously by the time of the 2004 Democratic presidential primaries. This difference in the partisanship associated with the Vietnam and Iraq Wars actually makes winning wars today more difficult than in the heyday of the Vietnam antiwar movement.

As described in chapter 2, the Vietnam War began with bipartisan support. President Kennedy sent the first American military advisers to Vietnam in 1961 and ultimately sent sixteen thousand American military advisers to Vietnam.[391] President Johnson dramatically escalated the war effort, with the first combat troops arriving in 1965 and troop levels peaking at 537,377 in 1968.[392] Only two

391 Arthur Schlesinger Jr., "What Would He Have Done?," review of *JFK and Vietnam* by John M. Newman, *New York Times*, March 29, 1992, https://www.nytimes.com/books/00/11/26/specials/schlesinger-newman.html.

392 Jeff Nisson, "Fifty Years Ago: Boots on the Ground in Vietnam," *Saturday Evening Post*, March 5, 2015, http://www.saturdayeveningpost.com/2015/03/05/history/post-perspective/50-years-ago-boots-ground-vietnam.html; Tim Kane and David D. Gentilli, "Is Iraq Another Vietnam? Not for US Troop Levels," Heritage Foundation, July 21, 2006, http://www.heritage.org/research/reports/2006/07/is-iraq-another-vietnam-not-for-us-troop-levels#_ftn2.

Democrats opposed the 1964 Gulf of Tonkin Resolution. The initial protests that grew in size and strength over the second half of the 1960s were protesting a Democratic president and a Congress with overwhelming Democratic majorities in both the House of Representatives and the US Senate. The Eighty-Ninth Congress from 1965 to 1967 included 295 Democrats to only 140 Republicans in the House and 68 Democrats to only 32 Republicans in the Senate.[393] The Ninetieth Congress from 1967 to 1969 included 64 Democrats and 36 Republicans in the Senate and 247 Democrats and 187 Republicans in the House.[394]

Protests grew tremendously against the Vietnam War during the period of solid Democratic control of Congress. The Students for a Democratic Society led the March Against the Vietnam War in April 1965 in Washington.[395] In October 1967, over one hundred thousand gathered to protest the war at the Lincoln Memorial and between thirty thousand to fifty thousand protesters then crossed the Potomac to protest at the Pentagon.

Protests continued after the election of Richard Nixon. On October 15, 1969, the first Vietnam Moratorium protest took place worldwide. Nearly one hundred thousand attended the protest in Boston, where George McGovern spoke. One of the organizers of the Moratorium protest in the United Kingdom was a young Bill Clinton, then studying at Oxford.[396] One month later, over five hundred thousand descended on Washington, DC, for the second Moratorium protest. The Kent State protest, at which four protesters

---

393 "Congress Profiles," History, Art & Archives, US House of Representatives, http://history.house.gov/Congressional-Overview/Profiles/89th/; "Senate History, Party Division," United States Senate, http://www.senate.gov/history/partydiv.htm.

394 "Senate History, Party Division," United States Senate, http://www.senate.gov/history/partydiv.htm; "Congress Profiles," History, Art, & Archives, US House of Representatives, http://history.house.gov/Congressional-Overview/Profiles/90th/.

395 Jeff Leen, "The Vietnam Protests: When Worlds Collided," *Washington Post*, September 27, 1999, http://www.washingtonpost.com/wp-srv/local/2000/vietnam092799.htm.

396 Michael Kelly with David Johnston, "The 1992 Campaign: The Vietnam War; Campaign Focus on Vietnam Reviving the Debates of the 60's," *New York Times*, October 9, 1992, http://www.nytimes.com/1992/10/09/us/1992-campaign-vietnam-war-campaign-focus-vietnam-reviving-debates-60-s.html?pagewanted=all.

were killed by National Guardsmen, occurred in 1970.[397] Massive protests on campuses and in major cities continued throughout Nixon's first presidential term.

In time, the Democratic Party would become the antiwar party, but only after a struggle over the party's leadership. As described previously, rank-and-file Democrats opposed to the war sought an antiwar presidential candidate, and Eugene McCarthy ran for president as an antiwar Democrat in 1968. Despite McCarthy's success in the early Democratic primaries and President Johnson's withdrawal from the 1968 race after the New Hampshire primary, the Democratic Party remained riven by divisions over Vietnam. Presidential nominee Hubert Humphrey continued to support the war effort, and opponents continued to protest the war, most famously and violently at the 1968 Democratic National Convention. The antiwar movement ultimately won the battle for the soul of the Democratic Party between 1968 and 1972. It took four years for the antiwar movement to take over the Democratic Party. But take over the party it did, and in 1972 the Democrats nominated George McGovern for president.

By contrast, the antiwar movement that arose during the Iraq War largely identified with the Democratic Party from the outset of the movement. The Iraq War began in March 2003, and, as described previously, the mainstream Democratic Party had largely adopted the antiwar position by the end of the 2004 Democratic primary process. As discussed in detail previously, the antiwar activists of the Democratic Party gravitated to the only vocally antiwar mainstream Democratic candidate for president, Howard Dean, in the late summer and fall of 2003—less than a year after the beginning of the Iraq War. Dean's success pulled the other 2004 Democratic presidential candidates toward the antiwar position. By March 2004—one year after the American invasion of Iraq—all of the leading candidates for the Democratic presidential nomination counted themselves in the antiwar camp.

---

397 "History—US Marshals Service and the Pentagon Riot of October 21, 1967," US Marshals Service, http://www.usmarshals.gov/history/civilian/1967a.htm; "This Day in History: October 21; Thousands Protest the War in Vietnam," The History Channel, http://www.history.com/this-day-in-history/thousands-protest-the-war-in-vietnam.

The evidence of how important anti-Republican partisanship was to the Iraq antiwar movement is most apparent by looking at how the movement fared after the election of Democrat Barack Obama in 2008. Following Obama's election, it became apparent that the fervor with which the antiwar movement denounced the Iraq War and called for the withdrawal of troops had diminished substantially. Gone were the marches on the Mall and in Manhattan of tens of thousands of people. Gone were the celebrity speeches, petitions, manifestos, and full-page advertisements opposing the war. Numerous articles and reports asked the question, "Whatever happened to the antiwar movement?"[398]

As early as August 2009, writers and commentators noticed the disappearance of the antiwar movement. Byron York, writing in the *Washington Examiner*, noted that the 2009 YearlyKos Convention—a convention of bloggers from and followers of the liberal website Daily Kos—had a much different outlook on issues than the 2006 edition of the YearlyKos Convention. At the first YearlyKos Convention in 2006, "activists spent hours discussing and planning strategies not only to defeat Republicans but also to pressure Democrats to oppose the war more forcefully."[399] By contrast, at the 2009 YearlyKos convention, the top issue in the minds of attendees (based on surveys taken at the convention by Democratic pollster Stanley Greenberg) was passing comprehensive health care reform, and the second most important issue was to enact and implement "green energy policies that address environmental concerns."[400] In the list of YearlyKos attendees' top concerns, "working to end our military involvement in Iraq and Afghanistan" fell to eighth place.[401]

---

398 Linton Weeks, "What Ever Happened to the Anti-War Movement?," National Public Radio, April 15, 2011, http://www.npr.org/2011/04/15/135391188/whatever-happened-to-the-anti-war-movement; David Boaz, "What Ever Happened to the Anti-War Movement?," *Encyclopedia Britannica Blog*, March 21, 2011, http://blogs.britannica.com/2011/03/happened-antiwar-movement/.

399 Byron York, "For the Left, War Without Bush Is Not War At All," *Washington Examiner*, August 17, 2009, http://www.washingtonexaminer.com/for-the-left-war-without-bush-is-not-war-at-all/article/93075.

400 Ibid.

401 Ibid.

Some of this change might have been attributable to the fact that, with Obama in the White House, activists were confident that he would, in time, withdraw troops from Iraq. However, pollster Greenberg also asked activists which issue "you, personally, spend the most time advancing currently." Health care reform came out on top, followed by "working to elect progressive candidates in the 2010 elections," and the very last issue—after several other issues—was "working to end US involvement in Iraq and Afghanistan."[402]

However, Obama did not immediately withdraw US troops from Iraq, and he surged troops in Afghanistan. In fact, in March 2011 a *Washington Post* / ABC News poll found that two-thirds of Americans no longer believed the Afghan War was worth fighting, and nearly three-quarters of those surveyed thought the United States should withdraw a "substantial" number of troops from Afghanistan in the summer of 2011.[403] Obama even entered the United States into another conflict, in Libya, though he deployed only airpower and no ground troops. Nevertheless, the antiwar movement was largely silent compared with the 2002–2007 period, in which marches of tens of thousands opposing the war in Iraq were de rigueur in Washington and other major US and European cities. In March 2011, with over forty thousand troops remaining in Iraq, only approximately one hundred demonstrators protested outside the White House on the eighth anniversary of the beginning of the war.[404]

Cindy Sheehan, after reading York's column, penned the following letter to York and his paper, the Washington *Examiner*:[405]

---

402 Ibid.

403 Scott Wilson and Jon Cohen, "Poll: Nearly Two-Thirds of Americans Say Afghan War Isn't Worth Fighting," *Washington Post*, March 15, 2011, https://www.washingtonpost.com/world/poll-nearly-two-thirds-of-americans-say-afghan-war-isnt-worth-fighting/2011/03/14/ABRbeEW_story.html.

404 Weeks, "What Ever Happened to the Anti-War Movement?"; "Chart: US Troop Levels in Iraq," October 21, 2011, http://www.cnn.com/2011/10/21/world/meast/chart-us-troops-iraq/index.html.

405 "What Happened to the Antiwar Movement? Cindy Sheehan Hits 'Hypocrisy of Left, Democratic Allies,'" *LiveLeak*, http://www.liveleak.com/view?i=86a_1250705724; http://www.washingtonexaminer.com/opinion/blogs/beltway-confidential/What-happened-to-the-antiwarmovement--Cindy-Sheehan-responds-53628177.html.

> I read your column about the "anti-war" movement and I can't believe I am saying this, but I mostly agree with you. The "anti-war" "left" was used by the Democratic Party. I like to call it the "anti–Republican War" movement.
>
> While I agree with you about the hypocrisy of such sites as the DailyKos, I have known for a long time that the Democrats are equally responsible with the Republicans. That's why I left the party in May 2007 and that's why I ran for Congress against Nancy Pelosi in 2008.
>
> I have my own radio show, "Cindy Sheehan's Soapbox," and I was out on a four-month book tour promoting the fact that it's not about Democrats or Republicans, but it's about the system.
>
> Even if I am surrounded by a thousand, or no one, I am still working for peace.
>
> Sincerely,
> Cindy Sheehan

In a subsequent phone call with York in which he confirmed that she had indeed sent this letter, Sheehan also noted that the press had lost interest in her opposition to the war. Sheehan told York, "I haven't stopped working. I've been protesting every time I can, and it's not covered. But the one time I did get a lot of coverage was when I protested in front of George Bush's house in Dallas in June. I don't know what to make of it. Is the press having a honeymoon with Obama? I know the Left is."[406]

An extraordinary study by Michael T. Heaney of the University of Florida and Fabio Rojas of Indiana University published in April 2011 confirmed the anecdotal evidence that much of the Iraq War's antiwar movement had been driven by anti-Republican partisanship. Heaney and Rojas studied why "the election of Obama appeared to be a demobilizing force on the antiwar movement, even in the face of his pro-war decisions" such as increasing troop levels in Afghanistan and keeping troops in Iraq through 2011 (the time when the

406 "What Happened to the Antiwar Movement? Cindy Sheehan Hits 'Hypocrisy of Left, Democratic Allies,'" *LiveLeak*.

article was written) despite promises to bring them home after his election.[407] The study conducted surveys of participants in antiwar protests that took place in the United States from 2007 to 2009.[408] During this time period, the Democrats regained control of Congress (in the 2006 midterm elections) and the White House (in the 2008 presidential election).

Heaney and Rojas found that attendance at antiwar protests dropped "by an order of magnitude" after January 2007 and again in 2008 and 2009.[409] Moreover, participation in antiwar protests by protesters that identified as Democrats dropped precipitously, from over 50 percent in January 2007 to 30 percent in April 2009 and 19 percent in November 2009.[410] In fact, *Slate* magazine's business insider, describing figure 3 of Heaney's and Rojas's study in which they showed the declining Democratic composition of the antiwar movement in 2007–2009, headlined a story, "In One Chart, Here's Why the Antiwar Movement Collapsed."[411] Heaney and Rojas concluded, "The withdrawal of Democrats from the [antiwar] movement in 2009 appears to be a significant explanation for the falling size of antiwar protests."[412] Moreover, Democrats deserted the antiwar movement as they achieved electoral success, not policy success.[413] What mattered to this segment of antiwar Democrats was winning elections and regaining power, not the management of the Iraq War.

It is also possible that the Iraq War, which began in George W. Bush's first term as president, reawakened the hard partisan feelings of the 2000 election, in which Vice President Al Gore won the popular vote and George Bush only emerged as the election winner after months of litigation and a

407 Michael T. Heaney and Fabio Rojas, "The Partisan Dynamics of Contention: Demobilization of Antiwar Movement in the United States," *Mobilization: An International Journal* 16, no. 1 (2011): 46.

408 Ibid., 49.

409 Ibid., Fig. 1 and p. 53.

410 Ibid., Fig. 3 and p. 54.

411 Joe Weisenthal, "In One Chart, Here's Why the Anti-War Movement Collapsed," Business Insider, *Slate*, September 2, 2013, http://www.slate.com/blogs/business_insider/2013/09/02/democrats_deserted_the_anti_war_movement.html.

412 Heaney and Rojas, "The Partisan Dynamics of Contention: Demobilization of Antiwar Movement in the United States," 54.

413 Ibid., 58.

Supreme Court ruling. The debate over the Iraq War took place in the fall of 2002, only two years removed from the bitter wrangling over the 2000 election's outcome. The bitterness of that election had been overtaken by the 9/11 attacks and the unity of Americans in the wake of those attacks but may never have fully gone away. Democrats who may not have reconciled themselves to the outcome of the 2000 election therefore may have seen the Iraq War as doubly illegitimate, illegitimate on its own and illegitimate because President Bush had not truly won the 2000 election. These feelings may have intensified the opposition to the war, both at home and abroad, where European and other foreign publics held President Bush in low regard and viewed him as a Wild West cowboy.

The collapse of the antiwar movement after 2009 represents a major difference between the antiwar movement of the 1960s and 1970s and the movement against the Iraq War. The antiwar movement in the 1960s and 1970s was less partisan and was influenced by other factors, including the draft. Regardless of who was in power, many of the protesters simply did not believe in the war and did not want to fight in Vietnam themselves.

Today's antiwar protests take place in an atmosphere in which there is no draft and college students are not faced with having to serve involuntarily in war. Therefore, the partisan features of today's antiwar movement are much more likely to be prominent in opposition to future armed conflicts than those of the antiwar movement of the 1960s and 1970s. In this sense, today's antiwar protests and protesters are not completely the result of Vietnam envy. Instead, however, they may represent something much more cynical: the use of antiwar opposition as a partisan weapon with which to attack and defeat political opponents. Policy makers must be aware of this fact when making the case of why a war is necessary and must continue to make this case through the course of an armed conflict. In this sense, policy makers must consider the possible need to mount a full political-style campaign to complement a military campaign, with regular and frequent reiterations of the rationales for the conflict and why the conflict must be won. Policy makers must meet antiwar opposition head-on and rebut it widely and forcefully at every turn, using a wide array of respected and articulate supporters of the conflict.

CHAPTER 10

The Wrong Lessons Learned and the Emergence of the Iraq Syndrome: The 2008 Campaign and the Iran Nuclear Deal

THE CONSEQUENCES OF THE ANTIWAR Sturm und Drang that began in 2003 with antiwar protests, French and German opposition in the United Nations, the explosion of protests in 2006, the garment rending from the Abu Ghraib scandal, and the failure properly to understand and assess the surge manifested themselves in the 2008 election. Rather than take a critical look at what had worked and what had not during the Iraq War, antiwar candidates during their campaigns etched in stone the lessons they believed they had learned. These lessons were the product of the factors described previously. However, the 2008 campaign effectively elevated these lessons into US foreign policy and national security doctrine.

By 2008, the antiwar movement had firmly moved the Democratic Party into the antiwar camp, and the party base was energized by the antiwar movement. In the Vietnam era, the antiwar movement took control of the Democratic Party between 1968 and 1972. Between 2004 and 2008, the antiwar movement took over the Democratic Party. It pulled the 2004 presidential candidates toward the antiwar position. It purged the party of elected officials who continued to support the Iraq War, most notably Senator Lieberman (who was reelected to the Senate as an "Independent Democrat" after losing his 2006 primary and retired in 2012). And, as the 2008 presidential campaign would demonstrate, it continued to hold Democratic officeholders' pro–Iraq War votes against them. By 2008, the antiwar movement drove Democratic Party foreign policy, just as it had a generation before in 1972. That is, by 2008, the antiwar movement's foreign policy was the Democratic Party's foreign policy. The antiwar movement's foreign policy and the Democratic Party's foreign policy had become one and the same.

Obama built his 2008 campaign in significant measure on the Iraq War and his opposition to it. He used his early opposition to the Iraq War to separate himself from his main primary competition, Hillary Clinton and John Edwards, both of whom had voted to authorize the war in the Senate in 2002. The combination of the antiwar movement's strength within the Democratic Party and Obama's strategy of using Iraq to distinguish himself as a candidate resulted in many of the positions the Democratic Party had taken in opposition to the war becoming the basis of what might be considered a new foreign policy "doctrine" of the Democratic Party.

The first major lesson that the antiwar movement and antiwar politicians took from Iraq was that no military solutions existed for situations such as those found in Iraq after the fall of Saddam and that only a political solution would bring a successful end to the conflict. As a candidate for president, in a major foreign policy speech to the Council on Foreign Relations in March 2008, Obama stated, "While we have a General [Petraeus] who has used improved tactics to reduce violence, we still have the wrong strategy. As General Petraeus has himself acknowledged, the Iraqis are not achieving the political progress needed to end their civil war."[414] Elaborating on his alternative Iraq policy, Obama stated,

> My plan to end this war will finally put pressure on Iraq's leaders to take responsibility for their future. Because we've learned that when we tell Iraq's leaders that we'll stay as long as it takes, they take as long as they want. We need to send a different message. We will help Iraq reach a meaningful accord on national reconciliation. We will engage with every country in the region—and the UN—to support

414 "Obama's Speech on Iraq, March 2008," Council on Foreign Relations, March 19, 2008, http://www.cfr.org/elections/obamas-speech-iraq-march-2008/p15761.

> the stability and territorial integrity of Iraq. And we will launch a major humanitarian initiative to support Iraq's refugees and people. But Iraqis must take responsibility for their country. It is precisely this kind of approach—an approach that puts the onus on the Iraqis, and that relies on more than just military power—that is needed to stabilize Iraq.[415]

Obama thereby reiterated the antiwar movement's position that US military power was insufficient to create a stable Iraq and that achieving political agreements and stability allowing the United States to leave Iraq should be the primary goal of US efforts in Iraq. Only such political agreements, combined with a US withdrawal, represented mission success. Reading between the lines and with the benefit of hindsight, it appears Obama believed he could force a political solution with the threat of removing US troops and that he believed in a time line with a defined end point for removing troops.

Missing from Obama's analysis of the surge's success were the reasons for its success. The surge succeeded, in part, because the United States was viewed as an honest broker and trustworthy interlocutor by all sides of the Iraq conflict—Sunni, Shia, and Kurds. By working with these various groups in Iraq to crush the insurgency and al-Qaeda in Iraq, the United States obtained a trusted position among and an ability to work with and navigate between each of these groups.[416] While they might not necessarily always be willing to work closely with each other, they were willing to work with the United States as a go-between. The United States' status among the various forces in Iraq actually put it in the best position to facilitate a permanent modus vivendi in Iraq.

Part of the reason for Obama's (and many antiwar Democrats') failure to acknowledge the reasons for the success of the surge was the fact that, by 2008, the Democrats largely had defined themselves by aligning with

---

415 Ibid.

416 For example, Rubin and Cave, "In a Force for Iraqi Calm, Seeds of Conflict," in which groups affiliated with the Awakening in Anbar Province and elsewhere express willingness to work with the Americans but not with Iraq's central government.

their antiwar supporters and opposing nearly any Iraq strategy or initiative of President Bush. Democrats effectively were forced to offer the caveat that the success of the surge was incomplete or nonlasting, as Obama had when he deemed the surge insufficient without a political settlement in Iraq and as Clinton had when she stated that the initial successes that General Petraeus testified to required a "willing suspension of disbelief."

However, the Democrats' political opposition failed to account for the lessons being learned on the ground. Emma Sky, the political adviser to Gen. Raymond Odierno, second in command in Iraq during the surge, wrote in 2011 that

> Petraeus and Odierno agreed that the essence of the struggle in Iraq was (and remains) a competition between communities for power and resources. By filling the power vacuum, the US military sought to buy the time and space for the Iraqi government to move forward with national reconciliation and improve its delivery of public services. US troops showed that they were willing to emerge from their bases and place the defense of the Iraqi people above all else, which sent a clear message to the Iraqi public that US forces would not be defeated. Many Iraqis stopped providing passive sanctuary to armed groups and, assured that the United States would protect them from reprisal, offered intelligence that enabled US troops to target insurgents more accurately. Meanwhile, the United States reached out to previously hostile tribal and factional leaders, coaxing them to turn against al Qaeda and participate in the political process.[417]

US troops put providing security first to allow the Iraqis space to develop politically. By making themselves trustworthy intermediaries, US troops won the confidence of the leaders of the various Iraqi communities. By demonstrating that the United States would not be defeated by the insurgents, the United States won the confidence of the Iraqi people. From that firm foundation, Iraqi reconciliation could take place. The antiwar Democrats, rather

417 Sky, "Iraq: From Surge to Sovereignty."

than recognizing that the prerequisite to their desired political settlement was the security the surge brought, chose to emphasize the inadequacy of the surge because it failed to achieve an immediate political settlement.

The second lesson that the antiwar movement and antiwar politicians took from Iraq was that the war had destroyed alliances and that, as discussed previously, only multilateralism, alliances, and diplomacy could achieve US national security objectives. In the same speech to the Council on Foreign Relations, Obama stated, "I also know that meeting these new threats will require a President who deploys the power of tough, principled diplomacy… And make no mistake—if and when we ever have to use military force against any country, we must exert the power of American diplomacy first."[418]

In the 2008 campaign and after, antiwar Democrats rarely, if ever, defined what they meant by "tough, principled diplomacy." One might take the position that it is diplomacy backed by the credible threat of force. But the fact that the antiwar Democrats never provided a clear, explicit definition of "tough, principled diplomacy" suggests that they deployed this phrase only as a means to draw a contrast with President Bush's supposed antidiplomatic, unilateral rush to war—despite spending six months at the United Nations seeking to demand Iraqi compliance with UN resolutions or face military action. That is, the antiwar Democrats' "tough, principled diplomacy" was defined not by what it was but what it wasn't: Bush's foreign policy.

Recall, however, that the notion that the United States "unilaterally rushed" to war primarily resulted from the opposition to the Iraq War of two countries: France and Germany. The idea that Bush's foreign policy had damaged or destroyed alliances and cost the United States friends around the world resulted from the strains on relations with France and Germany that resulted from the protracted six-month-long effort at the United Nations. In fact, as described previously, many countries—Great Britain, Spain, Poland, Australia, New Zealand, and others—supported the US position. Also, as described previously, France and Germany had numerous parochial, self-interested reasons for opposing US intervention in Iraq that did not relate to the merits of the action with regard to global and US security.

418 "Obama's Speech on Iraq, March 2008."

Nevertheless, in this way, the myth of the Iraq War as a unilateral action and the opposition to it—as crystallized in the 2008 Democratic presidential campaign—represented Democrats' elevating diplomacy, alliances, and multilateralism as a tool to deploy in any circumstances. Moreover, it provided cover for the unwillingness of the Democratic Party base and the Obama administration to support the use of force, a position that has become clearer in the Obama administration's dealings with Iran on the nuclear issue. Most troublingly, this plank of the 2008 Obama campaign ultimately had its roots in the self-interested opposition of France and Germany to the Iraq War. That is, the self-interested opposition of two foreign nations to the Iraq War in 2003 is the basis of a key component of the foreign policy of the Democratic Party to this day.

The Democrats reflected their commitment to multilateral solutions for Iraq in the 2008 Democratic platform, which called for "launching a comprehensive regional and international diplomatic surge to help broker a lasting political settlement in Iraq, which is the only path to a sustainable peace."[419] The Democrats' 2008 platform does not explain why a regional and international diplomatic surge was "the only path to a sustainable peace." From every appearance, the Democrats' reflexive support of multilateralism was a reaction to the supposed "unilateralism" of the Bush administration that morphed from a convenient antiwar movement talking point to a fundamental plank of the antiwar movement and Democratic foreign policy.

In fact, as described previously, many regional actors were directly responsible for the violence in Iraq. Iran provided support to Shia militias and other Iraqi insurgents. Iran was responsible for the increased lethality of IEDs targeting US troops and Iranian intelligence and Qods Force personnel were active in Iraq. Syria permitted foreign fighters to cross the Syria-Iraq border to enter Iraq to join the anti-US insurgency.[420] Turkey cast a wary eye toward the Kurds in northern Iraq, concerned about the possibility of their declaring

419 "2008 Democratic Party Platform," The American Presidency Project, University of California, Santa Barbara, August 25, 2008, http://www.presidency.ucsb.edu/ws/?pid=78283.

420 Alfred B. Prados and Jeremy M. Sharp, "Syria: Political Conditions and Relations with the United States after the Iraq War," Congressional Research Service, February 28, 2005, https://www.fas.org/sgp/crs/mideast/RL32727.pdf, at 15–16.

independence. The idea that an international conference including regional actors such as Iran, Syria, and Turkey would result in a pacified, friendly Iraq that could serve as a model for the Arab world was fanciful. Iran, Syria, and Turkey all had interests in Iraq, but their interests were diametrically opposed to those of the United States.

The Democrats' platform begged the question: why *would* an international diplomatic surge be "the only path to a sustainable peace"? What about a US diplomatic surge that followed and built upon the gains of the military surge? As a result of the surge, the United States, against all odds, had won the trust of the Sunni tribes and the Kurds and demonstrated that the United States wanted to defeat the insurgency. The United States enjoyed a dominant diplomatic position following the surge. Why not take advantage of the opportunity the success of the surge presented to broker a political settlement in Iraq, a settlement that reflected US and Iraqi interests but excluded regional troublemakers such as Iran, Syria, and Turkey? The Democrats never addressed this question; by 2008, multilateralism had become a sacrosanct shibboleth of the antiwar movement and the Democratic Party that required no defense and no explanation.

The 2008 Democratic platform regarding Iran also incorporated the supposed lessons on the importance of multilateralism in responding to the threat posed by the Iranian nuclear program. The 2008 Democratic platform stated that the effort to end the Iranian nuclear threat would start "with tougher sanctions and aggressive, principled, and direct high-level diplomacy, without preconditions."[421] The platform went on to state, "We will pursue this strengthened diplomacy alongside our European allies, and with no illusions about the Iranian regime…By going the extra diplomatic mile, while keeping all options on the table, we make it more likely the rest of the world will stand with us to increase pressure on Iran, if diplomacy is failing."[422] In 2004, the "global test" was a gaffe; by 2008, the Democrats proudly elevated it to policy by requiring that "the world stood with us" before the United States took military action against Iran.

421 "2008 Democratic Party Platform, August 25, 2008."

422 Ibid.

Once again, the Democrats' platform was long on shibboleths and supposed lessons from Iraq. What does it mean to engage in "aggressive" and "principled" diplomacy? The platform does not say. What does it mean to "go the extra diplomatic mile"? Again, the platform provides no explanation. How would one even decide at what point the United States has gone the "extra diplomatic mile" such that those other "options on the table" would need to be considered? Finally, how would the United States assure itself that "the rest of the world" would define "the extra diplomatic mile" in the same way as the United States, such that "the world would stand with us" if diplomacy was failing? Why wouldn't one or two countries opposed to military action against Iran—say, Russia and China or France and Germany again—argue that the United States hadn't yet gone the "extra diplomatic mile" and so they could not support military action against Iran? What then? By the Democrats' lights, the United States still would not be in a position to take military action against Iran even if the United States and many of its allies had determined military action was the only viable remaining option.

The nebulous phrases of the 2008 Democratic platform on Iran and their inherent ambiguity make plain the fact that the antiwar movement and the Democratic Party it captured took the wrong lessons from the Iraq War. As noted previously, many European countries backed the United States' invasion of Iraq. Two European countries—France and Germany—loudly and ostentatiously opposed the Iraq War. Why wouldn't there be diplomatic holdouts regarding military action against Iran in the same way France and Germany were holdouts on the Iraq War?

Finally, the Democrats' 2008 platform included this statement on the United States' with the world:

> To renew American leadership in the world, we will rebuild the alliances, partnerships, and institutions necessary to confront common threats and enhance common security. Needed reform of these alliances and institutions will not come by bullying other countries to ratify American demands. It will come when we convince other governments and peoples that they too have a stake in effective

> partnerships. It is only leadership if others join America in working toward our common security.
>
> Too often, in recent years, we have sent the opposite signal to our international partners. In the case of Europe, we dismissed European reservations about the wisdom and necessity of the Iraq war and their concerns about climate change. In Asia, we belittled South Korean efforts to improve relations with the North. In Latin America, from Mexico to Argentina, we failed to address concerns about immigration and equity and economic growth. In Africa, we have allowed genocide to persist for over five years in Darfur and have not done nearly enough to answer the United Nations' call for more support to stop the killing. Under Barack Obama, we will rebuild our ties to our allies in Europe and Asia and strengthen our partnerships throughout the Americas and Africa.[423]

This section of the Democrats' 2008 platform demonstrates, in a nutshell, just how completely the antiwar movement had captured the Democratic Party and defined the Democrats' view of the United States' use of force to achieve national security objectives. The United States had more European allies than opponents of the Iraq War. The Democrats effectively viewed France's and Germany's opposition to the war, along with the public demonstrations against the war (many of which, as described previously, were anti-American, anti-Western, or anticapitalist at heart), as a fundamental failing of US foreign policy.

Additionally, the language the Democratic platform used is instructive. The platform used words like *bullying*, *dismissed*, and *belittled*. These are soft words more appropriate for a therapy session or after-school special than for the world of foreign policy. They certainly do not convey the image of "aggressive" diplomacy. It is unlikely that Vladimir Putin, the Chinese Communists, Kim Jong Un, or Ayatollah Khamenei use words like *bullying* or *belittled* in determining their foreign policy strategies or that they are concerned about being perceived as bullies belittling or dismissing other nations. Bullying,

423 Ibid.

belittling, and dismissing nations are what they do. Standing up to the hard men of Russia, China, North Korea, and Iran and opposing US enemies and opponents requires a level of firmness and strength that worries about bullying and belittling do not convey. Nevertheless, the lesson the antiwar movement and Democrats took from Iraq was that having allies and world support was the sine qua non of a legitimate military action or foreign policy initiative.

Another flawed lesson the antiwar movement and the Democrats took from the Iraq War was that it was not a war fought in America's self-defense. The 2008 Democratic platform stated, "We believe we must also be willing to consider using military force in circumstances beyond self-defense in order to provide for the common security that underpins global stability—to support friends, participate in stability and reconstruction operations, or confront mass atrocities. *But when we do use force in situations other than self-defense, we should make every effort to garner the clear support and participation of others. The consequences of forgetting that lesson in the context of the current conflict in Iraq have been grave.*"[424]

The facts of the debate over the invasion of Iraq and the Iraq War belie this supposed "lesson of the current conflict in Iraq." As described in great detail previously, the Bush administration acted—in the aftermath of 9/11 and the 2001 anthrax attacks—on a sincere belief that the Iraqis had a WMD stockpile and an active weapons program. (Some members of the Iraqi military apparently held the same view, given the chemical suits and antidotes coalition troops found on the battlefield.) In stating that the United States acted in Iraq out of motives other than self-defense, the antiwar movement and the Democratic Party it had captured revealed they had a limited and crabbed view of what constitutes US self-defense. The previous Democratic administration of Bill Clinton believed the Iraqi weapons threat was significant enough to launch Operation Desert Fox in 1998—a time prior to 9/11 when the international community believed that the threat Iraq and its weapons program posed was little different than in 2002. Yet in 2008, the Democrats repudiated such preemptive strikes to degrade Iraq's weapons capacity. In effect, the Democrats redefined *self-defense* to mean "responding to and retaliating for an

424 "2008 Democratic Party Platform," August 25, 2008 (emphasis added).

attack." That way, as 9/11 demonstrated, the United States would ensure "the world stood with us," and it would have the "clear support and participation of others." The cost of obtaining this support, however, would be to absorb an attack on US interests and possibly the homeland again.

Moreover, as described previously, the United States indisputably obtained the support and participation of others: the United Kingdom, Spain, Australia, South Korea, Poland, and numerous other nations that committed troops after the major combat phase of the war ended. The United States just didn't win the support of France or Germany. To suggest the United States did not "make every effort to garner the clear support and participation of others" was not only false but a calumny against those nations whose troops did fight in Iraq.

A major error antiwar politicians made in assessing the war was to mistake tactical failures for strategic errors. In effect, the antiwar movement and antiwar politicians forgot one timeless maxim of war: that battle plans never survive contact with the enemy. Antiwar activists and politicians mistook the setbacks in the US occupation strategy as failures of foreign policy strategy. In hindsight, the US occupation strategy had numerous flaws. The decision to disband and reform the Iraqi Army along with the de-Baathification of the government led to many unemployed, disgruntled Iraqis who joined the insurgency. The United States also failed to anticipate Iraq becoming a magnet for foreign fighters, many of which were responsible for the most brutal attacks during the insurgency. In addition, the United States did not foresee the extent to which neighboring countries hostile to the United States, particularly Iran and Syria, would facilitate the efforts of foreign fighters, homegrown Iraqi extremists, and Iraqi insurgents to fight the US occupation. Finally, the United States did not develop an aggressive response to Iranian interference with US efforts to stabilize and reconstruct Iraq.

However, the antiwar movement and the elected officials who opposed the Iraq War see these errors not as tactical errors that could be and were rectified with new military strategy (e.g., the surge) but as an indictment of the entire Iraq enterprise. They have denied or downplayed the effectiveness of the surge and the American military's counterinsurgency capabilities. As a result, they are extremely susceptible to the argument that any future prolonged military action will result in the same type of insurgency and intractable, unending conflict they perceive Iraq—and Vietnam before it—to have been.

The consequence of this error is the reflexive, unthinking rhetoric when the United States is faced with new threats that it cannot go to war again, cannot rush to war, and cannot have "another Iraq" just as a generation before Americans said they could not have "another Vietnam." One writer has stated that the most powerful lesson from history Obama has learned is "No more Iraqs."[425] When faced with threats such as the Iranian nuclear program and Russian aggression in Ukraine, the North Sea, and elsewhere, the knee-jerk response is, "We can't have another Iraq." The result is inaction in the face of threats.

The antiwar movement's and Democrats' lesson that the Iraq War was not sufficiently multilateral and that only an international diplomacy "surge" could lead to a permanent solution in Iraq led them to another fateful conclusion: that the United States should not maintain a permanent troop presence in Iraq. It is a lesson that haunts the United States to this day.

Stationing troops in Iraq beyond the end of the Bush administration became a major campaign issue in January 2008, when the Bush administration was negotiating a Status of Forces Agreement (SOFA) with the Iraqi government. The Democrats, including 2008 presidential candidates Hillary Clinton, Joe Biden, and Barack Obama, vocally opposed the SOFA. Clinton said that the SOFA was President Bush's attempt "to try to bind the United States government and his successor to his failed policy."[426] Echoing Vietnam-style worries, Biden stated that the SOFA "would mire us in an Iraqi civil war indefinitely."[427] Approximately 250,000 antiwar activists signed a MoveOn.

425 Dominic Tierney, "The Obama Doctrine and the Lessons of Iraq," Foreign Policy Research Institute, May 2012, http://www.fpri.org/enotes/05/201205.tierney.obama-doctrine-iraq.html.

426 Michael Abramowitz, "Democrats Attack Iraq Security Proposal," *Washington Post*, January 24, 2008, http://www.washingtonpost.com/wp-dyn/content/article/2008/01/23/AR2008012303473.html.

427 Ibid.

org petition opposing the SOFA.[428] Having pacified Iraq from a security standpoint, the antiwar movement and antiwar Democrats were unwilling to maintain troops to consolidate the successes.

The third major lesson that the antiwar movement and antiwar politicians took from Iraq was the need to react to threats rather than identify and deal with them before they became overwhelming and impossible to deal with effectively. The attacks on the Bush administration's decision to invade Iraq even though many perceived it not to pose an "imminent" threat elevated the need for an "imminent threat" to be present before the United States would be willing to take military action. The 2008 Obama campaign, much like the 2004 Kerry campaign before it, viewed Afghanistan as the "good war" and the United States as having "taken its eye off the ball" in Afghanistan to fight in Iraq. Afghanistan had been the training, planning, and launching ground for the 9/11 attacks; the threat was beyond imminent, as the attacks had already occurred. By making Iraq into the "bad war," one begun without a sufficient casus belli, the antiwar movement made an "imminent threat" the test of the legitimacy of US military action.

The Iran Nuclear Deal

Having won reelection in 2012, Obama and the Democrats continued to seek opportunities to define their foreign policy in opposition to the supposed "cowboy" unilateralism of the Bush administration. The longstanding challenge posed by the Iranian nuclear program provided the clearest opportunity to show how their policy of diplomacy, first, last, and always was smarter and better than that of the supposedly bellicose Bush administration.

Obama and his secretary of state, John Kerry, along with France, the United Kingdom, Russia, and China, reached a widely criticized deal with Iran to rein in its nuclear program in July 2015. Critics of the deal argued that it failed to end the Iranian nuclear program, failed to require Iran to come clean about its past weapons-related work, and failed to create an inspections regime sufficiently robust to determine if Iran was cheating on the

428 Ibid.

deal. Moreover, critics charged that a time-limited deal would leave Iran as a threshold nuclear state when the deal expired.

The Obama administration's response to those who criticized the deal demonstrates just how important the supposed lessons of Iraq were in formulating the deal. Obama himself claimed that the only alternative to his deal was war with Iran and therefore that those opposing the deal supported war with Iran.

The speech Obama gave at American University on August 5, 2015, in defense of the deal shows just how devoted Obama and the antiwar Democrats were to reversing the supposed foreign policy that led the United States into the Iraq War. He stated,

> Now, when I ran for President eight years ago as a candidate who had opposed the decision to go to war in Iraq, I said that America didn't just have to end that war—we had to end the mindset that got us there in the first place. It was a mindset characterized by a preference for military action over diplomacy; a mindset that put a premium on unilateral US action over the painstaking work of building international consensus; a mindset that exaggerated threats beyond what the intelligence supported. Leaders did not level with the American people about the costs of war, insisting that we could easily impose our will on a part of the world with a profoundly different culture and history. And, of course, those calling for war labeled themselves strong and decisive, while dismissing those who disagreed as weak—even appeasers of a malevolent adversary.[429]

As with so much of the Obama administration's foreign policy, the American University speech is more evidence that the Democratic Party, now implementing the antiwar movement's preferred foreign policy, was fixated on proving that diplomacy can work under any circumstances and that Obama was not George W. Bush. Invoking the supposed "rush to war" in Iraq, Obama

429 "Remarks by the President on the Iran Nuclear Deal," White House, August 5, 2015, https://www.whitehouse.gov/the-press-office/2015/08/05/remarks-president-iran-nuclear-deal.

said the following: "In the end, that should be a lesson that we've learned from over a decade of war. On the front end, ask tough questions. Subject our own assumptions to evidence and analysis. Resist the conventional wisdom and the drumbeat of war. Worry less about being labeled weak; worry more about getting it right."

By inking a deal with Iran, Obama clearly viewed himself as demonstrating his and his party's preference for diplomacy over military action, the need to achieve international consensus to ratify US foreign policy decisions, and the need for the United States to be humble in its foreign policy dealings. The Iran deal was the vehicle by which Obama could expurgate all of the Bush foreign policy sins and mistakes associated with the Iraq War. Having elevated Iraq to a major, Vietnam-level mistake, Obama used the Iran deal to redefine US foreign policy and cited the failures of Iraq in doing so. Obama sought to prove that diplomacy could solve the Iranian nuclear issue and to make explicit how his approach differed from the purportedly failed "unilateral" Bush approach. The Iran deal was the apotheosis of Obama's foreign policy; one Obama policy adviser said it was "the biggest thing Obama will do in his second term on foreign policy" and compared it to health care reform in its importance to Obama.[430] The Obama administration viewed the Iran deal as its crowning foreign policy achievement, and given the statements made in defense of the deal, at some level it was intended to be an unmistakable, categorical rebuke to the Bush foreign policy. The Iran deal was to be everything the Iraq War was not.

In fact, observers expressly concluded that the Iran deal was Obama's direct repudiation of the Bush administration's war in Iraq and war on terror after 9/11. Julian Zelizer, a Princeton University professor of history and public affairs, wrote that the Iran deal represented "a repudiation of the Bush doctrine."[431] According to Zelizer, the Iran nuclear deal combines three elements that demonstrate this repudiation: (1) "Internationalism rather than

430 Justin Sink, "White House Official: Iran Nuclear Deal Top Priority," *The Hill*, October 31, 2014, http://thehill.com/blogs/blog-briefing-room/222417-white-house-official-iran-deal-top-priority.

431 Julian Zelizer, "The Iran Deal, a Repudiation of the Bush Doctrine," CNN, September 2, 2015, http://www.cnn.com/2015/08/31/opinions/zelizer-iran-deal-stakes/.

unilateralism is the basis of this deal"; (2) "More information is better than less information" (a reference to the incorrect intelligence regarding Iraq's WMD programs); and (3) "This deal repudiates the mechanism of regime change that the Iraq war embraced."[432] Others have noted that Obama's arguments in favor of the Iraq deal effectively represent a relitigation of the Iraq War debate, as he regularly claims that the same people who opposed the Iran nuclear deal today supported the Iraq War in 2002.[433]

The Iran deal represented the beliefs of the antiwar movement in Iraq, and Vietnam before it, implemented as policy. It elevated form—diplomacy and multilateralism—over the substance of the agreement and whether the agreement upheld Obama's promise in the final 2012 presidential debate with Governor Mitt Romney that "the deal we'll accept is they end their nuclear program. It's very straightforward."[434] The deal effectively swore off any US military action; indeed, the administration had, in practice, foresworn any military action against Iran well before reaching the final deal (despite the repeated statements from the Obama administration that the military option remained on the table). Whether the Iran deal is a success will be borne out in time, but a strong impetus behind the deal was to demonstrate, once again, that the Bush administration had resorted to war in Iraq under false pretenses and without sufficient international support and that diplomacy and multilateralism—*smart power*—were the proper means to deploy US influence in foreign affairs. In short, the Iran nuclear deal is one final rebuke of the Iraq War.

Journalists, commentators, and scholars have spilled much ink attempting to explain the motivating ideas and doctrines behind the Obama administration's foreign policy. They point to Obama's academic experiences,

---

432 Ibid.

433 Rebecca Kaplan, "Obama Links Support for Iraq War to Those Who Oppose Iran Deal," CBS News, August 5, 2015, http://www.cbsnews.com/news/obama-defends-iran-deal-american-university/; Kevin Liptak and Hilary Krieger, "Obama's Nuclear Deal Rhetoric Troubles American Jews," CNN, August 10, 2015, http://www.cnn.com/2015/08/10/politics/jewish-concern-obama-rhetoric-iran-nuclear-deal/.

434 Transcript of final 2012 presidential debate, pt. 2, CBS News, October 23, 2012, http://www.cbsnews.com/news/transcript-of-final-2012-presidential-debate-part-2/.

particularly at Occidental and Columbia. They note his relationship with Bill Ayres and Bernardine Dohrn of the Weather Underground. They even look to his Kenyan roots and family members in Kenya that opposed British colonialism in that country.

There may be grains of truth in these, but, in the spirit of Occam's razor, the answer may be simpler. It may be that the Democratic Party simply adopted the antiwar movement's ideal foreign policy—unbending faith in the power of diplomacy, the need to consult closely with allies, and the need to engage enemies diplomatically and directly—lock, stock, and barrel. Obama, as an opponent of the Iraq War untainted by any earlier vote in favor of the war, was the perfect candidate to bring the antiwar movement's foreign policy platform to fruition. In effect, Obama's foreign policy may be a case of dancing with the girl that brung him—he distinguished himself in 2008 as the consistent antiwar candidate who had never cast a vote in favor of the war, he adopted the antiwar movement's foreign policy platform, and he won the Democratic Party's support. He won the nomination and election as an opponent of the Iraq War against other candidates that had previously supported the Iraq War and a supporter of negotiations with enemies without preconditions. He promised he would work multilaterally, in concert with the world community, and place extraordinary emphasis on diplomacy. And, most importantly, he promised he would end the Iraq War. Obama's foreign policy has faithfully applied the statements in the 2004 and 2008 Democratic Party platform, which were highly influenced by the antiwar movement. In short, the Obama administration did exactly what it and the antiwar movement that captured the Democratic Party said they would do.

The Iraq Syndrome Today

Today, the United States appears to be suffering from an emerging Iraq syndrome, just as the United States suffered from a Vietnam syndrome for years after the Vietnam conflict ended. The Iraq syndrome involves a reflexive, publicly expressed unwillingness to commit ground troops to battle in the same numbers as were deployed in Iraq. Instead, it calls for a heavy reliance on air power and drone strikes. It relies upon highly trained special operators to conduct raids and one-off missions against high-value targets. It also seeks to internationalize combat, seeking ground forces from local countries, which the United States is prepared to train and possibly advise in combat. As occurred in the aftermath of Vietnam, the Iraq syndrome circumscribes the deployment of American ground troops under any circumstances.

The Iraq syndrome cuts across all political parties and is not confined to just Democrats or Republicans. Ron Paul's surprising success in the 2008 Republican primaries and the libertarian moment within the Republican Party that ensued reflected the Republican Party's partial retreat from a muscular, forward-leaning foreign policy that included the doctrine of preemption to a more isolationist foreign policy. Paul argued that it was American intervention abroad that led terrorists to target the United States, and he contended that Iraq was a terrible mistake. The durability of the libertarian moment of Ron Paul and his son, Rand, elected to the Senate in 2010, demonstrated the strength of the isolationist streak within a segment of the Republican Party.

Some of the 2016 presidential candidates in both parties have also embraced foreign policies that suggest they have absorbed and continue to suffer from an Iraq syndrome. Both Democratic and Republican candidates have categorically rejected the use of American ground troops (other than small numbers of special operators) in any action against ISIS.

On the Republican side, Sen. Ted Cruz has stated he supports arming the Kurds and making them the United States' boots on the ground.[435] Cruz said that "we need boots on the ground, but they don't necessarily need to be American boots. The Kurds are our boots on the ground."[436] He called for the United States to initiate carpet bombing of ISIS territory to defeat the terrorist caliphate and that the United States would support the Kurdish boots on the ground with overwhelming air power.

---

435 Nia-Malika Henderson, "How Republican Candidates Would Respond to ISIS," CNN.com, November 16, 2015, http://www.cnn.com/2015/11/16/politics/republican-isis-2016-election/.

436 Philip Elliott, "How Republican Candidates Want to Fight ISIS," Time Magazine, November 14, 2015, http://time.com/4113042/paris-attacks-islamic-state-republican-positions/.

Marco Rubio, one of the more hawkish Republicans in the race, stated that he would use American special operation forces whose size "would depend on our military tacticians to outline a strategy and tell us what the commitment would be. Whatever it is, we're going to do that. If you're going to engage militarily, you have to ensure you have the resources to win, not simply to have a symbolic gesture."[437] However, even Rubio made clear that he would avoid another Iraq War. He called for a primarily Sunni Arab ground force to fight ISIS supported by embedded US special operators. But he emphasized that "this is not a return to Iraq. We are not talking about 100,000 or 50,000 armed soldiers, but we are talking about [a] force with specific missions that will be embedded that this president and the United States must put together if we are to defeat ISIS on the ground. It's the only way to do it. They have to be defeated by a ground force and have to be made up primarily of Sunnis."[438]

It was of all people Dr. Ben Carson, a candidate widely criticized for having an insufficient understanding of foreign affairs, who hinted at a diagnosis of the emerging Iraq syndrome in the December 2016 Republican debate when he said, "We've got a phobia about boots on the ground. If our military experts say, we need boots on the ground, we should put boots on the ground and recognize that there will be boots on the ground and they'll be over here [in the United States], and they'll be their [the enemy's] boots if we don't get out of there now."[439]

Likewise, Democratic candidate Hillary Clinton stated that tens of thousands of American troops on the ground was not the right tool for the United States to use to influence the situation in Syria or to defeat ISIS. Like a number of the Republican candidates, she called for the United States to "support

---

437 Sabrina Siddiqi, "Marco Rubio Vows US Troops Will Inflict 'Humiliating Defeats' on ISIS," The *Guardian*, November 22, 2015, http://www.theguardian.com/us-news/2015/nov/22/marco-rubio-isis-strategy-us-troops-exclusive-interview.

438 Curt Mills, "Arab Troops Needed to Beat ISIS," *Washington Examiner*, November 22, 2015, http://www.washingtonexaminer.com/rubio-arab-troops-needed-to-beat-isis/article/2576926.

439 Michael Gormley, "Republican Presidential Candidates Debate in Las Vegas," Newsday, December 15, 2015, http://www.newsday.com/news/nation/republican-presidential-candidates-debate-in-las-vegas-1.11233329; Stephanie Condon, "Obama defends counterterrorism strategy to columnists," CBS News, December 17, 2015, http://www.cbsnews.com/news/obama-defends-counter-terrorism-strategy-to-columnists/.

those who take the fight to ISIS." However, she stated that "this cannot be an American fight, although American leadership is essential."[440] She expressed a willingness to increase the number of special operations troops in Iraq and Syria supporting groups fighting ISIS.[441] However, she stated unequivocally that she would not support another American ground war in the Middle East. She stated, "Like President Obama, I do not believe that we should again have 100,000 American troops in combat in the Middle East. That is just not the smart move to make here. If we've learned anything from 15 years of war in Iraq and Afghanistan, it's that local people and nations have to secure their own communities. We can help them, and we should, but we cannot substitute for them. But we can and should support local and regional ground forces in carrying out this mission."[442] In a December 2015 speech at the University of Minnesota laying out her counterterrorism policy, Clinton stated,

> It will require skillful diplomacy to continue Secretary Kerry's efforts to encourage political reconciliation in Iraq and political transition in Syria, enabling more Sunni Arabs and Kurdish fighters to take on ISIS on both sides of the border, and to get our Arab and Turkish partners to actually step up and do their part. It will require more U.S. and allied airpower, and a broader target set for strikes by planes and drones, with proper safeguards. It will require Special Operations units to advise and train local forces and conduct key counterterrorism missions. What it will not require is tens of thousands of American combat troops. That is not the right action for us to take in this situation.[443]

---

440 Eric Bradner and Dan Merica, "Hillary Clinton Calls for U.S. to 'Intensify and Broaden' Efforts to Fight ISIS," CNN, November 19, 2015, http://www.cnn.com/2015/11/19/politics/hillary-clinton-isis-speech/.

441 Ibid.

442 Transcript of "Hillary Clinton on National Security and the Islamic State," Council on Foreign Relations, November 19, 2015, http://www.cfr.org/radicalization-and-extremism/hillary-clinton-national-security-islamic-state/p37266.

443 Transcript of "Hillary Clinton Lays Out Comprehensive Plan to Bolster National Security," December 15, 2015, https://www.hillaryclinton.com/briefing/statements/2015/12/15/comprehensive-plan-to-bolster-homeland-security/.

Not to be outdone, Sen. Bernie Sanders has cited the Iraq War decision as a reason to support his candidacy for the 2016 Democratic presidential nomination over Hillary Clinton. Remarkably, over a decade after the Iraq War authorization vote, a Democratic presidential candidate is distinguishing himself from his opponent based on his opposition to the Iraq War. Sen. Sanders has stated that the decision to go to war in Iraq was "the crucial foreign policy issue of our time" and that "Secretary Clinton – with all of her experience – was wrong and I was right."[444] And Sanders expressly stated that opposition to the Iraq War was a hallmark of being a true progressive, stating, "the key foreign policy vote of modern American history was the war in Iraq. The progressive community was pretty united in saying, 'Don't listen to Bush. Don't go to war.' Secretary Clinton voted to go to war."[445] Sanders's statement is effectively an acknowledgement that opposition to the Iraq War was part of the progressive movement and not an independent foreign policy question. Like so many other progressive causes, it got caught up in the culture of protest that began in the sixties with Vietnam and, as chronicled herein, continues to this day.

The 2016 campaign makes plain the fact that the Iraq War, like the Vietnam War before it, has deeply influenced current policy makers from both parties who are devising policies to respond to the threats from ISIS, other terror groups, and Iran. Nearly every candidate, Democrat or Republican, has sought to distance himself or herself from the Iraq War and to state that they will not take any foreign policy actions reminiscent of the Iraq War. In this way, the antiwar movement's long efforts to erode the credibility of those who supported the Iraq War and the ability of the United States to fight the Iraq War succeeded. Most of the 2016 Republican candidates for president and all of the Democratic candidates have made clear that there will be no more Iraqs. Nearly every major candidate calling for some Untied States intervention against ISIS has stated that the "boots on the ground" must be a non-American force, be they the Kurds, a Sunni army (possibly led

444 Adam Gabbatt and Lauren Gambino, "Sanders Upends Foreign-Policy Critique by Clinton Experts: 'I Was Right" on Iraq," The Guardian, January 19, 2016, http://www.theguardian.com/us-news/2016/jan/19/bernie-sanders-foreign-policy-experts-hillary-clinton.

445 M.J. Lee, "Clinton, Sanders Clash Over What it Means to be a Progressive," CNN, February 4, 2016, http://www.cnn.com/2016/02/03/politics/democratic-town-hall-highlights/.

by regional Sunni powers such as Saudi Arabia and Egypt), or some other local force. Thus, the antiwar movement's efforts to discredit the Iraq War have had a lasting effect on American foreign policy, just as the Vietnam antiwar movement's efforts left a generation of Americans deeply ambivalent about projecting American military power abroad.

President Obama's final State of the Union address demonstrated that the antiwar movement has indelibly linked the Vietnam and Iraq Wars. In his address, President Obama stated,

> We also can't try to take over and rebuild every country that falls into crisis, even if it's done with the best of intentions. That's not leadership; that's a recipe for quagmire, spilling American blood and treasure that ultimately will weaken us. *It's the lesson of Vietnam; it's the lesson of Iraq—and we should have learned it by now.*
>
> Fortunately, there is a smarter approach, a patient and disciplined strategy that uses every element of our national power. It says America will always act, alone if necessary, to protect our people and our allies; but on issues of global concern, we will mobilize the world to work with us, and make sure other countries pull their own weight.
>
> That's our approach to conflicts like Syria, where we're partnering with local forces and leading international efforts to help that broken society pursue a lasting peace.
>
> That's why we built a global coalition, with sanctions and principled diplomacy, to prevent a nuclear-armed Iran.[446]

President Obama, an opponent of the Iraq War from its beginning, thereby neatly encapsulated the antiwar movement's view that Vietnam and Iraq are indelibly linked as "quagmires." President Obama expressed the antiwar movement's conclusion that the lesson of Vietnam and the lesson of Iraq are one and the same; namely, that any foreign intervention will inevitably immerse the

446 "Remarks of President Obama—State of the Union Address as Delivered," The White House, https://www.whitehouse.gov/the-press-office/2016/01/12/remarks-president-barack-obama-%E2%80%93-prepared-delivery-state-union-address#annotations:8513516 (emphasis added).

United States into local battles and civil wars that the United States cannot win and that will only drain American resources and cost American lives. In his address, Obama also paid a final tribute to the importance of diplomacy and the need for international support for American foreign intervention. He effectively reiterated the principle that only after building a global coalition is American military intervention legitimate. Obama thus once again implicitly criticized the Bush administration's supposed unilateral "rush to war." Finally, Obama and the antiwar movement expect that other countries will be willing and able to "pull their weight," neglecting the possibility that other countries simply do not have much to contribute militarily. The antiwar movement does not provide a strategy for responding to crises in those cases in which the United States believes intervention is necessary but allies are unwilling or unable to pull their weight.

Current circumstances may be such that a large American ground force would not be the right method for confronting ISIS or removing Assad from power in Syria. It may well be that the strategy of embedding American special operators with local ground forces coupled with American air power, advocated by numerous candidates and experts in both parties, will be the most effective strategy for combating ISIS and reversing the Syrian government's murderous rampage against its own citizens in the Syrian civil war. (The United States followed a similar strategy in Afghanistan, embedding small numbers of ground troops with the Northern Alliance and quickly routing the Taliban.) However, what is important from the standpoint of the thesis of this book is that the 2016 presidential candidates of both parties are taking pains to assure Americans that they will not get the United States into another Iraq, just as a generation earlier politicians sought to avoid another Vietnam. Candidates opposing the use of ground troops against ISIS are making an affirmative effort to tell the American public that he or she will not get the United States into another Iraq War well before they have assessed all of the available options for action against ISIS. That is, whatever the candidate would do as president to battle ISIS or other foreign crises, it will not be an Iraq-style war. In this way, both Republican and Democratic candidates are ruling out the types of action the United States is willing to take before the

United States has engaged in the fight. They are not leaving open the possibility of significant numbers of American ground troops. They are telling everyone—American voters, American allies, and American foes—that they simply will not repeat the Iraq War. Policy is being determined as much by what the United States will not do as what it is willing to do. By stating limitations on American involvement up front and eliminating any ambiguity about the limits of what the United States is willing to do to defeat ISIS, the United States signals to both friend and foe alike the level of American commitment to the fight.

The emerging Iraq syndrome risks another several years of American insularity from the world. In the wake of Vietnam and the United States' retrenchment in the 1970s, the Soviet Union invaded Afghanistan and made inroads in Central America and Africa. Cuba sent troops to Angola. The Iranian Revolution deposed the Shah and led to the Iran hostage crisis, beginning almost forty years of unrestrained hostility toward the United States. The period of the late 1970s saw the unleashing of dangerous anti-American forces, the effects of which the United States feels to this day. The onset of an Iraq syndrome and an accompanying American retrenchment risks repeating this difficult period in American and world history with consequences extending far into the future.

CHAPTER 11

Consequences: The Enduring Aftermath of the Antiwar Movement, the Emerging Iraq Syndrome, and Recommendations for the Future

THE ANTIWAR PROTESTS OF THE Bush presidency have had a deep, lasting, and almost wholly negative effect on US foreign policy and national security. These consequences have not been limited to the United States. Rather, one can argue strongly that the most negative consequences of the antiwar protests of the Bush presidency were felt first and most acutely by countries other than the United States. Nevertheless, the consequences are deep and abiding and even today have not been realized fully.

The first and perhaps worst long-term consequence of the antiwar protests was the practical neutering of the United States' ability to use military force against the Iranian nuclear program during the second term of the Bush administration. Antiwar activists successfully convinced much of the country that the US government "lied" the United States into war over the issue of Iraq's WMD, despite the Democrats' hawkish prewar positions on Saddam's WMD programs. The "Bush lied, people died" ethos had sunk too deeply into the American public's psyche for the United States credibly to threaten military action against the Iranian nuclear program.

Ironically, one writer, *Haaretz* columnist Ari Shavit, charged that the Bush administration should have pressured Iran, not Iraq, over WMD in the aftermath of 9/11.[447] Shavit went so far as to say that Bush "let Iran go nuclear" and because "he failed to target Iran a decade ago, and created a climate that made it very difficult to target Iran" today.[448] That is, Bush should have targeted Iran and not Iraq over WMD concerns, and having targeted Iraq wrongly, the United States could no longer target Iran. It may well be true that the Bush administration should have targeted Iran rather than Iraq after 9/11, though Bush did include Iran in the (frequently mocked) "axis of evil." However, to say that Bush "created a climate" in which the United States was unwilling to pressure Iran to terminate its nuclear program ignores the overwhelming pacifist forces the antiwar movement brought to bear on the US government prior to and during the Iraq War.

Moreover, there is no reason to believe targeting Iran in 2003 would have played out any differently than targeting Iraq did. Iran undoubtedly would have denied that it was seeking WMD, just as Iraq did. The United States might have pushed for tougher sanctions and a tougher inspection regime. The United States and Iran likely would have disputed the extent to which Iran cooperated with any inspection regime, just as occurred at the United Nations in the months preceding the Iraq War and throughout much of the 1990s with Iraq. The United States would then face the same choice as it did with Iraq—accept the incomplete inspection of possible WMD sites or threaten military action against Iran. There is no reason to believe the world community and United Nations would have reacted any differently to a proposed US military action against Iran in 2003 than it did to the Iraq War.

Post-9/11, Bush faced a Hobson's choice with Iraq and Iran—both were believed to have WMD programs. However, it was only in 2002 that the West publicly became aware of the existence of Iran's Natanz uranium enrichment plant and Arak heavy water reactor, through revelations made to the United Nations by the Mojāhedīn-e Khalq (MEK) Iranian dissident group.[449] As de-

447 Ari Shavit, "How Bush Let Iran Go Nuclear," *New York Times*, November 20, 2013, http://www.nytimes.com/2013/11/21/opinion/how-bush-let-iran-go-nuclear.html?_r=0.

448 Ibid.

449 Shreeya Sinha and Susan Campbell Beachy, "Timeline on Iran's Nuclear Program," *New York Times*, last updated April 2, 2015, http://www.nytimes.com/interactive/2014/11/20/world/middleeast/Iran-nuclear-timeline.html#/#time243_7210.

scribed previously, the Iraqi WMD programs had been the focus of concerted world attention and, at times, military action throughout the 1990s. Under the circumstances, that Bush chose to pressure Iraq instead of Iran is not surprising.

The relentless attacks on the Bush administration's credibility badly obscured some significant and beneficial corollary results of the Iraq War. First, the Libyan government, long a pariah state, voluntarily terminated its WMD program and relinquished the program's materials.[450] The United States' demonstration of a willingness to use force to terminate rogue regimes' WMD programs led the Libyan regime of Muammar Gaddafi to rethink the value of having a WMD program. Hans Blix, the UN weapons inspector, stated that he could "only speculate but [he] would imagine that Gadhafi could have been scared by what he saw happen in Iraq."[451] US intelligence analysts also thought that Iran suspended work on WMD-related technologies, possibly as a result of the US invasion of Iraq.[452]

The consequences continue right through to the present day. In the early stages of the 2016 presidential campaign, the media asked 2016 presidential candidates almost from the get-go whether they believed the Iraq War was a mistake. Many Republican candidates asked this question today disowned the Iraq War, saying if they knew in 2003 what they know today, they would not have supported the war. It may be that Republican presidential candidates took this position because they believed to do otherwise would be fatal to their presidential hopes. Early in the 2016 Republican primary race, Jeb Bush suffered significant damage for saying that knowing what we know now, he would still have voted for the invasion of Iraq.[453] The candidates also may have been grappling with the inherent ambiguity in the question; namely, whether

---

450 "Bush, Blair: Libya to Dismantle WMD Programs," CNN, December 20, 2003, http://www.cnn.com/2003/WORLD/africa/12/19/bush.libya/.

451 "Blix: Iraq War May Have Triggered Gadhafi Deal," CNN, December 20, 2003, http://www.cnn.com/2003/WORLD/africa/12/20/libya.blix/index.html.

452 Sinha and Beachy, "Timeline on Iran's Nuclear Program."

453 Jose A. DelReal, "Jeb Bush on Iraq War Comment Controversy: 'I Interpreted the Question Wrong, I Guess,'" *Washington Post,* May 12, 2015, https://www.washingtonpost.com/news/post-politics/wp/2015/05/12/jeb-bush-on-iraq-war-comment-controversy-i-interpreted-the-question-wrong-i-guess/.

"if they knew in 2003 what they know today" includes their knowing definitively in 2003 that Iraq did not possess WMD or the means for producing them. Jeb Bush actually identified this ambiguity when he first answered the question when he said, "In retrospect, the intelligence that everybody saw, that the world saw, not just the United States, was faulty."[454] He later clarified his initial comments about supporting the war in the face of a firestorm of criticism, noting that the United States had made intelligence mistakes and mistakes in governing Iraq during the occupation. Nevertheless, his campaign arguably never recovered from this debate.

But the media is asking the wrong question and, indeed, is asking an unimportant question from the perspective of choosing a president. Indeed, it is unlikely the Bush administration would have invaded Iraq had it *known definitively* in 2003 that Iraq did not have WMD or the means for producing WMD. The highly relevant and important question the media should ask candidates is this: if you were faced with the same set of circumstances as President Bush was in 2003—the 9/11 and anthrax attacks still fresh in the country's mind; videos of al-Qaeda leadership vowing to again strike the US homeland; terror bombings in other countries, such as the 2002 bombings in Bali; the consensus of all Western intelligence agencies that Iraq maintained nuclear, biological, and chemical weapons programs; Saddam Hussein's demonstrated noncooperation with United Nations inspections; Saddam's providing financial rewards to the families of Palestinian suicide bombers; and the potential consequences of a nuclear, biological, or chemical attack on the US homeland—what would you do?

Recommendations for the Future

As much as Americans would like for the world to just leave them alone, it is impossible to keep the world's forces of disorder at bay in perpetuity. The United States fought two world wars in the twentieth century, a time in which nations were far less interconnected economically, culturally, and socially. The global economy of the twenty-first century features nations that depend upon

454 Ibid.

one another for natural resources, food, and finished goods; routine travel between nations that is relatively inexpensive; and communication and entertainment shared globally through the magic of the Internet. The twenty-first century also includes rogue states like North Korea and Iran developing ICBMs and nonstate terrorist organizations able to infiltrate national borders. The oceans are no longer a buffer against outside influences, good or bad. Shutting the world out is simply not an option for the United States.

The world, however, is not always going to cooperate and provide a peaceful stage on which to conduct business affairs and share cultural productions. To preserve the benefits of the interconnected world, the United States must be prepared to defend these benefits. Future American leaders must be prepared to use force to protect American interests. The final portion of this book is devoted to proposals and recommendations for future American leaders who will face the difficult decision of whether to use force to defend American interests.

The overarching theme of this book is that the antiwar movement and its various strands—the anticapitalist organizations such as ANSWER and United for Peace and Justice; the veterans of the 1960s anti–Vietnam War protest movement; the current generation of antiwar young people, singers, actors, artists, and others looking for their own 1960s-style protest movement; and antiwar politicians belatedly opposing wars after the United States has committed to the fighting—are ever present in American society. The protests that accompanied the Iraq War—the largest, longest, and most comprehensive hot war since Vietnam—are likely to reappear whenever the United States determines it must go to war. The antiwar playbook will likely include plays similar to those run by the antiwar movement during Vietnam and Iraq: systematically undermine the credibility of policy makers; emphasize setbacks and planning failures; and stir enough of a storm so that when the inevitable setbacks do occur, the American public's confidence in the war will erode. Policy makers must account for this fact whenever considering whether to go to war or otherwise deploy force.

The several points below form the basis of a strategic response by policy makers who have determined that American national security interests require that the United States take military action against an enemy. Policy makers should embed each of these points in their presentations preparing the American public for military action and for sustaining the public's support during the military action, especially when unanticipated setbacks arise and the United States must adapt to changed circumstances on the ground.

1. *Accept that a level of poorly founded and bad-faith criticism will accompany any real threat to use force.*

   Almost immediately upon the United States expressing its intention to increase pressure on Iraq to come clean regarding its WMD programs, antiwar opposition reared its head. As described previously, a not-insignificant proportion of this opposition was rooted in factors other than an analysis of the merits of imposing pressure, backed with force, on Iraq. As noted previously, these factors included anticapitalist organizations seizing an opportunity to oppose the United States; Vietnam antiwar movement nostalgia and Vietnam envy; opposition to George W. Bush; and foreign politicians using anti-Americanism to boost their domestic standing.

   American leaders simply need to accept the fact that no matter how strenuously the United States attempts to avoid military action and makes military action a true last resort, any threat of the use of force will be criticized by a segment of the US and world population. Much of this undeserved criticism tells as much, if not more, about the sources of the criticism as its targets. As this book has shown, much of this criticism is reflexive, opportunistic, or made in bad faith. It is essential that policy makers carefully evaluate opposition to a proposed use of force and identify self-aggrandizing antiwar elements before giving them credence in developing policy.

   Policy makers should also look carefully at the protesters' actions in response to other world events. Many of the protest groups—ANSWER, United for Peace and Justice—that bewailed American actions in Iraq have uttered nary a peep at Russia's invasions of Georgia or Ukraine. They are silent regarding Chinese human rights.

They do not protest the gulags of North Korea. They do not vocally fight the human slavery that still exists in countries in North Africa. They would not know Cuba's Ladies in White from Chris de Burgh's Lady in Red.

Moreover, as shown throughout this book, protest is trendy. A military conflict gives those inclined to protest and searching for a cause the best cause possible for recreating the protests of the 1960s—the same cause that roiled American campuses, cities, and culture a half century ago. Policy makers must carefully evaluate protests to determine whether the protests are more about the events supposedly underlying the protest or the protesters themselves. It is one thing for protesters seeking notoriety or desiring to recreate the 1960s protest movement to force out university presidents and professors. It is another thing entirely to allow such protesters to alter American foreign policy and America's assertion of its fundamental national security interests. American foreign policy and national security decisions should not be dictated by those protesting for their own reasons—to enhance their personal visibility and celebrity, to recreate for themselves the protest experience of the 1960s, to give voice to innate anticapitalist, anti-Western tendencies, or to simply relive old glories.

Rather than react to this opposition or attempt to placate it—for example, by seeking diplomatic solutions or the blessing of military actions in the United Nations—American leaders should make decisions based on what they determine to be US national interests. Moreover, American policy makers should go on the offensive and publicly recognize what many already understand: that many antiwar protesters and groups selectively criticize the United States while giving a pass to worse regimes regularly committing the worst types of crimes.

This is not to say that American leaders should discount public opinion wholly. However, American leaders need to be prepared to see through unfair criticism made reflexively or in bad faith and make decisions based upon the evidence before them. They need to recognize that the antiwar activists have a strategy too and counter it.

Tom Hayden, the veteran activist and ardent opponent of the Iraq War, wrote a piece in the *Nation* in November 2011 describing the lessons he took from the anti–Iraq War movement. He noted that the most effective demands of the anti–Iraq War movement rested on three "pragmatic" factors:

- the moral dimension, especially the opposition of the clergy to America's descent into secret and tax-subsidized torture, which also tarnished the government's global reputation;
- the casualties suffered in a stalemated, seemingly endless war, which allowed growing outreach to military families; and
- the budgetary costs, which amounted to trillions for decades to come. An overall demand for the truth emerged as well, as Americans realized that the administration was lying about its intentions, the casualty numbers, and the true taxpayer reckoning.[455]

Hayden's analysis reflects many of the observations of this book. The antiwar movement sought to discredit the war effort, and it did so through a number of avenues. The "moral dimension" and the "secret and tax-subsidized torture" hearken back to the use of the Abu Ghraib scandal to undermine the moral justification of the war. By making the Abu Ghraib scandal a major element of the critique of the Iraq War, with Sen. Ted Kennedy going so far as to say Saddam's torture chambers had reopened "under new management," the antiwar movement tarnished the Bush administration and significantly weakened part of its rationale for war: freeing the Iraqi people from Saddam's tyranny. Similarly, the endless stories about "grim milestones" of casualties and the vocal protests of antiwar activists and politicians claiming the United States was mired in an Iraqi civil war neatly reflected the second point of Hayden's thesis. Finally, the

455 Tom Hayden, "Heart-Attack Iraq: Lessons from an Antiwar Movement," *The Nation*, November 1, 2011, http://www.thenation.com/article/heart-attack-iraq-lessons-antiwar-movement/.

notion that the government "lied" about its intentions and the likely cost of the Iraq War further undermined the Bush administration's credibility and soured Americans on the war effort.

Hayden also described an "inside-outside" strategy, in which antiwar groups would drive the protest movement and this movement would ultimately "enter and blend with mainstream opinion and institutions."[456] As described in this book, the anti–Iraq War movement largely employed this "inside-outside" strategy. It seized on every negative aspect of the war to slowly discredit it. First, the antiwar movement claimed that the war was unilateral because of the opposition of the French, Germans, and Russians at the United Nations. Then, after no WMD were found in Iraq, they claimed that the Bush administration deliberately lied about Iraq's WMD capabilities so it could invade Iraq and topple Saddam. The antiwar movement then seized upon the Abu Ghraib scandal to indict the entire American effort in Iraq. As the Iraqi insurgency increased in strength, the antiwar movement declared the war a lost cause, with America stuck in the middle of an Iraqi civil war, just as America had been in Vietnam three decades earlier. Finally, as the surge unquestionably began to lower the casualty rates in Iraq, the movement downplayed these successes, attributed them to factors other than the new surge strategy, ignored them altogether, or alleged they were based on false statistics.

As described previously, the antiwar movement also employed this "inside-outside" strategy by driving the Democratic Party firmly into the antiwar camp, particularly between 2004 and 2008. In 2002, all of the Democratic Party's major potential presidential candidates—Senators Kerry, Edwards, Lieberman, and Clinton and Representative Gephardt—voted to authorize the use of force in Iraq. By 2008, Kerry, Edwards, and Clinton had moved fully into the antiwar camp, Lieberman had been repudiated by his party, and Gephardt had retired. By 2006, the antiwar movement had reinvigorated the Democratic Party and drove it to victory in the 2006

456 Ibid.

midterm elections. In the span of four years, between 2004 and 2008, the "outside" antiwar movement had entered the "inside" by effectively taking control of the Democratic Party, just as Hayden suggested.

The effort to undermine the war effort by seizing upon and emphasizing each setback shifted public opinion against the war. This, in turn, gave politicians more breathing space to oppose the war. This cycle continued, as more and more politicians slowly came to the antiwar cause as the antiwar movement gave them the space to do so. By 2007, the entire mainstream Democratic Party opposed the war, and the 2008 primary season focused on the failures of the war in Iraq. Thus did the antiwar movement—the "outside"—bring the "inside" to opposition of the war.

To effectively prosecute a war, American leaders must counter the antiwar movement's strategies to discredit a war. First, American leaders must regularly remind Americans of whom their opposition is. In Saddam's case, it meant reminding Americans of what Saddam did to his opponents—gassing the Kurds, throwing opponents into wood chippers, and subsidizing Palestinian suicide bombers. It also means reminding Americans of what happened on September 11 and what would happen if a future rogue state or entity provided access to weapons of mass destruction to terrorists bent on committing future attacks on the US homeland.

American leaders must also emphasize that just because a country may not have perpetrated an attack on the United States does not mean that it will not, especially if it shares a world view with those who have attacked the United States. The antiwar movement regularly reminded Americans that Saddam Hussein was not involved in the 9/11 attacks despite the Bush administration's never having claimed otherwise. Yet Saddam, Iran, al-Qaeda, and today ISIS all shared the same anti-American world view. It is fair to conflate them, rather than waiting for one of them to perpetrate a 9/11 or share WMD with terrorists seeking to perpetrate another 9/11 (and attempt to obtain plausible deniability of involvement) before the United States strikes back. American leaders should make no apologies for conflating equally anti-American allies who share a similar world view of supporting terrorism and targeting civilians, including in the United States, and who actively seek WMD.

It is also essential that inaccurate themes are countered immediately, repeatedly, and forcefully. When an administration is attacked for lying where it has not, as in Iraq, it must forcefully and repeatedly push back against the accusation. Once the accusation takes hold in the public's mind, it is difficult to dislodge it.

2. *Do not accept the canard that the United States is a big, lumbering oaf—the proverbial bull in a china shop—on the world stage.*

   Americans often perceive themselves as being viewed by others as ugly Americans in their dealings with the world. The bien-pensants of the foreign policy elite sometimes look upon the United States as the clumsy, unsophisticated oaf of world affairs, making a mess everywhere it goes. The Iraq War and its aftermath, unfortunately, have reinforced this notion. It does not help when presidential candidates take the same position, as John Kerry did when he described the "Pottery Barn rule" of foreign affairs in a 2004 debate with George W. Bush: "You break it, you bought it."[457]

   Yet the United States, far from being a clumsy oaf, has been the most benevolent hegemon human civilization has ever known. Our national impulse, from Washington's Farewell Address to the present day, has been to avoid world conflicts whenever possible. Compared with other world powers at the height of their powers over the course of human history, the United States has not gone abroad in search of lands to conquer and resources to plunder.

   In fact, the United States has always been defined by its deep ambivalence about involvement in foreign conflicts. America is the world's libertarian; Americans have a live-and-let-live approach to the world and, all things being equal, would tend to their own affairs

457 "September 30, 2004 Debate Transcript," Commission on Presidential Debates, http://www.debates.org/index.php?page=september-30-2004-debate-transcript.

without involving themselves in foreign conflicts. (Even those exceptions, such as the Spanish-American War of 1898, focused on the Spanish presence in the Caribbean, America's near abroad. Moreover, the United States fairly quickly gave up full control of Cuba and the Philippines after its short bout of imperialism and attempted to install local governments in both places.) It took the bombing of Pearl Harbor to fully move America off the dime of nonintervention in World War II, despite knowledge of the atrocities perpetrated by Germany, Italy, and Japan and the fact that Britain remained the only major European power not to have fallen to the Third Reich. While Americans are eager and glad to do business with the rest of the world—exemplifying another fundamental American trait, the American love of dynamic economic, commercial, and inventive activities—Americans throughout their history have been, in principle, extremely reluctant to involve themselves in foreign conflicts.

At the outset of the Iraq War, many protesters complained about the war being a "war for oil." The United States easily could have appropriated Iraq's oil resources for itself, as the war's opponents claimed it intended to do. In 2008 and 2012, many of those same antiwar critics blamed the burgeoning US debt on paying for the Afghanistan and Iraq wars "on a credit card."[458] Of course, had the Iraq War truly been a war for oil, Iraq's oil revenues would have found their way into the US Treasury, and infrastructure contracts would have been awarded solely to American companies.

It is tiresome to hear complaints about the United States being a lumbering oaf in foreign policy and to hear from the foreign policy

---

458 Sen. Bernie Sanders (D-VT), "Sanders: If Republicans Want Another War, They Have to Pay for It," press release, March 20, 2015, http://www.sanders.senate.gov/newsroom/press-releases/sanders-if-republicans-want-another-war-they-have-to-pay-for-it; Rep. Jay Inslee (D-WA), statement on the House floor, Congressional Record—House, July 19, 2004, 16174, Google Books edition, https://books.google.com/books?id=oWMZh1nqt3sC&pg=PA16174&lpg=PA16174&dq=national+debt+because+paid+for+iraq+war+on+credit+card&source=bl&ots=rALaFgWcS5&sig=gzKhypg3S5G-zEY07aOievROGC4&hl=en&sa=X&ved=0CC8Q6AEwAzgKahUKEwjysZSgrN7IAhWDWz4KHY2xBIk#v=onepage&q=national%20debt%20because%20paid%20for%20iraq%20war%20on%20credit%20card&f=false.

establishment about the various flavors of the month nimbly asserting themselves on the world stage. It is wearing to hear about how the Chinese, the Russians, the BRICs, or the Europeans are going to outsmart the big, dumb, clumsy United States in foreign affairs and economic strength. In the 1980s the fad was Japan Inc. taking over America, buying Rockefeller Center and other American icons, and becoming the world's economic powerhouse to replace a decaying America. Since then Japan has endured two decades of stagnation while the US economy has grown significantly and given the world the Internet revolution.

The fact is that, alone among history's world powers, the United States has deployed its best troops and treasure to preserve and, in some cases, impose peace where only war existed. In the last twenty-five years alone, the United States has gone to war in Kuwait, Bosnia, and Kosovo to protect persecuted innocent people (Muslims, in fact) from death and destruction. The United States has deployed its military in the aftermath of tsunamis, earthquakes, and innumerable tragedies. In many ways, the US military is the world's first responder.

No matter what America's faults, past or present, in the end, deep down, the people of the world recognize just how lucky Americans are to be Americans. People do not risk life and limb to cross the straits to go from Miami to Cuba. People do not take dangerous train rides and pay criminals to smuggle them out of the United States and into Mexico. People are not banging down the door to enter China or Russia. There is a reason why the United States has an *immigration* problem, and it isn't because the United States is perceived as the "ugly Americans." The only people who view the United States that way are the people who can afford to. The American leftists who visit the "socialist paradises" of Cuba, and before that the Soviet Union, are like grandparents with grandchildren—they get all the enjoyment and benefits without having to deal with the difficult side of life in those countries, and they can always go back home when they have had their fill or when things start to become unpleasant.

3. *Understand that the world recognizes the United States as uniquely susceptible to international pressure and does not hold other countries to the same standards as the United States.*

   Over the last several years, a number of countries have engaged in significant military interventions beyond their borders. Saudi Arabia intervened in the Yemeni civil war to oppose the Iranian-backed Houthi rebels. The Russians intervened in the Syrian Civil War on the side of the Syrians, first backing the Syrian government with arms and financial aid and later with air support and troops on the ground. The Russians also fomented civil unrest in Ukraine, invading and annexing Crimea and continuing to support rebels in eastern Ukraine fighting the Ukrainian government.

   The international community reacted to each of these engagements with a collective yawn. The streets of major American and European cities have not filled with millions of protesters opposing the Russian and Saudi military activities in Ukraine, Syria, and Yemen. Nor, it goes without saying, have the streets of major Russian and Saudi cities filled with antiwar protesters. This despite the fact that the Russian and Saudi rules of engagement were considerably more relaxed that those of the United States in Iraq. The Saudis have bombed the Houthis with extraordinary imprecision, leading to widespread civilian casualties. The Russians, similarly, backed an Assad regime responsible for the deaths of an estimated 250,000—including through the use of chemical weapons and barrel bombs—and the worst refugee crisis since World War II. Human Rights Watch has alleged that Russian and Syrian soldiers have extensively used cluster munitions, inherently indiscriminate weapons, which have allegedly killed numerous civilians, including women and children.[459] Amnesty International has reported that Russian airstrikes in Syria have killed

459 Human Rights Watch, "Russia/Syria: Extensive Recent Use of Cluster Munitions," press release, December 20, 2015, https://www.hrw.org/news/2015/12/20/russia/syria-extensive-recent-use-cluster-munitions.

over two hundred civilians between October and November 2015 alone.[460] Yet the world has been mum.

Why the world is silent in the face of these atrocities is not entirely clear. Part of the reason for this silence may be that the Russians and Saudis did not seek the approval of world opinion before taking action in Syria, Ukraine, and Russia. The Russians did not seek UN approval before invading Crimea and eastern Ukraine or deploying air and ground forces in Syria. The Saudis did not seek international support for their intervention in Yemen. Unlike in Iraq, where the United States sought the approval of the United Nations before taking action and gave the world's antiwar community six months to mobilize before the Iraq War began, the Russians and Saudis simply assessed their interests and took action. The Russians and Saudis never gave the antiwar movement a chance to mobilize and gather strength.

However, this does not fully explain why the world has remained silent in the face of the Russian and Saudi interventions. Another part of the reason the world the world reacts with a shrug to the military interventions of non-US countries—even when on behalf of dictators responsible for carrying out attacks on civilians using chemical weapons and barrel bombs—may be that the world understands that protests of the Russian and Saudi actions will have no effect. Moreover, the antiwar movement recognizes that the Russian and Saudi actions will not result in the same level of vocal opposition and concomitant media coverage that resulted from opposing the United States in the Iraq War.

By contrast, as shown previously, the United States is uniquely solicitous of world opinion. The antiwar movement, embodied by the Democratic Party, has repeatedly expressed in public remarks, platforms, and other venues that it believes in having the support of the "international community" to legitimize the United States' international interventions. The United States is an easy mark for the world's

460 BBC News, "Syria Conflict: Russian Airstrikes 'Killed 200 Civilians,'" December 23, 2015, http://www.bbc.com/news/world-middle-east-35162523.

antiwar movement because the United States appears to so desperately want world opinion to ratify US foreign activities.

Finally, there is an element of Third World-ism and anticolonialism at work. US intervention in the Middle East and elsewhere easily can be caricatured as a neocolonial endeavor. Interventions by Russia and Saudi Arabia—both non-Western countries—are not as easily caricatured as neocolonial activities. Ironically, the Russian invasions of Syria and Ukraine are much closer to neocolonial activities that the US intervention in Iraq. Russia is actively trying to create a supportive puppet state in Syria in which it can base air and naval assets to project power from the eastern Mediterranean and is annexing Ukrainian territory to create new regions of Russia. The world simply is more concerned with neutering the United States and the West and less concerned with the activities of non-Western countries.

The United States needs to recognize that its activities will be opposed by many people throughout the world predisposed to opposing American interventions in world affairs, particularly military interventions. American leaders must price this realization into their assessment of taking military action and, ultimately, discount much of the world's antiwar opposition in favor of taking a cold-blooded, analytical assessment of US interests in a given situation to determine the correct course of action.

American leaders must be prepared to vocally and repeatedly challenge the "international community," particularly its antiwar movement, on this rank hypocrisy. American leaders intervening internationally based on American interests should quickly and vociferously challenge the antiwar movement's failure to protest atrocities of other countries. The United States should not feel above taking on these antiwar critics, because as shown previously, these antiwar critics can erode support for a military intervention over time and, indeed, delegitimize it. The silence of the antiwar movement in the face of real atrocities—Russia's invasion and annexation of Crimea, Russia's invasion of Syria and use of cluster munitions there, Assad's use of chemical weapons and barrel bombs in Syria, Russia's and Iran's support for the Assad regime, the gulags of North Korea—should be used to question the legitimacy and motives of the antiwar movement in the same way the antiwar movement attempts to delegitimize American military interventions.

4. *Fight wars to win them, and spare no expense or consequence.*

   Napoleon's axiom—"When you set out to take Vienna, take Vienna"—is as true today as it was in Napoleon's day. War has been a part of the human condition since the dawn of humankind. The United States would be guilty of deep hubris if it believed it could permanently alter this state of affairs. But the United States is truly a humanitarian nation, devoted to protecting human life whenever possible.

   The best way to reconcile the inevitability of war with America's fundamental benevolent, humanitarian instincts is to fight wars in as humanitarian a way as possible. But this does not mean fighting wars in a limited, halfhearted way or fighting them in a way that is designed to minimize casualties with no thought to achieving the goals of the conflict. Rather, it means fighting a war that achieves its ends completely in the shortest amount of time.

   This proposition may seem counterintuitive. Over the last twenty-five years, Americans have gotten used to an antiseptic way of warfare—unmanned drones, cruise missiles, campaigns limited to the use of airpower and smart bombs. The deployment of troops is limited, and an "exit strategy" is expected before the United States even commits troops to combat. Committing ground troops, particularly in the wake of the Iraq War, has been viewed as a bridge too far.

   Unfortunately, such campaigns fail to yield lasting results more frequently than not. Despite heavy bombing, the United States did not quickly roll back ISIS; ISIS's barbarity continues, to this day. The Saudis are having great difficulty dislodging the Houthi rebels in Yemen with airpower alone. Even what may be the greatest example of a successful airpower-alone campaign, the assault on the Serbs to defend Kosovo, had limits. The US and European air campaign in Libya removed Gaddafi but created a vacuum filled by equally or more brutal Islamist groups, including ISIS. When the United States' air campaign failed to stop the Serbian atrocities on the ground in Kosovo, it began bombing targets in Belgrade—that is, the bombing campaign only began to succeed when it was taken to civilian population areas. Only after the United States subjected Belgrade to aerial assault did the Serbs end their attacks on Kosovo and sue for peace.

By contrast, the ground forces of our enemies are frequently no match for the combined might of US air, naval, and ground forces. The first Gulf War lasted less than two months. In the Iraq War, the United States began bombardments on March 19, 2003; on April 9, Baghdad fell.

The same mentality informed the use of the bombs on Hiroshima and Nagasaki. While the casualties were tremendous, the casualties both the United States and Japanese would have experienced had the United States chosen to invade the home islands rather than use the atomic bombs may well have been significantly greater and the war significantly longer.[461] The United States was dealing with an enemy in Japan that based on the United States' experiences at Iwo Jima and Okinawa, among other places, was prepared to fight to the death. Kamikaze planes—World War II's version of the suicide bomber—wreaked havoc on US naval vessels. American policy makers who authorized the atomic bombing of Japan decided to do so because of their fears of massive American casualties that might result from an invasion of the Japanese home islands. Even after the atomic bombs were dropped, several members of the Japanese war cabinet opposed surrender. Under such circumstances, policy makers concluded that the only way to end the war was to win it decisively. And the way to end the war with as few casualties as possible—certainly on the

---

461 For example, see Karl T. Compton, "If the Atomic Bomb Had Not Been Used," *The Atlantic*, December 1946, http://www.theatlantic.com/magazine/archive/1946/12/if-the-atomic-bomb-had-not-been-used/376238/.

American side, and likely on the Japanese side as well—was to do everything in America's power to end the war as quickly as possible.

In the end, for a military campaign to be successful, it must be viewed by the American public as a success. Holding back to satisfy or placate the antiwar movement will not enhance support and will only make it more difficult to achieve the objectives of a military engagement. Far better to suffer the protests of a portion of the public and fight fiercely to achieve quickly the aims of the engagement.

Restrictive rules of engagement and antiseptic airpower-only warfare also increase the likelihood of a longer and more protracted conflict. Imposing extremely restrictive rules of engagement or limiting the nature of the force the United States is willing to deploy (for example, airpower only) will tend to lengthen a conflict. The longer a military engagement lasts, the more time antiwar movements will have to organize and to undermine the rationale for the war. A major setback, scandal, or accidental collateral damage can kick-start an antiwar movement that can undermine the ability to prosecute a war to victory. Although this should not necessarily be the case—once committing troops, the United States should do all it can to see the effort through—any prolonged conflict can lead to an antiwar movement that could undermine continued prosecution of a war.

In addition, highly restrictive rules of engagement provide enemies advantages on the battlefield that leads to more American casualties than might otherwise occur. The increased casualties from fighting in a more restrictive manner leads to more popular discontent with the war, which further undermines the mission. It also lengthens the war, which provides more time for the enemy to inflict more American casualties. This positive feedback loop would be muted if the United States fought under less restrictive rules of engagement that allow for a more rapid crushing of the enemy. American enemies know that in a one-on-one fight on a battlefield, they would be crushed. So they take steps to limit the United States' ability to wage this one-on-one fight—by hiding among civilians, for example—which they know will provide them protection because of the United States' restrictive rules of engagement. Deny the enemy this advantage, and military conflicts will end more quickly and more decisively.

By tying itself down in its rules of engagement, the United States weakens the deterrent effect of its unparalleled military might. The United States could send Iran or ISIS back to the Stone Age if it were so inclined. However, the United States is restrained because of its moral objections to such indiscriminate slaughter, its compliance with the laws of war, and its concerns for world opinion. Though the United States may not want to go so far as to bomb a country into the Stone Age given the clear moral and legal objections to such tactics, in the United States' case, the pendulum has swung very far to the opposite side—the United States is more worried about being loved than being feared. By demonstrating a willingness to deploy more of our arsenal, the United States may make countries less willing to challenge it and tempt fate as to whether the United States will deploy that arsenal against them.

5. *Never forget: Americans are the good guys.*

As noted previously, opponents of American military intervention often apply a moral equivalence to US actions and the actions of US enemies to prevent the United States from taking action against those enemies. The antiwar movement will magnify crimes American soldiers commit or mistakes American soldiers make in order to discredit American military interventions. Abu Ghraib is one example. Another example is the accidental bombing in 2015 of a hospital in Afghanistan that killed workers with the humanitarian organization Doctors Without Borders.

What the antiwar movement fails to admit—or deliberately obscures—is the fact that these unfortunate events are not American policy. The US military commissioned several investigations of the events at Abu Ghraib and punished those who committed the crimes at that facility. The US military acknowledged that the bombing of the Doctors Without Borders hospital was an accident. Nevertheless,

Doctors Without Borders rejected America's apology, vociferously and repeatedly argued that the bombing was a war crime, and demanded an independent investigation.[462] The United States has spent billions of dollars trying to build countries such as Afghanistan and Iraq into modern, functioning states. It has built roads, schools, and other public works. It has fought to protect the right of women and girls to obtain an education and work. As noted previously, the United States imposed restrictive rules of engagement on its military to protect Afghan and Iraqi civilians even though this increased the risk to American troops. In short, the United States has gone to extraordinary lengths—unparalleled in the annals of human history—to better the lives of the civilians of countries it (temporarily) occupies. The notion that the United States somehow targeted the Doctors Without Borders hospital with the knowledge that the facility was, in fact, a civilian hospital that was not occupied by enemy fighters flies in the face of all of this evidence and suggests bad faith on the part of the United States' accusers.

The US military should have the benefit of the doubt from the world that it does not commit war crimes. Indeed, it has *earned* the benefit of the doubt from the world. The US military has been the first responder for countless natural disasters, from the 2005 Indian Ocean tsunami to the 2010 earthquake in Haiti to Typhoon Haiyan in the Philippines in 2013.[463] American aid feeds countless people throughout the globe. When disasters strike, the world does not call on China, Russia, or anyone else. The world calls on the United States. And the United States responds. A 2013 RAND Corporation

---

462 "Statement on Kunduz Hospital Bombing," Doctors Without Borders, October 4, 2015, http://www.doctorswithoutborders.org/article/statement-kunduz-hospital-bombing; Thomas Gibbons-Neff, "US Military Struggles to Explain How It Wound Up Bombing Doctors Without Borders Hospital," *Washington Post*, October 3, 2015, https://www.washingtonpost.com/news/checkpoint/wp/2015/10/05/afghan-forces-requested-airstrike-that-hit-hospital-in-kunduz/.

463 Travis J. Tritten, "When Disaster Strikes, US Military Assets Often Key to Relief Efforts," *Stars and Stripes*, November 16, 2013, http://www.stripes.com/news/pacific/when-disaster-strikes-us-military-assets-often-key-to-relief-efforts-1.253245.

report noted that the US military has participated in over forty humanitarian assistance and disaster-response actions in the past two decades in the Asia-Pacific region alone.[464] As the report noted, the US military has unmatched air and sealift capabilities to deliver large amounts of humanitarian supplies, expertise in logistics and supply-chain management, emergency medicine, communications, debris clearing, and infrastructure repair. The United States does not have to make these assets available to the world. But it does—even at the cost to its taxpayers and risk to its servicemen and servicewomen. (Indeed, six Americans were killed in a helicopter crash during earthquake response efforts in Nepal in 2015.[465])

Moreover, whatever else one thinks of the Iraq intervention, it is apparent that the United States did not have designs to conquer Iraq for its oil or for American aggrandizement. The United States spent significant blood, treasure, and time trying to develop a pluralistic, democratic, stable Iraq in which minority and women's rights were protected, and Iraqis enjoyed freedom they had not experienced in decades. In fact, implicit in the arguments the antiwar movement makes that the Iraq War exacerbated the national debt is the fact that the United States did not seek to plunder Iraq's natural resources. Whether one believes America's efforts were successful or not, American motives were noble. The malicious motives the antiwar movement ascribed to the United States helped discredit America's intervention in Iraq, unfairly but effectively.

By contrast, the vicious brutality of ISIS and al-Qaeda are official policy. Those organizations' raison d'être is to impose a brutal form of Islamic law on their subjects and, ultimately, the world. Beheadings,

---

464 Jennifer D.P. Moroney, Stephanie Pezard, Laurel E. Miller, Jeffrey Engstrom, and Abby Doll, "Lessons from Department of Defense Disaster Relief Efforts in the Asia-Pacific Region," 2013, RAND Corporation, 1, http://www.rand.org/content/dam/rand/pubs/research_reports/RR100/RR146/RAND_RR146.pdf.

465 Kimberly Hutcherson and Kevin Conlon, "Marines Died Helping Hard-to-Reach Quake Victims," CNN, May 17, 2015, http://www.cnn.com/2015/05/17/asia/us-helicopter-found-nepal/.

slavery, sex slavery, and extermination of Christians, Yazidis, and other religious minorities are not accidents or aberrations—they are the foundation of ISIS's rule.

Yet opponents of US military intervention are quick to jump on any crime or mistake American servicemen and servicewomen commit to delegitimize entire American military efforts. Americans must steadfastly defend their actions and remind the world of their enemies' beliefs. The United States must shame its opposition if necessary, reminding this opposition of its silence and inaction in the face of the true brutality of ISIS and al-Qaeda and the flagrant violations of international law by China, Russia, Iran, Cuba, and others.

6. *The burden of proof should always—always—rest with the rogue state, and American political leadership must forcefully make this point to the American people to avoid a fatal undermining of its credibility.*

   Statisticians speak in terms of type I and type II errors. A type I error is one for which a proposition is believed to be true but in fact is false (a false positive). A type II error is the opposite: a proposition believed to be false that in fact is true (a false negative). In the context of WMD, believing that a country has WMD when in fact it does not is a type I error; believing a country does not have an active WMD program when in fact it does is a type II error.

   The risk and consequences of a type II error regarding questions about a country's WMD program are too great to contemplate. As catastrophic as the attacks of September 11 were, the United States was able to rebuild from those attacks. The consequences of a nuclear, chemical, or biological device going off in a major metropolitan area would be unimaginably devastating. Large swaths of the area would be uninhabitable for years. Casualties would range in the tens to hundreds of thousands.

   Although the Bush administration is roundly pilloried for its supposed mistake in invading Iraq, the administration in fact employed the correct philosophy for assessing and handling twenty-first century threats. The administration demanded that Iraq completely come clean regarding its WMD program. Coming clean meant a comprehensive and intrusive inspection regime that granted inspectors unfettered access to any site, anywhere, at any time. Before launching the invasion of Iraq, the United States allowed six months of UN weapons inspections from October 2002 to January 2003 in order to determine whether and to what extent Iraq was developing WMD.

Indeed, the US and allied buildup of forces in fall 2002 convinced Saddam Hussein to allow greater inspections, demonstrating that the credible threat of force can yield diplomatic results. However, even with this force buildup and the credible threat of invasion, Saddam Hussein continued to resist unfettered inspections, denying inspectors access to his palaces across Iraq and other sensitive sites. In short, the Bush administration demanded that Saddam Hussein prove, once and for all, that he had no WMD. He refused.

By launching the Iraq War, the United States set forth a new principle of foreign affairs: rogue states that refuse to demonstrate beyond a reasonable doubt that they are not sponsoring WMD programs run the risk of regime change. That principle is not a bad one to apply to the rogue regimes of the world. It does not require the United States to topple every rogue regime. But it places in the minds of those at the helm of rogue regimes the tremendous risk they take if they embark on a WMD program.

Rather than take that risk in dealing with Iraq, the Bush administration could be said to have made a type I error, believing Iraq had an active WMD program when no substantial WMD were found after the invasion. However, in the wake of September 11, the Bush administration reasonably concluded that the risk and potential consequences of a type II error were too great to accept.

With the benefit of hindsight, it is possible to say that Saddam Hussein's Iraq no longer maintained WMD capacity and infrastructure. And in retrospect, the failure to find WMD appears to have undermined the case for war. However, those who more or less said, "I told you so," when the United States and its allies failed to find

WMD in Iraq fail to consider what might have happened if the Bush administration was correct. After all, most of the world's intelligence services believed that the Iraqis had some form of ongoing WMD program, and the strongest arguments opponents made against the invasion was that Iraq did not pose an "imminent" threat. What if Iraq did have WMD? What if three, five, or ten years down the line, Iraqi WMD ended up in the hands of al-Qaeda or some other terrorist organization?

Moreover, we know that neighbors of a hostile rogue state will seek their own WMD if they believe the rogue state has its own WMD program. In the wake of the Iran nuclear deal, Iran's most powerful neighbors, Saudi Arabia and Egypt, are considering whether to develop a nuclear weapons program or acquiring nuclear weapons from another nation. Prince Mohammed bin Nawwaf bin Abdulaziz al-Saud, the Saudi ambassador to the United Kingdom, stated in June 2015 that Saudi Arabia "hopes [it] receive[s] the assurances that guarantee Iran will not pursue this kind of weapon [a nuclear weapon]... But if this does not happen, then all options will be on the table for Saudi Arabia."[466]

However, the Bush administration failed to anticipate that the failure to find WMD would lead to accusations that it "lied" the United States into war. It did not strike back forcefully enough against accusations that it was so determined to go to war in Iraq for any number of reasons—oil, Halliburton, Bush's supposed desire to finish what his father started—and that it cherry-picked and skewed intelligence to make a case for war. Future administrations must take every step to preserve their credibility in the face of accusations of "lying" the United States into war. As Vietnam and later Iraq demonstrated, once a substantial segment of the American public believes that the president "lied" the United States into war, the war becomes extremely difficult to prosecute. Antiwar protesters grow in strength,

---

466 Con Coughlin, "The Saudis Are Ready to Go Nuclear," The Guardian, June 8, 2015, http://www.telegraph.co.uk/news/worldnews/middleeast/saudiarabia/11658338/The-Saudis-are-ready-to-go-nuclear.html.

and politicians once fearful of challenging the decision to go to war are emboldened to oppose the war publicly. The antiwar movement thereby becomes a runaway train that overpowers the ability to prosecute the war, as occurred in both Vietnam and Iraq.

In some ways, the fact that the United States went into Iraq without absolute proof that Iraq had an active WMD program reinforces the important principle that the rogue regime bears the burden of proving it is not developing WMD. It reminds rogue states contemplating developing or obtaining WMD that the United States is not going to wait forever for proof that the rogue state is not developing WMD before taking action. Rogue leaders who enjoy the benefits and spoils of leading their countries will think twice before embarking on a WMD program. This leads nicely to the next important principle for America's use of military force.

7. *It does not hurt to be unpredictable in the use of force.*

   One salutary effect of the Iraq War that is sometimes forgotten is that rogue regimes reassessed the possibility of US military action against them in the post-9/11 world. By stating that the paradigm for deploying the US military had changed and that what was perhaps tolerable in the pre-9/11 era was no longer tolerable in the post-9/11 era, the United States injected an element of unpredictability into world affairs. The United States forced rogue regimes that previously felt comfortable engaging in illicit WMD programs and other nefarious activities to reassess the risks and benefits of such activities. The best example is Libya, which voluntarily gave up its entire WMD program, including its WMD stocks, precursors, supplies, and equipment in the wake of the Iraq War.[467] The US even reported that Iran temporarily halted some nuclear activities in 2003 after the Iraq War began.[468]

---

467 "Bush, Blair: Libya to Dismantle WMD Programs," CNN.

468 Mark Mazzetti, "U.S. Finds Iran Halted Its Nuclear Arms Effort in 2003," *New York Times*, December 4, 2007, http://www.nytimes.com/2007/12/04/world/middleeast/04intel.html?_r=0.

Being unpredictable in using force does not mean always using force. In fact, having a level of unpredictability associated with a country's actions lessens the need to employ force for each and every circumstance that might demand it. Rogue regimes considering whether to embark on a WMD program or sponsor international terrorist acts must consider the possibility that the United States might respond harshly. When the threat of force is credible and realistic, these calculations may lead rogue regimes to conclude it is not worth engaging in further provocative behavior. In this way, problems that might require the use of force are stopped before they even begin and before any overt threat of force is needed.

Ironically, in this one sense, the use of force particularly to deal with rogue regimes is similar to law enforcement, the paradigm so often cited by the antiwar movement and antiwar Democrats for responding to terrorist acts. One of the underlying principles of law enforcement is for it to provide a deterrent effect on others. Law enforcement resources are finite, and officers cannot arrest every criminal and investigate every crime in detail. However, the possibility of being caught and suffering the potentially severe consequences deters most people from engaging in crime. It is in the most high-profile circumstances that the full resources of law enforcement assuredly are brought to bear. Similarly, it is in the face of an implacable rogue regime threatening the civilized world with WMD that the full resources of US power should be brought to bear.

Viewing the deployment of military forces in the narrow manner of the antiwar movement—only to be deployed in the face of an imminent threat—weakens the deterrent effect of US military action. By demonstrating a willingness to deploy troops in the event of a potential threat that cannot be defined fully because of the unwillingness of a threat to come clean and be transparent, particularly in the area of WMD, the United States may actually have to deploy its forces less frequently. The mere threat of the use of force, if credible, would be sufficient to achieve the United States' aims and bend an adversary to its will without actually having to deploy troops.

8. *Stop fetishizing multilateralism. Do not get caught up in seeking the approval of the international community.*

   The meaning of the term *international community* is extremely nebulous. In fact, the idea of a single "international community" is primarily a myth. The United States is hardly a member of the same community as North Korea, Syria, or Iran, and to suggest otherwise is insulting and offensive. Even countries much closer in values and interests to the United States, particularly in Europe, nevertheless have a different outlook on world affairs. Some of this is historical; there is a deep pacifist strain in Europe (and Japan) owing to the wars of the twentieth century. Some of this may be because European countries have been living under the American defense umbrella since World War II and have gotten out of the habit of considering international events and their effects on global security. Some of this may be the result of different countries' differing national interests.

   Regardless of the source of the differences, the fact is these differences exist. In the absence of a world government with enforceable laws, countries' actions in the international arena will be defined primarily by self-interest. The United States must recognize that differences among countries and their national self-interests exist and influence countries' calculations on how to respond to individual international events, threats, and concerns. Countries' self-interests will cause them to take different and sometimes oppositional stands from the United States. Such opposition does not, ipso facto, make US military action wrong or illegitimate.

   In addition, the same international issue or concern likely subjects different countries to different levels of threats and risks. The United States, by virtue of its size and importance in world affairs, is naturally a larger target than other countries. As described previously, France's differing conception from the United States of the threat Saddam

Hussein's Iraq posed to the world played a role in France's opposition to the Iraq War. That the United States perceived Saddam's Iraq to be a greater threat than France did does not make the United States a warmonger or an opponent of the international order. However, US policy makers have a solemn obligation to consider US national security in determining whether to deploy military force. US deployment of military force should be based on American conceptions of the threat and risk to the US population and not any other country's or international organization's perception of the threat.

Moreover, the United States is more consumed with how it is viewed by the rest of the world than any other country. In making decisions in foreign affairs, the United States considers world opinion more than any other country. Does Russia worry about outbreaks of anti-Russianism when it acts aggressively on the world stage, such as when it invaded Georgia or Ukraine? Does China worry about outbreaks of anti-Chineseism when it takes aggressive actions against its Asian neighbors in the South China Sea and elsewhere? Of course not—the very words *anti-Russianism* and *anti-Chineseism* sound strange to the ear because no one uses those words. These countries do not care about how the rest of the world perceives them, and world public opinion does not affect their decision making, and so the rest of the world does not engage in "anti-Russianism" or "anti-Chineseism." Paradoxically, in time, the less solicitous the United States is of world opinion in making foreign policy decisions, the less likely massive outbreaks of anti-Americanism may be.

9. *Do not value some allies over others; get allies where you can.*

The United States is blessed with numerous allies throughout the world. Many US allies recognize the United States' commitment to freedom, equality, justice, free enterprise, and respect for the rights of the individual. Countries that lived under the yoke of Soviet Communist domination have a special appreciation for the United States' commitment to these ideals. As such, these countries are particularly inclined to support the United States in defending and promoting these ideals around the world. The United States should never elevate the support of France over the support of Poland or the support of Germany over the support of Lithuania or the Czech Republic. And by all means, the United States should not elevate the support of the United Nations over the support of coalitions of individual countries. The concept of a "coalition of the willing" is not only wise but the best way to defend American interests and ideals in the world. As noted previously, America's history and underlying ethos is to avoid international conflict as much as possible. When the United States decides to go to war, it has strong and righteous reasons for doing so. Countries that support the United States share our beliefs and interests and should be encouraged and welcomed, not belittled as insignificant.

It is counterproductive and, at some level, offensive to undervalue alliances with some countries and overvalue the support of others. When a country like Poland wholeheartedly backs US foreign policy objectives, the United States must value that support in the same way it would value France's support. Countries like Poland and the Czech Republic also have a history of being sacrificed by larger powers to support these larger powers' interests; by not valuing these alliances, the United States risks losing them altogether. When the United States pulled missile defenses out of Poland and the Czech Republic in 2009 to curry favor with the Russians, it dramatically undermined those alliances.

10. Regime change *is not a dirty word.*

The world has lectured the United States endlessly that its policies of regime change, most recently in Iraq but also during the Cold War, are neocolonial and immoral. President Obama has endlessly repeated apologies for the overthrow of Mohammad Mossadegh in Iran in 1953 and the shah's return to power. Nevertheless, the Bush administration implemented regime change in Afghanistan and Iraq.

Regime change has become a dirty word because, according to the antiwar movement, it smacks of neocolonialism, of Western nations subjugating and plundering non-Western nations. Colonialism, in the antiwar Left's lexicography, is perhaps the deadliest sin, imposing Western values on others.

And yet when the United States ostentatiously removed itself from the Middle East under the Obama administration, almost seemingly as penance for the United States' having meddled in the region since the end of World War II, the whirlwind indigenous forces have unleashed is arguably worse than any colonial regime the West ever imposed. ISIS is marauding through Syria and Iraq, burning and beheading men and boys and selling women into slavery. Religious sects that survived for two thousand years are on the verge of becoming extinct. Priceless antiquities—the common inheritance of humanity—are being destroyed. Chaos reigns supreme. No colonial regime in its heyday—not the British, not the French, not the Ottomans—would have allowed ISIS to rampage with impunity.

Even though regime change got a bad name during the Cold War and Iraq, the time has come to reassess whether regime change should once again be a part of our foreign policy. Clandestine subversion of hostile governments could be a cost-effective strategy to put foes off-balance and force them to play defense. Such subversive activities do not involve large-scale invasion forces. They do not involve the vast sums of money associated with a full-scale military operation and occupation. Rather, these activities involve identifying friendly elements within the country and providing them with financial, moral, and material support, while simultaneously waging economic warfare against the enemy state.

Perhaps the greatest opportunity for such regime change is Iran. Iran is the single most malignant actor in the Middle East. It is the head of the snake, the body of the octopus. Its tentacles include Hezbollah in Lebanon and Syria, Hamas in Gaza and the West Bank, the Houthi rebels in Yemen, and the opposition in Bahrain. It is the leading state sponsor of terrorism in the world. And yet the United States knows that the Iranian government is despised by its people, as the thwarted

Green Revolution of 2009 made clear. Iran's government is ripe for being undermined by the United States, and doing so would not require an invasion. It would be more effective than one-off drone attacks against terror leaders. It would halt, at least temporarily and without a military strike, Iran's march to a nuclear weapon. And it would save Iran's people from a tyrannical government they despise. Yet because of the fear of appearing to be a "colonial" power meddling in the affairs of others as part of a modern "Great Game," the United States has refrained from such tactics. It is time to reconsider this position.

11. Imperialism *and* colonialism *aren't dirty words either.*

Americans are by nature idealistic. We aspire to a free and open civil society, where the state is but a small portion of one's overall existence. We strive for religious pluralism, freedom of speech, an open political system, and non-state-based centers of society, such as churches, synagogues, and charitable and service organizations, which play large roles in American life. All of these different centers of life thrive because the United States successfully maintains the security of its citizens, providing them the space to build a civil society.

Many of the countries in which the United States has recently gone to war, such as Iraq and Libya, were totalitarian dictatorships in which the state was all-powerful and all-consuming. Iraq's civil society had suffered through over thirty years of Saddam's rule and even more years of Baathist rule. Saddam's tyrannical regime destroyed Iraqi civil society. Removing his regime left a tremendous vacuum. Iraq had not had an open civil society for more than three decades, and suddenly it had to reconstitute its civil society.

The United States, by its nature, wants others to live free lives with fair elections and open, pluralistic societies. However, having made *colonialism* and *imperialism* dirty words, the antiwar movement has caused Americans to fear being accused of being a neocolonial or imperial power. However, it is not neocolonial or imperialist to say that a ruined society needs to be managed by an outside power to give it the breathing space it needs to get back on its feet. A ruined civil society like Iraq cannot simply be rebooted like a crashed computer. And if that is imperialist or colonial, so be it—it is still the correct approach to take. Iraqis who lived under Saddam Hussein's regime were victims, and their society needed time to be nursed back to health.

After removing a regime that threatens the United States, the United States should ensure that the aftermath does not result in a greater threat. But in doing this, the United States should make no apologies for running a country until it is ready to handle its own affairs. This means providing ample, robust security; using overwhelming force to crush any residual enemies; and, with security achieved, helping slowly rebuild the institutions of civil society. This also means waiting until the society is ready for self-government and independence, sectarian or other rivalries have had time to cool down, and citizens have had a chance to slowly acclimate themselves to cultural freedom in a secure environment only the United States can provide.

The United States should realize that it may not take as much as it thinks to "win hearts and minds." Most people in a country like Iraq are simply glad to be relieved of the tyrannical regime that governed them. Nothing the United States might do in running a country would be worse than what Saddam did to his own people. The United States should realize this fact and not apologize for having to install an all-powerful viceroy to run a country for as long as it takes to rebuild it physically, spiritually, and culturally.

An excellent model is postwar Japan. The United States ran Japan for five years after the end of World War II, with Gen. Douglas MacArthur serving as the all-powerful viceroy governing the country during this time. MacArthur gradually gave more and more power back to Japan over time. The United States never intended to make Japan the fifty-first state or a permanent American colony. Yet within twenty years of the end of World War II, Japan was a recovered nation, a full part of the Western economic system, an Olympics host, and a reliable American ally.

Ironically, one of the reasons the Bush administration chose to occupy Iraq with a light footprint after the combat phase of the war ended may have been to minimize American casualties. In this, again, the shadows of Vietnam are apparent. The United States committed hundreds of thousands of troops to the Vietnam War. The massive military force and the draft needed to maintain it were dominant forces driving the antiwar protests in the 1960s and 1970s. In effect, the Bush administration's decision to use a relatively small force reflected the fear of entering another "quagmire," another stalemate, another unwinnable war. In short, another Vietnam.

Another rationale for the small occupation force may have been the desire to preempt the inevitable criticisms that the United States was acting like a colonial power in occupying Iraq. This rationale demonstrates the effect that a generation of antiwar, anticolonial sentiment had on the United States' way of waging war and peace. A generation's worth of sympathy for Third World dictators (particularly the anti-American kind such as Castro in Cuba, Ortega in Nicaragua, and "Uncle Ho" in Vietnam), of supposed blowback for US support for right-wing dictators and the removal of left-wing dictators (Allende and Pinochet in Chile, Mossadegh and the shah in Iran, and General Park in South Korea), and of anticolonial sentiment generally took their toll on America's willingness to wage war and manage peace. The United States could not be seen as an occupying, colonial power, this logic went. Nor could the United States be seen as interested only in Iraq's oil reserves and other natural resources.

Instead, the United States would have been better served by maintaining a strong, visible presence in Iraq, swatting down any signs of resistance with overwhelming force, and achieving security and stability before embarking on the task of rebuilding Iraqi civil society. Countries such as Japan, South Korea, and Taiwan have followed this model to prosperity. Japan was occupied and governed by the United States and Gen. Douglas MacArthur for several years before returning to full independence. South Korea and Taiwan both were run in the postwar years by dictatorships that maintained security and gave their populations the space to create vibrant, successful economies before democratizing their systems. Neither of these countries had rich democratic histories or traditions. Yet both experienced successful transitions to democracy and are fully democratic states today.

Moreover, it is likely that, no matter what type of footprint the United States used in Iraq, the United States would be denounced as a colonial, imperialist occupying power by the antiwar movement.[469] Some viewed the resistance that arose after the occupation phase of the Iraq War as beginning a war of national resistance.[470] Antiwar filmmaker Michael Moore referred to the insurgents as "Minutemen."[471] However, much of the violence in occupied Iraq was sectarian in nature and influenced by outside forces, including Iran and al-Qaeda.

What was needed in Iraq, more than anything, was space—space to build governing institutions, space to build private enterprise, space to allow an economy to take root, and space to rebuild Iraqi civil society. This space exists only when the environment is secure and citizens are confident that they can engage in civil and economic activities without risk to life or property. In practice, in future situations similar to Iraq, this means that the United States needs to overcome its inherent inhibition around appearing to be a colonial power and impose security. If that means a larger, more visible occupying armed force in the near term in order to impose security on a country, that is preferable to trying to impose security with one hand tied behind its back in the hopes that Europeans, the United Nations, and the antiwar movement will not accuse the United States of being a neo-colonial power.

---

469 See, e.g., "Iraq and the New American Colonialism," Cal Poly, April 1, 2003.

470 Richard Falk, "Lessons to be Learnt from the Iraq War," Al Jazeera, March 14, 2013, http://www.aljazeera.com/indepth/opinion/2013/03/2013361029140182.html.

471 Michael Moore, "Heads Up . . . from Michael Moore," MichaelMoore.com, April 14, 2007, https://web.archive.org/web/20040501040852/http://www.michaelmoore.com/words/message/index.php?messageDate=2004-04-14.

The Israeli experience is instructive. Accused of being a colonial power, Israel unilaterally left the Gaza Strip, lock, stock, and barrel, in 2005. The Israelis left no installations behind—not one Israeli settlement, not one army post, nothing. Israel continues to be criticized routinely by the antiwar movement in the United States and Europe as a colonial occupying power in Gaza, most recently during the August 2014 war. As another example, when Israel left south Lebanon in 2000, Hezbollah immediately made claims for more territory, the disputed Shebaa Farms region; as an aide to former Lebanese prime minister Fouad Siniora put it, "most Lebanese had never heard of it until Hizbullah brought it up in 2000."[472] No matter what the Israelis do, in the eyes of the US and European antiwar movement, Israel is accused of colonialism and occupation. The United States is in the same position. No matter what it does in the Middle East, if it involves visible troops on the ground, some segment of the United States and Europe will accuse the United States of colonialism. Therefore, US policy makers ought to ignore such accusations and simply take the actions they believe are in the best interests of American national security.

12. *Not every world conflict can be solved only politically; sometimes a military solution must precede a political solution.*

    For the antiwar movement and many antiwar Democrats, it is axiomatic that world conflicts cannot be solved militarily but only politically and diplomatically. However, history—including very recent history—teaches quite the opposite. Military solutions creating facts on the ground are essential to negotiating a satisfactory political and diplomatic outcome.

    The Russians have most recently given this thesis expression in Georgia and Ukraine. They have occupied portions of Georgia and Ukraine (Crimea and parts of eastern Ukraine) before agreeing to any political or diplomatic settlement of any disputes with these smaller,

472 Joshua Mitnik, "Behind the Dispute over Shebaa Farms," *Christian Science Monitor*, August 22, 2006, http://www.csmonitor.com/2006/0822/p10s01-wome.html.

weaker countries. The Chinese are busy creating facts on the ground, and indeed literally creating ground itself, as they build islands in the South China Sea. China undoubtedly will use these islands to press territorial claims and expand its sphere of influence in the South China Sea. Even the United States has imposed its military will in recent conflicts to achieve desired political aims. For example, as described previously, the United States launched a bombing campaign against Serbia to stop the ethnic cleansing in Bosnia and Kosovo, which included bombing the civilian city of Belgrade to force Serbia's president, Slobodan Milošević, to sue for peace. Similarly, the United States forcibly ejected Saddam Hussein from Kuwait before considering ending the first Gulf War.

This same theory has held throughout history. The Union did not eradicate slavery and unify the country by achieving a "political settlement"; it forcibly defeated the Confederacy and imposed a political solution, ending slavery and the secession efforts of the Confederate states. The United States achieved its independence by forcing the surrender of Cornwallis at Yorktown, not by negotiating a political settlement of the disputes between the American colonists and the British Crown. World War II ended not with a political settlement but with Allied troops in Berlin, Hitler dead in his bunker, Japan reeling from two atomic bombings, and the resulting unconditional surrenders of Germany and Japan.

The expression "Possession is nine-tenths of the law" did not arise in a vacuum. It neatly makes the point that a stronger power can achieve its ends practically by deploying superior force, and no amount of international law can truly restore the status quo ante. Military solutions, therefore, are frequently necessary to achieve acceptable political solutions to disputes.

13. *Remove the term* exit strategy *from the vocabulary of politicians and policy makers.*

When policy makers make the difficult decision to use force in a particular situation, they have made a judgment that American national security and economic security demand that the United States risk the lives of its soldiers to defend those interests. The goals of any such military action should be clear. Americans should go to war to achieve particular goals. The "exit" from the theater of battle should occur when those goals are achieved.

At some level, the concept of an "exit strategy" is downright offensive. If a goal is so important to the United States that it is willing to commit the lives of its soldiers to achieving that goal, policy makers should contemplate only how to achieve that goal through victory. Determining how to remove troops at a time when a goal has not been achieved—and, indeed, before combat has even begun—calls into question how vital the goal of the military operation is. No military plan survives contact with the enemy, and the idea that the United States can plan how it will leave a theater of battle demonstrates a lack of commitment to friend and foe alike.

Rather, American policy makers should define an "exit state"—the end state of a military conflict that the United States deems meets the objectives of the conflict. The United States should then take those actions needed to achieve the exit state, altering strategy as needed.

Former British prime minister Tony Blair, in his address to the House of Commons in March 2003, may have put it best when describing the need to have a realistic, credible threat of force to support foreign policy. In describing the consequences of not credibly threatening force against Iraq, Blair stated,

> Our fault has not been impatience.
>
> The truth is our patience should have been exhausted weeks and months and years ago. Even now, when if the world united and gave him an ultimatum: comply or face forcible disarmament, he might just do it, the world hesitates and in that hesitation he senses the weakness and therefore continues to defy.

> What would any tyrannical regime possessing WMD think viewing the history of the world's diplomatic dance with Saddam? That our capacity to pass firm resolutions is only matched by our feebleness in implementing them.
>
> That is why this indulgence has to stop. Because it is dangerous. It is dangerous if such regimes disbelieve us.
>
> Dangerous if they think they can use our weakness, our hesitation, even the natural urges of our democracy towards peace, against us.
>
> Dangerous because one day they will mistake our innate revulsion against war for permanent incapacity; when in fact, pushed to the limit, we will act. But then when we act, after years of pretence, the action will have to be harder, bigger, more total in its impact. Iraq is not the only regime with WMD. But back away now from this confrontation and future conflicts will be infinitely worse and more devastating.[473]

Today, with the successes of the antiwar movement and the current vessel through which the antiwar movement expresses itself politically, the Democratic Party, the United States may have reached the point of permanent incapacity of which Prime Minister Blair spoke: The point at which the only military actions the United States is willing to take are drone strikes and air strikes, which give the United States limited control over the broader outcomes of these actions. The point at which, without the unanimous support of the world, Americans view any military action as illegitimate. The point at which the United States is willing to deliberately diminish its world footprint, even at the risk of the Middle East erupting in flames and countries like Iran, avowed enemies of the United States and the West, obtaining nuclear weapons. The point at which the United States delays taking action in the present, ensuring any future action will have to be harder, bigger, and more total in its impact.

473 "Full Text: Tony Blair's Speech," *The Guardian*.

CHAPTER 12

Being Prepared for the Next War

THIS BOOK OPENED BY ASKING the following questions: Will an Iraq syndrome reminiscent of the Vietnam syndrome take hold of the United States? Has the Iraq War experience, like Vietnam before it, created a generation of antiwar activism that will color America's involvement in world affairs and its deployment of force for years to come? What will this mean for the United States' ability to counter threats in the coming years? In truth, it is impossible to answer these questions not knowing what the next war will be or who will be the adversary. This book focuses primarily on one aspect of war: the domestic front and domestic opposition and whether an Iraq syndrome has developed as a result of the Iraq War and the opposition to it.

The history of the antiwar movement during Iraq has much in common with its Vietnam-era predecessor. Much of the Iraq antiwar movement borrowed from and was animated by the Vietnam-era protest movement. In other ways, the Iraq protests represented an updated, more modern version of the Vietnam-era protests, from sophisticated, professional organizing by groups like ANSWER, to the ability to spread the message through social media and videos, to treating veterans not with contempt but as additional victims of a reckless, misguided foreign policy. Both the Vietnam and Iraq antiwar protests had a significant effect on the waging of the respective wars, in both cases making the wars more difficult to prosecute. Moreover, in both cases the political leadership was unprepared to respond to the protests effectively. In the case of Iraq, factually inaccurate claims that Bush deliberately "lied" the United States into the Iraq War, actually went to war for oil, and was falsifying statistics showing the success of the surge took root and undermined the credibility of the administration as it sought new strategies to win the war.

If America is to win the next war and avoid the effects of an Iraq syndrome, American leaders must be prepared to counter an antiwar movement that is likely to oppose the war no matter how righteous the cause, short of a cataclysmic attack on the homeland such as 9/11. To do that, policy makers must understand the antiwar movement to effectively respond to it. The common threads of the antiwar movement from Vietnam and Iraq likely will be the threads of the next antiwar movement that will arise the next time the United States determines it must take military action. American political leadership must be prepared to maintain and defend the government's credibility. American leaders should consider strategies that lead to strong, decisive victories and forceful consolidation of gains made. They should be prepared to ignore criticism from foreign governments who have a dog in the fight and whose opposition is driven by their own political or strategic considerations. Finally, American political leaders must be willing to firmly, comprehensively, and publicly reject disingenuous criticism from protesters who, at root, are anti-American (such as ANSWER) and more interested in neutering American power than in promoting human rights.

Most importantly, American policy makers must consider developing a strategy for building and maintaining public support of military action every bit as important as the military strategy for the action. No longer can American presidents and their administrations allow opposition to wars and incendiary allegations regarding these wars to go unchallenged. From the moment an administration begins considering military action, it must begin developing a strategy for obtaining *and* maintaining public support for the war. The strategy should include rapid responses to false allegations and accusations, repeated as often as necessary to ensure that false allegations do not become accepted truth. It should also include a measure of transparency, providing both good and bad news to ensure policy makers retain credibility with the public.

The next antiwar movement need not derail the next military action the United States takes to protect its national security and national interests. The

Iraq War need not result in an Iraq syndrome that causes timidity and reluctance in deploying US forces to support American national security and foreign policy objectives, as the Vietnam syndrome did a generation earlier. But political leadership must be prepared in advance with a strategy to respond to antiwar opposition and any nascent Iraq syndrome outbreak. This book, hopefully, will contribute to that strategy and to American victory in the field.

About the Author

Michael E. Ginsberg is an attorney in Washington, DC. He holds an undergraduate degree in engineering sciences from Harvard and a Master's degree in aeronautics and astronautics from Stanford and is a 2002 graduate of Harvard Law School. Ginsberg has been in practice for the past thirteen years, including in the areas of international law, export controls, and economic sanctions. He is an expert on the implementation, enforcement, and effects of US economic sanctions on Iran, Syria, and non-state terrorist groups.

www.ingramcontent.com/pod-product-compliance
Lightning Source LLC
Chambersburg PA
CBHW060449280326
41933CB00014B/2713

* 9 7 8 0 9 9 7 2 3 3 7 0 4 *